"Thomas Merton wrote that contemplation is the spiritual life 'fully awake, fully active, fully aware that it is alive.' In *Beguiled by Beauty*, Wendy Farley develops a remarkable account of contemplation that demonstrates the truth of Merton's insight. Drawing extensively on the historical wisdom of the world's contemplative traditions, Farley describes the Christian contemplative life as one open and attuned to divine beauty and immersed in everyday joy, sorrow, delight, suffering, and routine. Not a 'how-to' book, this work is nonetheless filled with practical wisdom for anyone who longs to more fully embrace and embody God's love, compassion, and justice in the world."

—Timothy H. Robinson, Lunger Associate Professor
of Spiritual Resources and Disciplines, Brite Divinity
School at Texas Christian University

"Lots of books ask questions, but few of them put us in question. By doing the latter, this book helps to make us who we hope to become. Contemplation leads to compassion, and Farley leads us toward both."

—J. Aaron Simmons, Professor of Philosophy,
Furman University

"Wendy Farley gently lures us into a world of wonder. We begin to sense the nuance of each detail, infused as it is with divine goodness. She pivots us from one scene to another, showing us ever more instances of inherent beauty even in heartache. She invites us to make a shift from a moral obligation to 'do right' to a deep desire for all beings to 'be right'—whole and beloved. As we follow her lead into this theology of compassion, we finally come to notice that the world we have fallen in love with is our own. We discover that the 'rich, courageous, generous, and joyful' life she describes can be our own. And she gives us tools to make it so, helping us into practices of contemplation to center and guide us, opening deep wells of respite in these times of grief. Dr. Farley's writing style has wide appeal—theologians, philosophers, pastors, parishioners, and practitioners will find themselves 'beguiled' by the experience."

—Marcia McFee, PhD, Creator and Visionary of the Worship Design
Studio and Ford Fellow Visiting Professor of Worship,
Graduate School of Theology, University of Redlands

# Beguiled by Beauty

*Cultivating a Life of Contemplation and Compassion*

Wendy Farley

WESTMINSTER
JOHN KNOX PRESS
LOUISVILLE · KENTUCKY

© 2020 Wendy Farley

*First edition*
Published by Westminster John Knox Press
Louisville, Kentucky

20 21 22 23 24 25 26 27 28 29—10 9 8 7 6 5 4 3 2 1

Unless otherwise indicated, Scripture quotations are from the New Revised Standard Version of the Bible, copyright © 1989 by the Division of Christian Education of the National Council of the Churches of Christ in the U.S.A., and are used by permission.

Scripture quotations marked RSV are from the Revised Standard Version of the Bible, copyright © 1946, 1952, 1971, and 1973 by the Division of Christian Education of the National Council of the Churches of Christ in the U.S.A., and are used by permission.

*Book design by Drew Stevens*
*Cover design by Allison Taylor*

Library of Congress Cataloging-in-Publication Data is on file
at the Library of Congress, Washington, D.C.

ISBN: 9780664266813 (pbk.)
ISBN: 9781646980079 (ebook)

Most Westminster John Knox Press books are available at special quantity discounts when purchased in bulk by corporations, organizations, and special-interest groups. For more information, please email SpecialSales@wjkbooks.com.

*To Scotty, Paul, and Yana*
*My best and most beloved teachers*

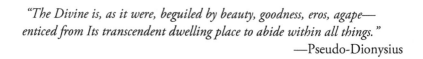

*"The Divine is, as it were, beguiled by beauty, goodness, eros, agape—
enticed from Its transcendent dwelling place to abide within all things."*
—Pseudo-Dionysius

*"All goodness is a participation in God and [her] love for [her] creatures."*
—Catherine of Genoa

# Contents

# *Preface*

I began this book a couple of years into Trump's presidency. Like many others, I have found the egregious assaults on truth, on women, on everyone and everything deeply disturbing. I have been aware for many years of the approaching environmental crisis, already deadly before we knew the effects of climate change. Now fires burn millions of acres of forest, soil is destroyed by corporate farming methods, bizarre weather destroys lives and ecosystems, toxins invade every part of our lives. An unchecked pandemic has taken over 200,000 lives in the United States and forced countless more into financial crisis. People of color are bearing the brunt of both of these. This, together with the on-air extrajudicial murder of George Floyd, has forced us toward a long overdue reckoning with the atrocities of our racial caste system. I type this on the day a grand jury declined to prosecute Breonna Taylor's killers.

We, especially white people, have found it difficult to acknowledge the realities of climate change, racism, and all forms of interhuman degradation. These are not political matters but spiritual ones. We cannot retain our humanity in these dark times if we do not discover the inner resources to live with nobility, compassion, and justice. I meant this book to provide tools to face the crisis of conscience that is upon us. I believe that if we reignite our ardor for the divine Beloved and fall in love with the beauty of all created beings, we will be inspired to act well, even as the world falls apart. I believe that interrogating our interior resistance to social and environmental justice will help unlock our power to act with the courage that is required of us.

Whoever you are, wherever you are, it is incumbent upon you to take concrete action, to contribute your widow's mite to the assaults on our humanity and our earth. Let us lament. But let us conspire together to embody the world we yearn for.

# Introduction

How difficult it is to maintain an open heart in these dark days! Climate change performs its destructive work even more quickly than we feared. Hatred is given permission to rage with impunity. Work, school, and religion are often alienating. Technology silently steals our ability to concentrate or think deeply. Our activism can make us sympathize with Sisyphus, condemned to endlessly push a stone up a mountain, only to have it roll back as it nears the summit. Religious commitments sometimes feel dry as dust. But the world remains so tender and lovely, so vulnerable and enigmatic. How can we keep opening our heart to the sorrow and tragedy of the world and yet remain alert to its endlessly proliferating splendors? How can we train ourselves to fall ever more deeply in love with the world without glossing over deception and cruelty?

This book began to percolate many years ago when I started teaching a freshman seminar at Emory University that I called "Contemplating Beauty." The idea came from nowhere and did not seem to be anything but a whim. We read Gregory of Nyssa and Dostoevsky, Natasha Trethewey and Simone Weil. Our readings continually exposed us to the paradoxical intertwining of beauty and compassion. Over the years the power of beauty as a threshold to the divine became deeply rooted in me, changing the way I experience the world. Tragedy and affliction do not operate in some other world, as if the truth of suffering were alien to creation, but are always present or just below the surface of awareness. Beauty does not stand apart, bright and unscathed, but permeates everything. It is heartbreaking to see the interdependence of these things; to acknowledge sacred beauty in the midst of disaster seems a betrayal. To allow in awareness of suffering in a moment of intoxication would seem to spoil it. But becoming aware of the radiance of beauty anoints all events—all people, beings, and environments—with the holy chrism of the sacred.

Like many Protestants, I thought of social responsibility as one thing and enjoying nature or poetry as something completely different.

I understood obligations to a public world but thought little of how the distortions of my mental habits would be mirrored to the world, whether I liked it or not. I did not appreciate how central intimacy or union with the Beloved was to earlier Christians' understanding of how the commandment of love could be practiced. I have studied many forms of contemplative practice and meditation, but I missed the connections between awakening to the beauty of beings, falling in love with the Beloved, and cultivating radical compassion. There are many paths, and for some reason, the path of beauty has called to me.

The beauty of beings is not their external "prettiness." The man on death row, the old woman dying in her bed, the bleached coral reefs are not pretty sights. But this man, this woman, this coral are beautiful and sacred. They are irrevocably woven into the family of being. Glimpsing the raw beauty of beings is a joy. It opens us to the eternal incarnate in time and in flesh. It is also a long sorrow. Beauty is constantly perishing. All things pass away, but too often the beauty of beings perishes because of violence, rapaciousness, indifference, and betrayal.

This book is about a contemplative way of life. It is not so much a description of particular forms of meditation, though the last chapter offers examples of concrete practices one might experiment with. This book describes some ways one might cultivate habits of wonder, attention, compassion, courage, joy. It offers a conversation that might spark your own ways of awakening to beauty and sustaining compassion.

Though there are many exceptions, descriptions of contemplation or meditation often imagine life with sufficient luxury that one can dedicate serious time and energy to religious practices.[1] The monk's cell is the traditional ideal for a contemplative life. I am the mother of three children, a professor, and have walked in dark valleys where hope seemed very dim. I know more than I wish I did about trauma. I mention this because it shapes the way I understand a contemplative way of life. I did not have the time or ability to follow the instructions of dedicated meditators. One can hardly meditate twice a day for twenty minutes or rise before dawn for an hour of practice when every second is dedicated to children, work, and keeping terror at bay. Or maybe you can. But I couldn't. I have no doubt that the ability to dedicate hours, days, and years to religious practice is an enormous gift and may deepen capacities for union and love in ways nothing else can. But that was not my life. There were not many signposts for people in my situation. I thirsted for the Beloved and longed to deepen and purify capacities for courage and compassion. But my dedication to being a mother and teacher, entangled with the lives of my family and friends, my community and nation, made a contemplative way of life difficult to cultivate.

Whatever your life is like, signposts may feel few and far between. You may be inspired by teachings about prayer, meditation, and contemplation only to crash against the constraints of a busy or difficult life. But whoever we are, we are made for the Beloved and made to share the Beloved's delight in and care for the world. The responsibilities of ordinary life do not alienate us from our nature. They are the environment in which we encounter it. Rather than imagine contemplation as an impossible ideal, it is possible to nurture your spirit within the terms your life is setting for you—whether you are an aging person whose wisdom expands even as your body or concentration diminishes, a delighted and exhausted mother, a person working more hours than there seem to be in a day, someone whose spirituality is damaged by a cruel church community, a trauma survivor who may be triggered rather than supported by meditation books or communities, a retiree with more time available to explore new things, or a pastor eager to find fresh approaches to faith.

For those of us who embrace life in the company of lovers, spouses, children, activity, and work, it may seem that a contemplative way of life is nothing more than a wish or dream. This is only true if we understand monasticism as the only model for spiritual life. If we split apart the world into various dualistic categories, then we tear apart aspects of ourselves that long to be together: activism / spirituality, prayer / work, interiority / public life, family life / contemplation, friendship / universal compassion. Life is a seamless whole. Every part is related to every other part, just as every being is related to every other being. There are no absolute divisions anywhere. Contemplation is not something separate and apart from ordinary life. It is a way to inhabit ordinary life. We might take periods of time for meditation or prayer or contemplative walks or working with a poem or piece of music, but these are not separate "contemplative" moments; they are simply part of the interweaving of life. Brother Lawrence said to a friend, "For me the time of action does not differ from the time of prayer, and in the noise and clatter of my kitchen, while several persons are together calling for as many different things, I possess God in as great tranquility as when upon my knees at the Blessed Sacrament."[2] This eye-of-the-hurricane calm may seem a fantastic dream, but it is possible because "God is everywhere, in all places, and there is no spot where we cannot draw near."[3]

A meditation pillow, a lit candle, a quiet corner, and a prayer circle are all very nourishing. These moments of silence and solitude help to cultivate a space within us that is less reactive and open a depth in our heart. When we are able to find moments of prayer and silence, we can become more centered in intimacy with the Beloved. But they do not make the divine Beloved present. They can only make us more aware of the presence, which is there in the pots and pans, at the sickbed, and present while we nurse or cry or type or protest. A contemplative way of life reorients our awareness to the presence that is always with us. There is a sacred energy—the Beloved, Holy Wisdom, the Divine Mother, God, chi, *prana*—that is nearer than our breath. "Everything in the world shares in this energy, contributes to it, benefits from it, is sustained by it. This energy connects us. . . . That is simply the way the universe is made."[4] The Spirit of Goodness is everywhere and always. When we integrate our awareness into it, in whatever ways make sense to our life as it is right now in this moment, we can participate in the beauty and compassion that endlessly flows throughout creation. We weave contemplative awareness into every moment, whatever is happening. We do this more naturally and spontaneously the more we practice it. It is not a duty or something that earns us salvation. It is not a way of perfection or of perfect holiness. It is simply being human, being a creature of spirit and flesh, bearing a flaming and broken heart, and constituted by our infinite connections to others.

This book may be part of the conversation as you think about how you want to nourish your heart's longing for—for what? This yearning may be hard to name. We are creatures of spirit and made for the Beloved, for the ultimate mystery that has no name. As creatures of spirit, our longing for the sacred is not only a private relationship with the holy other. It is a call to honor the sacred worth of every creature. Our inchoate longing is a desire to love more deeply, feel more unconstrained compassion, wonder at the glorious creativity of nature and art. We long to be alive to all that is—the Good beyond all names, the beings that inhabit the world, the creativity of the human spirit, the inconsolable tragedies of our lives and of the world. We desire to be fully alive, but the world does not always support this desire. We are entangled in things that dull our senses and distract us from our loves. Suffering or witness to suffering make us want to become numb to the world and shielded against our own heart.

We cannot love the world without accepting its tragic suffering as part of the whole. I do not know why these are woven together and have no theories about it. But beings are beautiful and they suffer. Contemplation requires that we intensify our awareness of both of these truths. We often dull down our capacity for beauty because we cannot bear to stay awake for the atrocities that we encounter when we love fragile creatures. It requires so much courage and strength to endure love for the beauty of the world. As Galway Kinnell points out, love requires courage: "perhaps it *is* courage, and even perhaps *only* courage."[5]

We cannot expect to live a contemplative life or to love the world or even love one single thing in it without courage and without sustained resources to feed our courage. The very word "courage" comes from the word for heart. If we want our heart to live, we must feed it and nourish it. Contemplating the beauty of beings is one way to do this—in the ordinariness of life, in the unending bodying forth of the divine goodness in the depth and width and height of creation.

I would like to express my gratitude to early readers, Liz McGeachy and Sue Gilbertson. Their suggestions and encouragement meant the world to me. I also am—again—still grateful to my editors: Robert Ratcliff who has seen this through and most especially to Dan Braden for his seemingly endless patience and kindness.

# 1

# *Contemplation on the Borderlands*

"Love all of God's creation, the whole and every grain of sand in it. Love every leaf, every ray of God's light. Love the animals, love the plants, love everything. If you love everything, you will perceive the divine mystery in things. Once you perceive it, you will begin to comprehend it better every day. And you will come at last to love the whole world with an all-embracing love. Love the animals: God has given them the rudiments of thought and joy untroubled."

"For we acknowledge unto You that all is like an ocean, all is flowing and blending, and that to withhold any measure of love from anything in Your universe is to withhold the same measure from you."[1]

"It is about the loveliness and beauty of the dance of God in the midst of this 'ball of confusion.' It is about God's love and compassion for this earth with all its creatures and for us human creatures with our beautiful and ugly ways."[2]

We live in a time of turmoil and possibility. "Things fall apart, the center cannot hold."[3] The Spirit must be engaged in a wild and desperate dance. One hopeful sign in these dangerous times is the recovery within Christianity—and beyond—of practices of contemplation and meditation. These practices are not an escape from turmoil but disciplines that open our hearts wider to the world's tragedy and beauty, however difficult times become.

Contemplative practices have accompanied Christianity from its beginnings: "whenever you pray, go into your room and shut the door" and pray to the Beloved (Matt. 6:6). Even though much of the rich history of Christian contemplation has been exiled to underground channels, in the last few decades contemplative practices have flowed out of monasteries and convents and into lay communities. Centering prayer and other forms of meditation—chant; contemplation of Scripture (*lectio divina*) or poetry, music, art, icons; wilderness experiences; retreats and prayer groups—all flourish.

This revival is partly due to contemplative Christianity reaching out to contemplative practices in other traditions. His Holiness the Dalai Lama and Thich Nhat Hanh have been inspiring ambassadors of Buddhist practices of compassion and meditation. Japanese Zen meditation has been around in the United States even longer. People are more aware of different Indian practices, including yoga, chant, and many forms of meditation. Sufi poetry has made us aware of a new kind of spiritual friendship with Islam. These conversations and crossover practices are a welcome way of enriching our understanding of the religions. As Pope John XXIII said in 1962, "In the present order of things, divine providence is leading us to a new order of human relations which, by human effort and even beyond human expectation, are directed toward the fulfillment of God's higher and inscrutable designs; and everything, even human differences, leads to the greater good of the Church."[4] These religious dialogues, though not entirely new to Christianity, have greatly expanded our spiritual imagination and reminded us of treasures in our past that we had forgotten.

Some people find their way to Christian contemplation through interreligious dialogue. Others are seeking a more experiential approach to their faith. In addition to worship and church community, they want to explore something of their own interiority and augment public worship with an opening of the heart in silent prayer. Still others find themselves unwilling exiles from the church. While many in the LGBTQ+ community find themselves in warm and welcoming church communities, there are too many others who have been rejected by their community. Forced to choose between hiding themselves from family and church or being told they are going to hell, they find a third way and simply leave their faith family. Many women have become fatigued by the effort to find themselves included somewhere in the church's patriarchal language, and the subtle—or not-so-subtle—disparagement of their voices. For some, the social conservatism of their church feels at odds with the gospel of love and the prophets' cry for justice. For still others, a liturgy built around a story of sin, punishment, and forgiveness fails to speak to their existential reality. On the other hand, someone might appreciate the theological and social openness of a more progressive church but find it dull or uninspiring. For these reasons and others, Americans are increasingly identifying themselves as spiritual but not religious or identifying with no particular religious community or tradition.

Whether one is fascinated by religious dialogue, enriching one's faith, or seeking to quench a spiritual thirst on the margins of organized religion, many are finding that there is a rich conversation about contemplative practice and meditation within Christianity and on its borderlands. This book is written for all these seekers and holy wanderers. My own background is Christian; I am a theologian and come from a long line of ministers and family members devoted to their church. I don't think of myself as an expert, but I have studied some of the great texts of Christian mysticism from its early days to the present moment. I have also studied Christian meditation practices for many years and have been incorporating silent retreats into my life for more than two decades. I have studied other traditions with some care and find much that enriches Christianity or allows me to understand it in a new way. The Buddhist emphasis on compassion is not new to Christianity, but it allows me to see things in the stories of Jesus that I had not noticed. Yoga's attention to bodily practices makes me rethink ways Christians have used and abused their bodies in the service of their faith. Slaves, Shakers, and others have danced and sang their faith. Hesychasts have used breath and visualization to pray. But Christians have also tormented their bodies with penitential practices or ignored them altogether. The recovery of bodily prayer is a great enrichment to contemplative practice. The centrality of the natural world to indigenous or Celtic spiritualities return me to the Bible and earlier Christian writings to discover a celebration of the earth as sacred, which I had not realized was there—even as it expands my thinking beyond these sources.

Every person and community of faith must reforge the gospel for their own time. Images and practices that make sense during one historical epoch or in response to some particular social challenge do not seamlessly translate to another era. The gospel is living and moving. This vitality of faith is anticipated in Jesus' farewell address to his disciples in the Gospel of John. He promises he will send the Paraclete, a comforter who will lead them in all truth (John 15:26). Early Christianity also knew of a mysterious holy Spirit who dances through time and space, weaving ancient and eternal truths into the ever-changing historical moment. Pope John emphasized the need to courageously embrace the living power of the gospel in a new way: "it is not the Gospel that changes; it is we who begin to understand it better. . . . The moment has arrived when we must recognize the signs of the times, seize the opportunity, and look far abroad."[5]

Contemplative practice is one ancient and novel way the Spirit is leading us into this moment of our history. We live in dangerous times, and they will only get more precarious as climate change takes its relentless toll, disrupting nature and societies, tempting us to turn to hatred and ideologies that offer an illusory sense of security. A commitment to a contemplative way of life may contribute to the capacity to endure these times with an open and courageous heart. Rosemarie Freeney

Harding, one of the great civil rights mothers, knew well what it was to live through outrages and the defeats of hope. Yet she describes the power of the Spirit to draw "circles of protection and power around us even as we look elsewhere. Teaching about how to be family. How to live like family. How to live with some strength and care in your hands. How to live with some joy in your mouth. How to put your hands gentle on where the wound is and draw out the grief. How to urge some kind of mercy into the shock-stained earth so that that good will grow."[6] A contemplative way of life can enable us to participate in this work of the Spirit more deeply, compassionately, and joyfully.

## A WORD ON LANGUAGE

About halfway through *The Color Purple*, Celie tells Shug she has rejected God—who allowed so many horrifying things to happen to her and who has never listened to any black woman. Wild and life-filled Shug is shocked and asks Celie what she thinks God looks like: "He big and old and tall and graybearded and white. He wear white robes and go barefooted . . . [eyes] sort of bluish-gray Cool. Big though. White lashes." Shug quickly disabuses her of the idea that God is a judgmental, harsh white man. She tells Celie that for her, the "first step away from this old white man was trees. Then air. Then birds. Then other people. But one day when I was sitting quiet and feeling like a motherless child, which I was, it come to me: that feeling of being a part of everything, not separate at all. I knew that if I cut a tree, my arm would bleed. And I laughed and I cried and run all around the house." Shug acknowledges it is hard to get this angry white-man-god out of one's head, but "You have to git man off your eyeball, before you can see anything a'tall."[7]

Contemplation can be a powerful antidote to our mental habit of thinking of God as an angry or royal (white) man. As one enters more deeply into the wordless mystery of the divine, language is less *about* God and more a poetical invocation *of* divine goodness. As the divine white man begins to lose his grip, we are able to see a bit better.

Our minds are deeply shaped by the ideas we carry around in our heads about "God," often images we absorbed in childhood. It is therefore important to use wildly creative language about divine reality, to use words and images that will help to unpin our minds from ingrained images. It is not that images are bad; we cannot think without images.

Though divine reality is mirrored in no earthly image, we cannot think of divine reality without images. But the attachment to images, especially oppressive ones, is unfortunate. If we forget that divine goodness is infinitely more than our small minds can hold, we will be anxious when our ideas begin to change. When an image is challenged or becomes toxic, we seem to lose "God" altogether. Contemplation helps us to open our minds to a number of images so that no one image is allowed to claim authority in defining who God is. Images modify each other: God is Father but also Mother. God is Lady Love but also Holy Wisdom. We become more open to new ways of thinking about our relationship to divine Goodness. We come nearer to relationship and are less dependent on static or barren images. I tend to avoid the word "God" for the most part. It is a fine word, but it is so freighted with predetermined meanings—a man reaching out to touch Adam's hand on the Sistine Chapel, a frowning judge, a justice-loving or cruelly arbitrary divine monarch. It is difficult to allow our minds to roam toward less manly images. I use a variety of terms: Beloved, Divine Mother, Goodness, Bright Abyss, Divine Emptiness, Dance, Spirit, Lady Love, Wisdom, as well as others.

As there are no adequate images for divine reality, neither is there a gender. The second commandment warns us against creating an image of God from anything in the earth, above the earth in the heavens, or below the earth (Exod. 20:4). This is a fairly comprehensive rejection of images, including gender, as appropriate to God. For that reason, I employ gendered language (She, He), nonbinary language (They), and nongendered language (It, Spirit, Dance, Good, Abyss) throughout the text. This may seem jarring if one is used to something more traditional. It may feel strange to use the nonbinary term "They" for God. As feminists argued a long time ago—and people of every color and ethnicity also knew—the words and images we use for divine Goodness carries over to the way we value human beings. If God is a man then only men are divine. If we believe that the utterly inclusive love of the divine Goodness created all of humanity, then our language must include everyone—women, nonbinary, men, gay, straight, trans, people of every color, ethnicity, and religion—everyone. I believe it is good for our minds and our spirits to adventure through language in ways that are deliberately jarring to our preconceptions and mental pictures. As Meister Eckhart says: "I pray God rid me of god."[8] That is, may divine reality displace the small thoughts about the divine that imprison my mind.

## RADICAL COMPASSION

Our images of the divine are reflected in how we treat others. Perhaps paradoxically, religion can train us to be hostile or indifferent toward others. For millions of Christians, belief in God has done little to stop them from despising groups of people they categorize as dangerous or inferior. For some, the gospel is consistent with racism; the domination of women; the exploitation of refugees, immigrants, and people of other faiths; and the colonization of other lands and of the earth itself. The gospel has done little to reveal the agony suffered by hungry children or impoverished families. It has turned a blind eye to the devastation of forests, oceans—whole species and ecosystems. The biblical prophets rail against the powerful institutions of ancient Israel who perform their cultic service but grind the faces of the poor into the dust (e.g., Deut. 27:19; Isa. 3:15). From a biblical point of view, this kind of worship is indistinguishable from idolatry. One might as well worship a golden calf as this cultic god that cares nothing for creation.

On the other hand, many people, including people of faith, become interested in meditation in order to obtain relief from stress or perhaps from the restless meaninglessness that haunts the edges of consciousness. Meditation promises a variety of benefits: lower blood pressure, healthier organs, a more relaxed attitude, an antidote to stress. These are all to be highly prized in our stressful world. Meditation also promotes a deeper level of peacefulness. A religious person may hope to feel closer to God. All of these are worthy goals and in our stressful world can contribute to improved mental, physical, even spiritual health. This is a significant good in itself.

But if we think of contemplative practice primarily in this way, we might come away with the stereotype of someone who remains preoccupied only with their own benefit. We might spurn contemplative practices as fundamentally selfish or a distraction from more active engagement in the world. Or we might seek it out for precisely that reason—it promises relief from the painfulness of life. As worthy as self-improvement, relaxation, and spiritual benefits are, they are not the purpose of a contemplative way of life.

When we love Divine Goodness more deeply, we love the world more passionately. When we love and care for the world, we fall more deeply into divine reality. "God" is not just a magical being in whom we are instructed to believe, but the unnamable, infinite goodness that Christians know as love. When we love one another more beautifully, we enter into the divine realm—whatever our names for it might be. Regardless of the words we use, the primary sign that one loves God is that one loves other people and the world itself. As Julian of Norwich instructs Margery Kemp, her religious experiences are only authentic if they "profit her fellow Christians."[9] Or as Marguerite Porete puts it, there is "no lesser way."[10]

*It is impossible to overemphasize that the core practice of a contemplative way of life is radical compassion.* One's concentration may be impossibly wandering. One may not be able to sing three notes of a chant. A headstand may prove impossible. Securing twenty minutes twice a day for prayer may be no more realistic than growing wings and flying to the moon. These things are instruments that a contemplative might use, but they are not themselves what constitute a contemplative way of life.

A contemplative way of life is motivated by a devotion to the welfare of others. However much we remain caught up in the inexorable demands of life, "seared with trade and bleared with toil," we may yet burn with a sense of sorrow for the world's suffering.[11] We may feel discouraging pain as we observe the hate speech, acts of violence, the calculated indifference of our times, the horrifying hostility to truthfulness. It may be that this concern for suffering and injustice inspires in you or your community participation in social activism. Or it may simply make you want to binge watch the most recent Netflix series. The difficulty and crisis of the world is overwhelming. It is virtually impossible to bear it without very deep resources. Without watering our roots in deep and life-giving waters, awareness of radical suffering, injustice, and turmoil is likely to distort our capacities for care and responsibility.

The feeling of tenderness toward others is rooted in the source of compassion, the Divine Beloved. This is why the twin love commandments are really the same. The possibility of radical compassion arises as we deepen our relationship with ultimate reality, known to Christians by many names, most often as "God." We can tell whether we are worshiping the divine Goodness or an idol of our imagination by the fruits of our worship. Love, compassion, and social justice are the fruits of loving God. Cruelty, hubris, selfishness, and hostility to creation suggest that, whatever names we are using, we are worshiping an idol.

Set your heart on radical compassion—a living desire that the suffering of others be alleviated, no matter who they are. Radical compassion does not impose conditions that say some are worthy of compassion and others are not. It does not limit compassion to certain groups of people. It does not indulge in hatred or demean opponents. We may feel the edge of compassion when we find it difficult or impossible to wish a particular person or group well or when we are motivated by rage at destructive people. But we can recognize this limitation of our heart as alien to our deepest desire, and we can work to weaken the resistance we feel. We do not have to wish that someone who has harmed us or others thrives in their evil-doing. Radical compassion resists harmful acts, but it also recognizes that to do evil is itself a kind of suffering, and therefore one can wish for their transformation.

When we begin any particular meditation, prayer, or contemplative practice, it is useful to remind ourselves that the deepest reason for practice is the generation of radical compassion. Likewise, we can use all of our daily practices—driving, laundry, work, rest, recreation, pleasure, obligations—as opportunities to increase joy in others and compassion for their suffering. We can gently and nonjudgmentally notice where we are stuck or limited. "Ah yes, I see you. Still enraged. Still terrified. Still distracted." The intention toward radical compassion is what distinguishes a spiritual or religious practice from a secular desire for one's own well-being. It is also the source of our greatest joy.

## CONTEMPLATIVE PRACTICE AS INTERIOR TRANSFORMATION

At the beginning, middle, and end we must remember that practice is always for the world. Something that concerns only one's private welfare or contentment may be useful and important, but it is not what I mean by a contemplative way of life. This does not mean that we do nothing that serves our private good or need for pleasure or relaxation. A balanced life is likely to include all the parts of ourselves. I suspect that we do more good in the world if we can also enjoy the small things that give us pleasure and if we carve out time to nurture our well-being. A gray-faced, righteous, and withered ascetic may not invite confidence. A contemplative way of life need not draw sharp lines between what is permitted or not permitted. But it does invite us to discern what is truly life-giving for ourselves and others.

While a contemplative way of life rests in a yearning for the good of all creation, it focuses on interior transformation as an important element of care for others. This attention to interiority as the source of radical compassion distinguishes a contemplative way of life from secular meditation, which may pay more attention to certain benefits such as relaxation or pain relief. It also distinguishes it from social activism, which so externalizes world engagement that it may fail to notice the ways negative habits infiltrate the work for justice.

Attention to interior transformation may decolonize our minds so that we choose better how to act and respond to the world. But another reason interior work is so important is that our effect on the world is not limited to the things we consciously choose to do or say. Our choices certainly matter, but we powerfully affect the world simply by the sort of person we are. A person might be rather taciturn and yet radiate such a deep kindness that they change the energy in a room. This kindness might be expressed in word and deed, but it is also conveyed unconsciously—it is like a sweet smell that comes off jasmine. Does the jasmine do something to spread its sent? More likely, by simply being jasmine its beautiful scent is effortlessly emitted.

We are not solitary mind-bodies jumbled together with others like old dolls in a closet, juxtaposed but disconnected. We are complex beings deeply interdependent upon an infinite number of other beings, some known, many not known to us. Neither are we rational beings freely choosing and acting in ways that we completely understand and control. We influence those around us in ways we are hardly aware of. Much of our mind and motivation is hidden from us. We are creatures of spirit and in the realm of spirit, everything is related to everything else. There are no hard boundaries separating "self" from "other." This means that what we do—and perhaps even more—what we *are* affects others. We cannot know all the ways we touch other lives. We cannot count on all of our acts or decisions being helpful or wise. But we can train in such a way that some goodness in us becomes more spontaneous. This goodness will be communicated to others in ways we do not control, just as what is limited or harsh or despairing is transmitted whether we wish it so or not—simply because it resides inside of us. We can train so that we might say or do the exactly right thing at a crucial moment to make an extraordinary difference. And we may never know we did it. What matters is that we prepare ourselves to act well, even though we will never perceive all the good (and bad) that we actually accomplish.

For this reason, though contemplative practice is for the world, it has to do with our interior lives. This can cause confusion. Because in contemplation we are attending to our interior life, it can seem as if our focus is self-centered, merely "navel-gazing." It can also be the case that we meditate only for some perceived benefit to ourselves and take no particular interest in the welfare of others. But the spirit in us craves liberation from selfishness and remains discontent and frustrated until we begin to open our hearts to others, even though this is emotionally dangerous. Removing obstacles to compassion and joy is interior work, but it is for the world and is expressed in the way we relate to the world: the cleaning products we buy and the clothes we wear; who we vote for and where our money goes; how we relax and refresh ourselves; how we treat family members, neighbors, coworkers, people who work for us, strangers. The fruit of a contemplative life will be realized in our decisions and actions, but it will also be expressed in what our eyes do when we look at someone. It will invisibly perfume off of us beyond what we consciously intended.

When we care for ourselves, we are better able to care for others. Mothers cannot care for the needs of their children well if they do not or cannot care for themselves. It is not selfish to care for oneself; it is necessary for the good of the world. But as we engage more deeply with contemplative practices, we discover that the membrane between ourselves and others is much thinner than we realized—for better and for worse. If a mother is under a great deal of stress and difficulty, however careful she is to protect her children from her stress, they will perceive it and be affected by it. None of us are free to eliminate stresses in our lives. But to the extent that we can nurture ourselves and find joy and contentment, we are better able to convey to others the courage and love we desire for them. Whatever our spiritual formation is, it will inevitably be released into the world, whether we wish it so or not. If our lives shape us in a way that makes us more selfish or more depressed or cynical, if we are formed to fear or demean others, all of these things will be released into the world and affect people in ways we do not necessarily recognize. But if we pursue practices that heal us and open our hearts, however imperfect we inevitably remain, the good we desire will also be released into the world, also in ways we may never know anything about.

It is rather terrifying to think that the causes of well-being and unhappiness lie deep inside us and we share them without knowing it. What loving mother wants to communicate her anxiety to her children? What dedicated teacher wants to convey their cynicism or anger to their students? We may wish to do good in the world, but we will communicate what we are, even if that is different from what we wish to be. We may feel real compassion, but if we are tyrannized by fear, we will not be able to convey our compassion as fully as we wish. We might wish to be open to all but convey a demeaning attitude because of internalized—perhaps unrecognized—habits of racism or homophobia. To become the people we yearn to be requires attention to what is invisible and unconscious. A contemplative way of life is therefore not a straightforward journey into the land of peace and love. It is an encounter with inner demons. It is much more like a fairy tale, replete with dangerous forests and wild beasts.

## THERE BE DRAGONS

The contemplative life presents many difficulties. It is a fantasy to imagine that a dedication to Lady Love will bring only happiness and equanimity. Some meditators are surprised to discover that meditation increases their unease by bringing to the surface bad memories, negative mental habits, even traumatic experiences. Or they find their understanding of God is challenged in disorienting ways they did not expect. This can feel like a betrayal of the purpose of meditation, as if they were promised candy and received bitter vegetables. Thomas Keating once scoffed at the idea that centering prayer gave one a deeper level of peace, saying that after the first few weeks or months, it made one less peaceful than ever. The work of "unloading the unconscious" is not pleasant.[12] Meditation and contemplation do not leave us unchanged. They force us to encounter things that might be painful. We learn more about ourselves. The blinders we have been wearing to the suffering of the world will begin to come off. It is as if our own minds and the world around us are being unwrapped from the gauzy covering we placed over them because the beauty and suffering of the world is just too intense. Because the interior journey is unpredictable and not always pretty, it needs to be undertaken with care and in the company of wise guides.

Sometimes it is suffering that awakens someone to the border lands of contemplation. Of course, suffering can make one more enraged, addicted, violent, or depressed. But it can also break us open to the realm of the spirit, enticing us toward deeper understanding and tenderness for others. If we think of spirituality as the region of light and purity, or if we think that only good things happen to good people, suffering will seem antithetical to spiritual practice. But suffering will inevitably arise—as democratic and universal as a heartbeat. Contemplation does not protect us from suffering nor does suffering or even trauma make us unfit for contemplation. Suffering is part of the untidiness of life and an inevitable part of contemplative commitments.

Suffering requires tending and care. But it can open up a depth in the soul, which can also make someone more available to the spiritual journey. I do not mean that suffering is inherently "good for us" or that we should seek out suffering as a spiritual exercise. The world is likely to be more than generous in this regard. Because suffering is an ever-present part of life, contemplation incorporates it into the journey. There is a way that the stories of saints have been told that may make us think of them as great heroes, filled with fiery and fearless determination. Unencumbered by doubts, impervious to suffering, onward they go like indominable soldiers of Christ. The historical record tells a different story. Many, perhaps most, of the great contemplatives, reformers, and agents of change experienced great suffering, serious illness, danger, or what we would now call trauma. Francis was a tortured soul, enduring great physical suffering and disappointed anguish until his dying day. Clare spent much of her life on a sickbed. Mechthild of Magdeburg, Marguerite Porete, George Fox, Mary Fisher, Fannie Lou Hamer, Martin Luther King Jr., and Desmond Tutu were among the countless devotees of the Beloved who were cruelly persecuted. Catherine of Genoa, Teresa of Avila, and Julian of Norwich took up their tasks only after near-death experiences. St. John of the Cross grew up hungry and often homeless and was cruelly tortured by fellow Carmelites. Sojourner Truth endured the cruelties of slavery. Howard Thurman faced the endless assaults of racism. And yet somehow for these and countless others, extremes of suffering broke them open to recognize the Beloved and the Beloved in all persons.

Suffering does not have to lead to spiritual exploration, but it can. Beautiful gifts of the human spirit sometimes arise when someone cracked open by affliction finds their way to the Beloved and to greater tenderness for creation. These witnesses may help us recognize ourselves as beloved, even when suffering or contempt tempt us to despise ourselves.

Suffering creates vulnerabilities that make the pursuit of a contemplative way of life both urgent and fragile. Contemplatives who are in the throes of deep suffering may need to take the advice from books with a grain of salt. A distinctive mark of past witnesses is that the path they ended up taking was one that had no markers and few guides. Suffering can take us off the beaten track of religious belief and practice, but it can also reveal amazing vistas.

It can also happen that the disciplines of meditation and contemplation become disconnected from the radical compassion and appropriate humility that moor healthy spirituality. The person may experience many benefits and perhaps gain a kind of charisma that makes them seem attractive and inspiring. But practices intended to generate inner freedom and kindness are put in the service of relationships of domination. You may know of people who meditate regularly or even are popular public teachers who sexually exploit followers; are cold, dismissive, arrogant; or who abuse family members. Meditation is not a magical wand, and one can be quite adept at a variety of contemplative practices and remain a jackass. Worse, a charisma may develop that gives someone greater power over people.

Every single thing in life can be an instrument of good or bad. Contemplation does not protect you from pain or mistakes. It does not guarantee steady "progress"—whatever that means. It does not guarantee that a teacher can be trusted. But "rooted and grounded in love" and in the healthy humility that does not attach too much importance either to mistakes or to accomplishments, it can contribute to a deeply meaningful and joyful life.

## CONTEMPLATIVE WAY OF LIFE, CONTEMPLATIVE PRACTICES, MEDITATION

I am using several terms that form a constellation of ideas. In earlier Christianity, contemplation meant a form of awareness in which the heart-mind became identified with divine reality. One was not only thinking about God but also becoming one with God. Meditation preceded this non-dualistic form of awareness. One meditated in the sense of holding one's attention on something. This was not thinking about something but was rather holding onto something in a more single-minded way. For example, one might engage in a period of prayer on Scripture. One would begin simply by reading the passage and perhaps thinking about it. But one would then begin to attune one's mind to the passage, not trying to figure it out but to begin to enter into it so the passage became on object of meditation. Eventually (ideally) the meditation would fall away, just as thinking about the passage had fallen away during meditation. The heart had opened to that dimension where divinity and humanity mingle and the separation of one from the other is not as vivid. One enters a space of unitive awareness.[13]

People who practiced this way very seriously did more than meditate for twenty minutes twice a day. A whole way of life emerged to produce a kind of synergy in which mind, emotion, body, service, relationships, worship, desire, and understanding all conspire to gradually clear away obstacles to unconstrained love of God and creation. The classical literature on Christian contemplation is filled with descriptions of this passion for union with the Beloved. In its purest sense, unitive consciousness may be something relatively few people fully experience. But we are all held together in the unity of being and so can enjoy the thought that such a thing is possible for human beings. And we can get glimpses and tastes of it in dramatic and in very simple ways. It is the path of elite spiritual athletes and also of ordinary people living unremarkable lives.

There are a number of good books that describe methods or techniques for learning how to meditate. They do not all propose the same way of thinking about meditation. But for our purposes, let us understand meditation as a period of nonverbal prayer in which the mind gently focuses on some object or state of openness. It is a kind of concentration in the sense one is giving focused attention to a period of prayer rather than day-dreaming and wool-gathering (as useful as these relaxed mental states are). But it also (as Cynthia Bourgeault insists) a kind of intention.[14] There are many kinds of meditation and various schools of thought that describe this focused state of prayer in different ways.

Contemplation in the older texts tends to refer to unitive consciousness. But in the contemporary period it has a more fluid meaning. Sometimes people use contemplation and meditation interchangeably. Contemplative studies is now a concentration in a number of universities.[15] Often these studies combine the neuroscience of meditative practices with an exploration of contemplative practices in various religions. For our purposes, contemplation refers to a wide variety of spiritual practices, including but not limited to meditation. One might take up a contemplative attitude toward cooking or walking or nursing a baby. One might sing or dance, chant or exercise in a contemplative way. One might engage in works of social justice from a contemplative frame of mind.

A contemplative way of life refers to a general attitude for integrating all the aspects of one's life into a spiritual whole. In this sense, one does engage in particular practices of prayer, service, and meditation. But more important, one engages all of one's life from a contemplative perspective. Commitment to a contemplative way of life emphasizes the possibility of experiencing a holistic approach. There is nothing that is not contemplative—or at least nothing that is excluded in principle from a contemplative life. One is guided by a general desire to weave ordinary life with the Beloved and see how ordinary actions contribute to a gentle transformation toward greater liberty, steadier joyfulness, and more courageous compassion. Contemplation can have positive effects on our minds and bodies. But its real power is to enflame us with love for the world.

Our deepest well-being arises when the anguish of egocentrism begins to give way to an ability to see and delight in others as really real. When we recognize the tender beauty of all beings, we find that we long for their well-being. We realize that our happiness and unhappiness is bound up with the happiness and unhappiness of others. Indifference is not an option. Contemplation requires a good deal of courage. It is the purpose of contemplation to provide concrete ways of living that will sustain an open heart to the world.

Work, sex, parenting, shopping, leisure, prayer, friendship can all be included within a sense of contemplative purpose. "Ultimate reality is in everything, not lurking behind it."[16] Or, as Richard Rohr wrote in his daily meditation, Christianity is about being at home in the world and loving the Beloved by loving the world. "*What you choose now, you shall have later* seems to be the realization of the saints. Not an idyllic hope for a later heaven but a living experience right now. We cannot jump over this world, or its woundedness, and still try to love God. We must love God *through, in, with* and even *because of* this world."[17]

And yet, it is not the case that a contemplative way of life is always more peaceful, joyful, free, courageous, compassionate. It means that in the ebb and flow of life, in the dark moments of experience and of history, in the horrifying acknowledgment of ways you might have harmed someone or been harmed, in the bracing awareness of how deeply embedded certain negative mental patterns are—one remains dedicated to the vast and mysterious, tragic and beautiful world cherished by the Beloved. This is not a "way of perfection." But it is a way of life worth living, whatever happiness and defeat one encounters along the way.

## BEAUTY

I am approaching such a life from the perspective of beauty. This is not because other ways are not just as good or better. But focusing on beauty brings to light things that are easy to overlook about spirituality.

Without remembering beauty, one might think of spirituality more in terms of beliefs or emptying the mind or ascetical disciplines. We might think of spirit disconnected from the body, art, and nature. But beauty is the threshold to Divine Goodness and a door into radical compassion. When we fall in love with the beauty of the world, we care all the more passionately about the well-being of the environment and all of the beings in the world. When our heart drops its barriers and perceives the great beauty that constantly surrounds us, we cannot help but respect and protect living creatures and their environments. We are each beautiful and cherished beings. Perceiving our own beauty and vulnerability, we are more inclined to seek our genuine well-being—driven neither by unhealthy self-sacrifice nor unhealthy habits.

Beauty here does not mean simply an aesthetic response to something pretty, though that is a very pleasant experience. When I asked my freshmen what they thought beauty meant, their examples tended to circulate around movie stars and sunsets. With respect to my dear students, this reflects a degeneration of beauty into nice experiences. It is a disenchantment of beauty that redirects it to the logic of the marketplace. But after we watched the film *Waste Land*, their ideas about beauty changed. The film is about the return of the artist Vik Muniz to Brazil, where he befriends the *catadores*. These people pick out recyclable material from mountains of trash in Jardim Gramacho, the largest landfill in the world. With their help, he created works of art in which the workers serve as models for incredibly powerful portraits, not with paint or charcoal but with trash.

This film moves the viewer far beyond prettiness toward the intense dignity of people at the far margins of society. The beauty of their spirits is all the more luminous as it emerges from the raw ugliness of their environment. The beauty of the art, created from trash but capturing some of the beauty of the models, allows us to witness an alchemy in which what is despised—trash and its pickers—is transformed into great art. At the same time, art prized by museums and collectors, expresses the moral beauty of the *catadores* and their community that is far removed from the business of art. Beauty of persons, of art, of community and justice awakens us not to prettiness but to something luminous and transforming.

Beauty is not something beheld primarily by the eyes. It is beheld by the spirit—it reveals the truth of beings. Something that might be considered physically unattractive, like a community of trash pickers, is revealed to be of sacred worth. In an unattractive and oppressive environment, the beauty of hard-won human dignity shines brightly. The eyes of the spirit perceive that art is not simply a business transacting cultural commodities. Art is a revelation of the spirit. It is beautiful because it moves the spirit and awakens it—not to moralism but to the depth of life's tragedy, playfulness, poignancy, loveliness.

Beauty is perceived by the spirit. As a spiritual matter, it must be cultivated. It requires energy and a kind of spiritual pedagogy. When we read the poetry of Gerard Manley Hopkins, William Blake, Gwendolyn Brooks, Lucille Clifton, or Mary Oliver, we encounter people who did not just open their eyes and see color and shape. We find in them people who perceived with eyes of the spirit and in seeing with physical and spiritual eyes, they entered into the truth of things in their raw and luminous beauty. In the absence of the practice of beauty, "These things, these things were here and but the beholder wanting."[18]

Beauty reveals the relationship between the divine goodness and the world. In the early sixth century, Pseudo-Dionysius described God as "beguiled by beauty."[19] Divine goodness fell in love with creation and so was compelled to bring it into being. The zeal and eros of God for creation is manifest in the beauty of beings, which are themselves expressions of the divine beauty. Beauty, sadly overlooked in our modern times, is a link between the human spirit and the divine goodness.

Through the doorway of beauty, we walk into the divine realm and begin to perceive creation—to speak poetically—more the way the Beloved perceives it. Creation is vastly complex, diverse, wild. It can be enslaved to human need, but it cannot be contained. The smallest patch of land is home to countless beings—plants, animals, and those strange creatures that are neither or both. If we pause and calm our minds for a moment, the natural world can appear to us not merely in its aesthetic wonder—though this is important. It appears to us as if a layer has been removed, and the inner light of the trees, moss, ocean tides, stars, flowing waterfall shine forth. This light reveals the truth of creation—we are beautiful, and for this we were made.

Human beings are a part of creation and are also complex, diverse, wild. For reasons neither religious mythologies nor scientific theories fully unveil, we are estranged from our place in creation, from one another, from ourselves, and from the Beloved. Moral ugliness scars the luminosity of our sacred goodness. But this goodness is created and cherished by the Beloved. It therefore participates in a kind of eternity. What is beautiful and sacred in us cannot be destroyed, however much it can be marred. Contemplating the beauty of human beings begins to open our eyes to the truth of who we are. In the perception of the beauty of beings we begin to dwell in the divine kingdom promised us when we see as Jesus did: seeing Christ in all beings, especially the "least of these" (Matt. 25).

Creation is interdependent. In a completely literal sense, everything is related to everything else so deeply that the well-being of one contributes to and depends upon the well-being of everything else. This is true in the human realm, too, but we are able to hide this truth from ourselves and believe that the sufferings of injustice, poverty, hunger, oppression, imprisonment, misogyny, racism, war, environmental harm, and a thousand other dismemberments cannot harm us. The practice of recognizing and cherishing beauty does not tolerate this lie. The loving eye pays attention to details and begins to glimpse the paradise of beauty that is endlessly unfolding throughout the cosmos. From its simplest beginning "endless forms most beautiful and most wonderful have been, and are being, evolved."[20] A contemplative way of life begins to taste this beauty and cherish the beauty of beings.

## A GENERAL OUTLINE OF THIS BOOK

This book will lay out some ways to think about why we practice and how we might practice a way of beauty. These are examples. Each person, given who you are at the moment, given your resources and challenges will discover for yourself what makes life rich, courageous, generous, joyful. My remarks may prod you to imagine for yourself how contemplation, beauty, and compassion might weave through life.

Contemplative practice arises from two aspects of our being. One is our natural tendency toward the good—both ordinary good things and also the ultimate Good—the Beloved, God. We are made for this—the desire for contemplation arises from our core identity. The next two chapters describe ways in which we are made for the divine goodness and for the beauty of the world. This created goodness makes us yearn for the Good we have barely begun to imagine. But obviously, this yearning runs into a thousand obstacles.

The second reason we practice is so that we can acknowledge and address those things within ourselves and our society that impede our desire to love Holy Wisdom and Her world. Our social world does not support spiritual values. We are deeply shaped by the conscious and unconscious patterns through which we experience the world: racism or sexism, a disposition toward anger or dispiritedness, judgmentalism or anxiety, workaholism and other addictions—and so on. We are all too busy, too overwhelmed by the pleasures and problems of an electronic age, too disconnected from human and natural contact. We might be laboring under the yoke of an oppressive, even cruel, religious upbringing, which makes religion dangerous and abusive. We may have experienced afflictive suffering or trauma that shadows us like a curse. We may be exhausted, demoralized, or angry activists whose moral indignation has overshadowed the reason we care about justice in the first place. We may find it difficult to accept that caring for ourselves is a good in itself and contributes to the good we want to do in the world. Or we may wish to learn to meditate as a way to seek private satisfaction—so spiritual practice becomes another device for separating ourselves from others. Chapters four through seven discuss ways to cultivate habits of courage, delight, and compassion and to address obstacles that are a natural and integral part of a contemplative path. Difficulties in ourselves and in our world will always be with us. Much of a contemplative way of life is training in ways to respond to obstacles with gentleness and tenderness. These chapters give examples of ways we might disempower unhelpful mental patterns and cultivate more wholesome ones. In addition to cultivating positive habits, it is useful to find time to dedicate to particular practices of prayer, meditation, and contemplation. The last chapter describes examples of how one might integrate contemplative practices into one's daily life.

When we think about a contemplative approach to life, we often see the brilliant light far ahead leading us on or the distant mountain top invisible in its crown of clouds. We read about great mystics, Tibetan lamas, and civil rights leaders and yearn for their greatness. We hear about a life that is more peaceful, compassionate, and filled with gentleness, wisdom, and courage. And then we wake up and find ourselves in the same old life we have been living all along. We try to meditate and "fail" because our thoughts are as busy as a traffic jam on Atlanta's I-285. We are still impatient with our children or hooked by the psychodramas at work. And so we renounce our desire and find the consolations nearest at hand.

The most perfect way to practice is the one that we actually do, with all its brokenness, false starts, mistakes, and confusions. This is life. Contemplation does not take us out of life but deeper into it. A contemplative way of life helps to enlarge the heart so that it has the courage to take in more. It gives us clearer eyes to perceive the beauty of the world. It increases our capacity for joy and compassion in difficult moments and in happy ones. It also contributes to a sense of acceptance when these virtues continue to evade us. We pursue a contemplative way of life to intensify spiritual capacities. But we also do this for the same reason we go for a walk. It might be good for us. But we do it because it enriches our life, whether we die in the next hour or not, whether we find ourselves more peaceful and compassionate or not. We are made for the divine Beloved. We are made to fall in love with Their creation. The "success" of our practice is only that we keep finding ways to show up for it as it evolves, even through arid patches, even in our confusion.

The source of life is deeply, unimaginably Good—but life is a hot mess. The Spirit sings to our spirits to join Her dance.

# 2

# *We Are Made for the Beloved*

"I have seen what you want; it is there: a Beloved of Infinite tenderness."[1]

Whatever we think meditation or contemplation may do for us, the primary reason we find ourselves called to contemplation is that we are made for the Beloved. God thirsts for us and will never be satisfied without deep intimacy with every human being. This intimacy already surges and dances through every molecule of the universe—pulsing through stars and tiny lipids. But for whatever reason, human beings have trouble keeping up with the dance. God's yearning for us is why we *can* practice, the difficulty of this intimacy is why we *must* practice. We keep forgetting who we are.

## FORGETFULNESS

Forgetting who we are does not mean we do not "believe in God." But it may be that even in our believing, our primary experience of ourselves is as ordinary people trying to make it in modern society, enmeshed in its satisfactions and frustrations. We believe in God, but we have tacitly accepted the identity that is given to us by school, work, family, and society. God is an appendage to this identity, reflecting the values of our church, nation, or society. But who are we really? What is this depth that stirs in our deepest loves and delights, in the anguish of human affliction, in our secret restlessness?

21

At the beginning of the dialogue bearing his name, Socrates asks Phaedrus: "Where have you been? And where are you going?"[2] Phaedrus is a wealthy citizen of a noble city who enjoys the pleasures available to young men: he plays at erotic encounters, enjoys civic influence, and likes drinking parties. Phaedrus believes Socrates has asked him where in the city he has come from, but Socrates is asking him where his soul been wandering and where it might be bound. What desires guide his actions and relationships? Is playing at pleasure and prestige all he can hope for? From the world's perspective he has everything a young man could wish for. But from Socrates' point of view, Phaedrus has forgotten who he is and lost the "divine madness" that urges one toward Good. His erotic pleasures are tinged with violence. His participation in the polis is laced with lies. Socrates does not suggest that Phaedrus renounce either love or political life. But he offers a counter-vision, which enables Phaedrus to reorient eroticism so that all of his ordinary desires become woven into and transformed by the crazy love for the True and the Beautiful. Phaedrus is not unlike many of us. Our private pleasures and social identity constitute our real life and we forget the depths of beauty and truth away from which we are wandering.

Teresa of Avila considered the absence of self-knowledge to be the root of our spiritual crisis. She describes the soul as a wonderful, beautiful, diamond-like structure with many chambers winding toward a center of inexplicable beauty. At the center of the "interior castle" the Bridegroom dwells, waiting for us. We hold the divine within us all the time, even if for the most part we do not know or remember it. For Teresa, our deepest problem is that we have forgotten the great beauty of our soul and who dwells there.[3] We lack self-knowledge. We may think it is a kind of humility to despise ourselves or to identify entirely with a socially constructed identity, but she believes this is false humility, a kind of "*ratero*": flying low, creeping, vile.[4] It can also mean petty theft. Our willingness to be satisfied with a low-flying understanding of ourselves is a theft of our true identity. The important moment of awakening is to relocate this identity in a larger context. We wake up to the beauty of our soul and to the unspeakable joy that Holy Goodness dwells within us. For Teresa, true self-knowledge is true humility. It is not self-hatred or unworthiness but a recollection that we are lovers of the divine. In light of this knowledge, preoccupation with our individual needs and anxieties becomes less intense.

Guigo, a twelfth-century monk, also describes the freedom humility brings. "Of what then does he think? Of that which is above him, his

highest good, his God. And the more he sees and loves Go
he sees and loves himself."[5] In wonderfully transgendere
Guigo sings out: "You who are filled with grace, what i:
you bear in your bosom? It is the Lord, and you say, "I ar
maiden, He who is mighty has made me great."[6]

It is our condition to live in illusion and confusion. We endure a
thousand sufferings and indignities, pursuing a thousand meretricious
pleasures, anxious over real and imagined difficulties. We believe in
God but often feel flat and cold toward "him" or alienated because of
"his" bipolar extremes of punishment and forgiveness. Perhaps we are
angry at his impotence in the face of the suffering and injustice that
soaks into every inch of our writhing earth. Contemplation invites us
to acknowledge and reframe these things. But it does so by challenging
many of our root religious ideas.

*faith*

## FORGETFULNESS OF GOD

A contemplative way of life is not simply adding on meditation or prayer
practices to our beliefs about God. It is a wild journey that unravels our
beliefs about God in order to drop into deeper relationship with the
Divine Beloved. I cannot pretend to know any more about God than
anyone else. But in conversation with ancient and modern contemplatives, I propose ways to stretch our holy imagination and to break up
old idols that may not serve us. As we explore what it means to be made
for the Beloved, we commence the adventure of abandoning what we
thought we knew and proceed into the unknown with courage and
determination.

Not understanding who we are, we are also confused about the
Good. We may forget God in the middle of our belief. That is, we
might believe in God but what we worship is more like a demon than
divine—cruel, untrustworthy, hostile to diversity and beauty. Sometimes LGBTQ+ people raised in conservative environments know
"God" only as a savage entity that despises them. Women may think
of God as a male deity for whom the feminine is always second best.
Or we may have a casual acceptance of God as creator and redeemer,
which does not affect our daily life very much. Our real life happens
somewhere quite separate from our religious beliefs. In our deep heart's
core, religion does not go far in consoling us when we are anxious or
despairing. It does not ignite in us a delight in the beauty of life. Our

beliefs may not challenge us to consider what activities genuinely feed us and which are distractions or even irritations.

Who we understand God to be is deeply related to who we believe ourselves to be. If I am primarily preoccupied with my own angers, frustrations, and desires, then I am likely to conceive of God as a divine dispenser of rewards and punishments. In my egotism or my anxiety, this dispensation is likely to follow my own assessments. Because my church rejected me, God, too, must have rejected me. Or perhaps God rejects those people I reject and rewards those I would reward. This punishing God turns us against each other and even ourselves. This God suggests that the world is filled with things for me to use but not care for. It is full of "enemies"—I forget that they are, like me, part of the single fabric of creation. I have learned to attribute to God hostility and condemnation, which is all too human. Or maybe God is just not that involved in daily affairs. I conduct my life more or less without him, even though I feel genuine devotion to and belief in him.

Julian of Norwich was a fourteenth-century anchoress who lived during one of the worst centuries in human history. The black death wiped out more than half of the population of Norwich. Famines and floods were worse than anything in memory. Wars ravaged the land, and wandering mercenaries ravaged its people. The church was roiled by corruption. The French king had removed the Pope from Rome to Avignon to be his puppet. The Inquisition, in all of its savagery, was introduced. Desperate peasants rebelled against crushing taxation only to be ruthlessly repressed. It was during this time that Julian offered an alternative theology "to her fellow Christians who were struggling with despair at the horrors of their surrounding world as well with their own sense of failure and guilt."[7] She believed that a significant part of their suffering was the belief that God was angry and had rejected them. She likened humanity to someone who has fallen into a ditch and cannot see where they are. Their body is full of pain and distraction. They feel isolated because they cannot see that they are intimately connected to God and to all beings. Julian says that the worst part of all of this is that such a person has forgotten God's tender and unconditional love for them and for all creation: "And of all this, the greatest hurt which I saw him in was lack of comfort, for he could not turn his face to look on his loving lord, who was very near to him, in whom is full comfort."[8]

Julian, like other contemplatives, acknowledges that there is a great deal of suffering that is simply part of being human. But what makes this suffering so soul-destroying is that we cannot see how beloved we are. We no longer remember that we are adored and cherished by God. If we could reconnect to God's love for us, we would still suffer, but it would not be so overwhelming. For Julian, self-and-God forgetfulness creates a terrible wound within us and contributes to our destructive behavior while intensifying our anguish. Just as divinity itself is immutable, our identity as beloved of God is immutable. Humanity experiences many difficulties. But our divine Mother cannot allow an ultimate separation to occur. As Julian puts it, "The mother may suffer the child to fall sometimes and to be distressed in various ways . . . but she may never suffer that any kind of peril to come to the child, because of her love. But even if our earthly mother could allow her child to perish, our heavenly Mother Jesus cannot allow us that are His children to perish."[9]

Awakening to this awareness is not only a piece of information to file away, it is a reconstitution of our core identity as well as our most basic sense of reality. When our fundamental experience of the divine nature and our own nature are so radically altered, we experience a *metanoia,* a turning and remaking that is a kind of resurrection not at the end of life but in its midst.[10] By remembering that Divine Goodness is love and loves us, we remember who we ourselves are: lovers of the Beloved, in love with the Holy One's much cherished creation. This *metanoia* is the heart of the contemplative way.

Utter and perfect, timeless goodness, pouring infinitely and eternally out as love and beauty, is the deep truth of reality. The abyss of divine goodness holds everything all the time: being and nonbeing, death and life, terror and happiness. We can fall nowhere but into the arms of this sweet savior. There is not any other place. This is the utopia—the no-place—and every place of creation: the Beloved's unending sweet goodness.

## AWAKENING THE HEART

In our confusion, we find it difficult to recognize the Beloved or see what we are in the sight of this Love. But our confusion does not change our nature; though we do not remember who we are, the divine Beloved has never lost sight of us. "Sweet bird, although you did not see me, I saw you."[11] The divine Mother and Lover waits in the wilderness for us, destitute until we find our way back to the love that is our source and destiny. Our doting Mother, tender Lord, Holy Wisdom, made humanity to be Their own dwelling place. "He wills that we know that this dearworthy soul was preciously knit to him in the making. Which knot is so subtle and so mighty that it is oned into God, in which one-ing it is made endlessly holy.[12] The contemplative path undertakes the journey with the Good back to Good.

We human beings are caught on the fangs of affliction, addicted to things that cannot satisfy us and lost in a thicket so we cannot find our real home. Religion tries to speak to us in our need and reminds us of the reality of something mysterious and sacred. It speaks to us as spiritual, not merely social or domestic or physical, beings. This whisper of the sacred is present in neolithic monuments like Newgrange and in the cathedral-like silence of old-growth redwoods. As spiritual beings we thirst for living water. We thirst not only for a message from our distant lover, not the dead letter of word and idea. We thirst for the living water of the Beloved's sweet presence to us in the inner chamber of our heart. We are made for the sacred and this sacred Spirit has made us a dwelling place for Her own heart. We hunger and thirst, panting in the wilderness, seeking water, and find none. However we try to satisfy this thirst with distractions, however much we love our family or perform good work in our jobs or vocations, we remain thirsty for the living water for which we were created. We cry in the dark, the lamp of our soul dim, the darkness pressing hard around us.

When we become aware of this pain, it is because our heart has begun to wake up and rub its eyes. Pain is the sign of the loss of something good, and when we feel spiritual pain it is because we begin to desire the good that is proper to us, the good for which we have been created. Contemplative practices and a contemplative lifestyle are nurses that tend to this pain. They do not bring pain-relievers, as the world does. They bring healing and life. These nurses are not the emissaries of our distorted self-will, as some of the Reformers seemed to think. The nurses of contemplative practice are the handmaids of the Beloved. If we feel called to contemplative practice, it is because the Beloved has begun to pipe a song to us already:

> The voice of my beloved!
>> Look, he comes, leaping upon the mountains,
>> Bounding over the hills . . .
> My beloved speaks and says to me:
> "Arise, my love, my fair one,
>> and come away . . ."
>
> (Song 2:8, 10)

If you feel any stirring interest in the contemplative way of life, you may thank the Beloved for showing you a way to continue your life of faith, for "What does a [person] possess that he [or she] has not received?"[13]

This awakening has many dimensions and will be unique to each individual. It may arise as a more fervent desire for intimacy with the Holy One. It may also be a more fervent desire to find within oneself the courage to love ever more inclusively and unconditionally or to engage in more activism. It may be the stirring of a new freedom or creativity or a call to shift something about one's life. It may be supported by a set of practices that feed these desires. But it is not primarily techniques like prayer and meditation, reading Scriptures, and so on. Life itself becomes a practice for loving the Divine Goodness and Her world ever more passionately and joyfully. In some sense, it is a call toward ultimate reality, which is known to Christians and other theists as something lovable and intimate. As Aelred, a twelfth-century English monk, wrote to his sister: a contemplative life is "to enable you to stir up the love of God in yourself, feed it and keep it burning."[14]

Spiritual practice can contribute to a stronger sense of vitality and an urgent desire to cast off consoling or terrifying ideologies. It brings us news of another world. Through liturgy and Scripture, prayer and worship, song and community, we are afforded some glimpse of another identity, another truth. A contemplative way of life is the part of religion that gradually transposes faith into experience. We not only believe that God is love, but this awareness also permeates our basic sense of everyday life. We not only affirm the possibility of transformation but also seek to live with unveiled face, reflecting the beauty of the divine, changed into its likeness (cf 2 Cor. 3:18).

Our ego minds may jump between feelings of unworthiness and excessive self-preoccupation. From a contemplative point of view, neither extreme represents our true identity. We human beings bear the divine image: as the desert fathers and mothers put it, we are God-bearers. Like Mary, we are *theo-tokos*, bearers of the divine life. God is love, and in all of our truest loves, we mingle with the divine love for all creation. This is how we are made and why we are made.

## MADE FOR THE BELOVED

Contemplation is distinctive because it shows us that we are not only in a subject-object relationship with God—parent to child, king to servant—but we are also in the process of reuniting our being with the divine reality. We are light. The "flowing light of the God-head" circulates from Love to each of us and through us to one another.[15] As Jesus insisted, this light was not made to be put in a basement or under a bushel.

"If then your whole body is full of light, having no part dark, it will be wholly bright" (Luke 11:36, RSV). In this saying Jesus invites us to remember who we are: we are light and are witnesses to the light. We are partakers of the divine nature (2 Pet. 1:3, 4). And what is this light but the Holy Wisdom dwelling within us? Christians call this light Christ. Other traditions have other names for it. Whatever its name, it is like the bright morning star of our divine nature arising in our hearts (2 Pet. 1:19; Rev. 22:16). Christ shows us what it means to be human, to bear this light in the flesh within and for the world.

> You make each person a home and You dwell within everyone, and You become a home to all, and in You we dwell, each one of us entirely, Savior, with You, entirely . . . listen now to things more awesome! We are made members of Christ, and Christ becomes our members and Christ becomes my hand and the foot of all-wretched me, and wretched I become the hand of Christ and the foot of Christ. I move my hand and my hand is Christ entire. . . . Do not say that I blaspheme, but accept these things. . . . He who is united with us, oh spine-chilling mystery! . . . and they shall see all the things that were previously defiled by corruption as holy, incorrupt, entirely healed over. They glorify the compassionate one, they yearn for the beautiful one, and they are all united to the whole of his love.[16]

Through images like these we are reminded that we are of a noble lineage and we are called to great things. We are beloved of the Beloved. Poor, troubled children of Eve, we have become confused and lost our way. If there is such a thing as sin, it is not the stain of guilt we cannot wash out but forgetfulness that we are held with tender mercy by our Beloved.

## CONTEMPLATION AS DESIRE

In creating us for intimacy with Herself, the Beloved implanted in us a silver thread that will lead back to Her—divine desire. This is the deep river from which flows all good eroticism. Prayer is the "heart's devoted turning to God."[17] But desire is deeper than prayer, more urgent, more insistent. Poet Anne Porter captures the poignancy of this holy desire. She remembers sobbing as her mother sang one day, because something in the song testified to a "solemn glory" her "smallness could not hold."[18] She associates this raw longing evoked by music to a memory of a beauty and intimacy mythologized as Eden. In her poetry, Porter evokes the longing that is well known to contemplatives of every tradition. Our longing for the Divine Beauty and Its longing for us mingle, ceaselessly drawing toward one another. Desire is this longing for what we never possessed except in dreams but which seems to be the essential food and water of the spirit.

Stodgy pastors and theologians have made us suspicious of desire. But the holiness of desire is as ancient as our most sacred texts. "As a deer longs for flowing streams, so my soul longs for you, O God. My soul thirsts for God, the living God" (Ps. 42:1). "Let him kiss me with the kisses of his mouth! For your loving is better than wine" (Song 1:2). If we think of ourselves primarily as reasoning animals, shaped by will and emotion, we will not understand our spiritual nature or this yearning, thirsting, weeping longing for something we have no name for.

One of the most powerful aspects of our mind is desire. We may not be able to wave a magic wand and become more patient, more courageous, more assertive, more compassionate, more balanced. But we can desire these things. We may not be able to translate our vague hope that God is loving into an adamantine certainty and trust. But we can desire this.

Desire is enormous soul energy. More than will power or good intentions, desire orients us to what is good. We can be confused about what is ultimately good or good for us in a particular situation, but the *desire* for the good is like a light that illuminates our steps. Even when we make mistakes, desire keeps desiring the good. Simone Weil insists that spiritual desire brings down the thing desired. It cannot be endlessly frustrated, however long we may yearn, seemingly in vain. Our desire for the Beloved is like a magnet, irresistibly drawing the divine and the human together.

> An Eskimo story explains the origin of light as follows: "In the eternal darkness, the crow, unable to find any food, longed for light, and the earth was illumined." . . . Desire directed towards God is the only power capable of raising the soul. Or rather, it is God alone who comes down and possesses the soul, but desire alone draws God

down. He only comes to those who ask him to come; and he cannot refuse to come to those who implore him long, often and ardently.[19]

The desirability of God is so intense partly because of the infinite sweetness of this love. But it is also intense because, unlike everything and anything in the world, divinity cannot be possessed. The common distortion of desire is to wish to possess the object of desire. Most literally, we digest it like food. But the divine goodness eternally evades our efforts to possess. Poets and mystics describe this yearning for what is most near and ever absent—or rather, whose seeming absence flees in the presence of our longing.

> Where have You hidden Yourself,
> And abandoned me in my groaning, O my Beloved?
> You have fled like the hart,
> Having wounded me.
> I ran after You, crying; but You were gone.[20]

We are bound to the beloved by yearning. When we attempt to possess the Beloved, They flee like a flying deer. But when we allow ourselves to reverse the flow and desire from possession to seeking, we suddenly find ourselves in paradise:

> The breathing of the air,
> The song of the sweet nightingale,
> The grove and its beauty
> In the serene night,
> With the flame that consumes, and gives no pains.[21]

Desire is our trustworthy magic lamp that never goes out. When we are led in a direction that does not serve us, desire stands back up, dusts itself off, and tries again. Desire desires our deepest good and will not give up through all of our crazy wandering. It is "the broken road" that leads us straight to our Beloved—and to all that the Beloved loves.[22] Of course, we do not know exactly how to follow this broken road and make countless (seeming) mistakes. But "if we would know how we shall do all this, let us desire it of our lord and he shall teach us, for it is his own desire and his honor."[23]

This is one reason why contemplatives considered enflaming and redirecting desire to be one of the most important aspects of faith. We all hold many mistaken and unhelpful ideas about God but desire leads us on despite all of our limited ideas. Desire loosens the hold of the idols and images of our small minds. Desire routes our soul energy in the direction of the living Goodness who draws us with the sweetness of desire.

If we think of faith as what we believe, when we are faced with something that makes us change our ideas about God it can seem as if we have lost our faith. What we had believed has proven unreliable, and we make the mistaken leap to the idea that it was God that was unreliable or religion or Christianity—or Judaism, Islam, Buddhism. Of course, nothing is more natural than that we human beings are mistaken about all kinds of things and that our ideas change and grow. My eldest child was a chemistry major and laughed to think that each year the teacher began by saying, in effect, everything you learned last year was either a lie or so simplistic that it completely distorted reality. Students had to learn things step by step, and the first steps were so simple that they were false compared to more mature understanding. What is true for chemistry is infinitely more true of divine reality. We begin with ideas so simple they are at best "loving lies." If we attach to the way we learned chemistry as freshman or the religious belief we learned as nine-year-olds, we will never move more deeply into the truth of these things.

Divine reality is infinitely more unlike our imaginings than our elementary understanding of electrons, and yet religions do not do a good job of teaching us *gladly* to move beyond earlier ideas. We are not taught that our fourth-grade understanding of who God is will constantly change. We leave behind those Styrofoam models of atoms and gain a less literal way of thinking about how electrons and protons work; likewise, we should be trained to leave behind ideas of God that made sense (or not) when we were children or young people and continue to move more deeply into our faith. Life experience, conversation with other religions, new books, and new communities constantly challenge and enrich our faith. When we identify our faith with whatever we happen to think at one time of life, this process can feel painful. We seem homeless with no place to go once our ideas about God or our religion fail us.

But if we connect our faith to desire then this process is exhilarating and delightful. We are less attached to particular beliefs because we are in love with Divine Goodness—not the God our mind has constructed but the ever mysterious and sweetly luring Holy Wisdom of faith. Our ideas may fail us. Our church may fail us. Everything in creation may fail us. But Holy Goodness will never fail us. The Beloved's love for us

faith

does not depend on our ability to get our beliefs just right. Everything about the human mind and heart are fallible. All the beauty of creation is temporary and partial, and in the end it dies; it is not permanently reliable. But we do not have to worry about this because Divine Goodness is not creation. It is not our mind or beliefs. It is not the church.

It is a great relief to know we do not have to be in control of our faith. If we relocate our primary spiritual energy to desire, we have a way to disconnect from the need to be certain and become open to the way faith evolves. We desire to trust God. We desire intimacy. We desire to love creation more sweetly and compassionately. We desire to be more courageous. We do not have to possess these things to kindle a life of faith. Desire will guide us because it is the thread that connects the depths of our own spirit to the abyss of divine love.

## "FLOWERING PARADISE OF MY HEART": GOD OF INFINITE GOODNESS

Desire is a distinctive mark of contemplative Christianity partly because of who we are. But we are who we are because of who Holy Wisdom is. There are many different kinds of contemplatives in the Christian tradition: ascetics, penitents, monks and nuns, beguines, laypeople, mothers, soldiers, slaves, sharecroppers, anchoresses, Quakers, Shakers, and more. But a common thread of all of this literature is the supreme desirability of God. That is, we seek our Beloved Lady Love not to avoid going to hell or to be rewarded in heaven. Dorotheos of Gaza identifies motivations like this as a kind of spiritual slavery: doing good to avoid punishment or seek reward.[24] God is sought because there is nothing sweeter. Tasting this divine sweetness makes the world seem sweeter to us.

Many of these writers evoke a sense of the mutual longing between humanity and divinity. Julian describes the Beloved as "thirsting" for humanity. "For the thirst of God is to draw all humanity into him. . . . And so drawing his living members, ever he draws and drinks and yet he thirsts and longs."[25] Mechthild of Magdeburg describes God's yearning for us in a lovely poem, which imagines the Holy Trinity conspiring in the creation of human beings: "a powerful desire stirs in my divine breast as well, and I swell in love alone. We shall become fruitful so that we shall be loved in return, and so that our glory in some small way shall be recognized. I shall make a bride for myself who shall greet me with her mouth and wound me with her beauty. Only then does real love begin."[26] This is a highly poetic way of speaking, but it captures this sense of the Beloved's ceaseless yearning for and delight in humanity.

Peter of Alcantara, a monastic friend of Teresa of Avila writing in the sixteenth century, described how to begin a meditation practice. He begins with ordinary pious intentions. He bids readers to love God with their whole heart, soul, and being. He encourages them to believe that God is their hope, glory, and refuge. But this advice quickly advances to an intoxication of extravagant love poetry. "O Best Beloved of all, Spouse emblossomed, honeyed and sweet: O Sweetness of my heart, Life of my soul, joyous Resting Place of my spirit! O Day of Eternity, beautiful and bright, Flowering Paradise of my heart, my Creator; most lovable and all sufficient for me!"[27] He asks that God make a dwelling place within his own heart and comes to rest in him. He begs to be wounded in his innermost soul by the arrows of divine love and to be inebriated by the wine of charity. "O Beloved, Beloved, Beloved of my soul! O Sweetness, Sweetness of my heart! . . . O my God, my Loved One and the Innermost Good of my soul! O Love so sweet to me! O Delight so great for me! O my Strength, help me; my Light, guide me!"[28] This almost delirious incantation continues for several pages.

Guigo, a Cistercian monk, also wrote a simple meditation manual that is part advice and part love poetry. He begs for "at least one drop of heavenly rain with which to refresh my thirst, for I am on fire with love." Through "burning words" the heart's desire is inflamed "and by such spells it seeks to call its spouse."[29] The desire for God is "sweeter than honey and the honeycomb." It is a sweet scent as well as a sweet taste—a "garden of delight filled with roses and lilies in its wonderful variety."[30]

The beguines often describe divine presence as Lady Love.[31] But they complemented the gentle wisdom of this divine Lady with erotic metaphors. Mechthild of Magdeburg describes prayer as a kind of divine pillow talk. In one love poem to God she describes a dialogue between the Soul and her divine Lover.

> "Stay, Lady Soul."
> "What do you bid me, Lord?"
> "Take off your clothes."
> "Lord what will happen to me then?"
> "Lady Soul, you are so utterly formed to my nature
> That not the slightest thing can be between you and me."

She is bid to cast off the clothing of fear and shame, leaving only the nakedness of her boundless desire, which her Lover will fulfill with "limitless lavishness."

> Then a blessed stillness
> That both desire comes over them.
> He surrenders himself to her,
> And she surrenders herself to him.[32]

Marguerite Porete portrays the inner stillness of divine goodness as a throne of peace, which nothing in the world can give or take from her. But this peace is not blank quietude; it is unspeakable joy. "Such a Soul, says [Lady] Love, swims in the sea of joy, that is in the sea of delights, flowing and running out of Divinity. And so she feels no joy, because she is joy itself. She swims and flows in joy, without feeling any joy, for she dwells in Joy and Joy dwells in her."[33]

From a contemplative point of view, there is nothing but goodness in God. There is no admixture of harshness. Julian of Norwich observes that notwithstanding the evil, sin, pain and blame we experience: "I saw truly that our Lord was never angry, and never shall be. For he is God, he is good, he is truth, he is love, he is peace. And his might, his wisdom, his charity and his unity suffers him not to be angry. For I saw truly that it is against the property of might to be angry, and against the property of his wisdom, and against the property of his goodness. God is that goodness which cannot be angry, for God is nothing but goodness."[34]

Marguerite Porete echoes this, praising the unimaginable and limitless goodness: "For the salvation of every creature is nothing other than the understanding of the goodness of God."[35] For contemplatives, divinity is a goodness that is entirely trustworthy, utterly enticing, and profoundly fulfilling.

## THE BRIGHT-DARK ABYSS

The bewildering paradox of falling in love with the divine is this: that which is so desirable and so infinitely satisfying remains always at a remove from our ideas about it. This is true in one sense of everything. My thoughts about my children are not the same as their experience of themselves. My thoughts about a bird in flight is not the same as

its living awareness. But the divine does not grant us the physical &
conceptual presence that things in the world offer. The contemplative
path is tolerating and then loving this radical non-possessability, this
intimate absence, this holy unknowing.

Made for the Beloved, we are created in such a way that we are
capable of a deep intimacy with our divine Beloved. This intimacy that
we write so much about is far beyond any words we have. We may
believe that without words there is hardly an experience, but in fact
this wordlessness inflects many aspects of life that we do not think
of as religious. We touch this part of our spirit in prayer, but we also
connect with it when we sing or dance or give birth. When we enter
into the total concentration of step dance, marching bands, rugby, or
golf we access this luminous darkness beyond thought; we are present
to what is happening, and words would only interrupt the singularity
of our attention. But the sweetness of the Good is beyond words in
an even deeper way. Much of our experience refuses to be captured by
language. But the Good is cloaked in impenetrable mystery. It is nonconceptual because no concept or image or word grazes the obscurity
of the divine reality. There is a depth where our names run out and we
meet a profound silence. Desire is endlessly aroused and yet never fully
quenched. It is an aching yearning for deep intimacy, surrounded by
the bright-dark abyss of divine unknowing. Even if we do not have a
name for this part of ourselves, we can know that this kind of unknowing is part of our very being.

The spiritual part of ourselves is a divine abyss. It is a dimension that
is not touched by words, thoughts, ideas, feelings. Divine Reality is not
a thing among things and therefore no word is adequate to God. This
is the part of ourselves capable of awareness not governed by words.
It is not the part that thinks or believes or even has emotional experiences. Writers evoke it with many images: manna, light, darkness, love,
the marriage bed, a wound. To awaken to the bright-dark abyss is to
be constantly hungering and fed at the same time. It is desire not for
possession or certainty or solid belief systems. It is a desire to dispossess
oneself of all of the thoughts and ideas that create obstacles between
oneself and God. Any thought, even a very holy thought, is still a
thought. Talking about a kiss is far removed from the tenderness of
touch. John of the Cross describes God conducting the soul in a secret
way, beyond senses and all creaturely knowledge, beyond all higher
faculties of awareness, beyond an "interior light of the intellect or any

Or as Pseudo-Dionysius chants: "It is not soul, not
ogos, not intellection . . . not likeness, not unlikeness
t at rest . . . It is not dark nor light, not error, and not
versally neither position nor denial of it . . . beyond
eeminence of that absolutely absolved from all and
...c whole."[37] Every image, every category, every affirmation,
every denial remains a word, an idea, a thing among things. These
cannot touch the abyss of wonder. Contemplatives use many images
to disenchant our identification with only our thoughts and feelings
as our only way of "knowing" the Divine Wisdom. Marguerite Porete
describes this unknowing as the disappearance of both ideas about God
and the self-reflection of ego mind.

> I have said that I will love Him.
> I lie, for I am not at all.
> It is He alone who loves me. . . .
> God is tranquil/undifferentiated and I am tranquil/undifferentiated.
> This is the essence and faithful love.[38]

These words are difficult to understand in part because they are point-
ing to an aspect of awareness beyond understanding. They disrupt our
ordinary way of thinking.

We are created so that we hear and touch, think and feel, but these
spiral around a deep abyss, a "precious one-ing" (Julian of Norwich)
because we are made for God. Our eyes can perceive the beauties of the
visible world. Our ears can hear music, voices, birdsongs. Our reason
can track the patterns of the stars, devise healing cures, decipher moral
dilemmas. But God is not something to be seen or heard or grasped by
reason. We manufacture images of God all the time. We become very
attached to our images. But Divine Reality created us in such a way
that we can move outside seeing, hearing, reasoning, feeling.

The abyss-like nature of our soul opens upon the abyss-like nature
of divine love and this can seem excruciating to our creaturely self.
Touching this tender longing is to open a wound that will not heal.
"Where has your lover gone, a fairest among women, where has your
lover turned that we might seek him with you?" (Song 6:1). The
Beloved is absent from our ordinary ways of experiencing the world,
and so we wander and seek. And at the same time, our deep heart
knows: "He has brought me to the house of wine and his banner over
me is love" (Song of Songs 2:4).[39]

## THE PATH OF UNKNOWING

Divine goodness is like the sweetness of honey, the loveliness of a garden, the intoxication of a lover, the tenderness of a mother, the wisdom of Lady Love. Though God's own self is clothed in wordless mystery, love is the first and last thing we know before the Holy One disappears into the darkness of unknowing. Let us adore in silence what remains beyond our understanding.

There is no metaphor or word or concept or paradigm or model or creed or Scripture verse that captures the reality of the divine. Holy eroticism is lured toward a darkness beyond light and dark, a cloud of unknowing, a paradise beyond the wall of reason.[40] If we were the greatest thinkers, theologians, scholars, adepts in the world, everything we know through our understanding is as nothing compared to the depth of the divine reality. As mind slips the noose of conceptual thinking and the will slips the bit of self-assertion, there is nothing left but the sweet nothingness of divine goodness.

God is utterly beyond thoughts and images but manifest in all that is. We love images and poetry just as lovers love to caress one another with their loving words. It is unspeakable, and yet we are driven to speak it over and over. The contemplatives are, in a sense, freed to swim and play in language because they know it does not limit their lover, just as human lovers chant one another's praises but know that it is life itself that is the expression of their boundless love. Because we cannot know or grasp the ultimate nature of the divine, we love the way the divine appears to us. And because we cannot possess final knowledge about the bright-dark abyss of Divine Goodness, we can be grateful rather than condemning of spiritual friends in other traditions. Maximus of Tyre gives generous advice about dwelling in this land between naming God and relinquishing all names:

God Himself, the father and fashioner of all that is, older than the Sun or the Sky, greater than time and eternity and all the flow of being, is unnamable by any lawgiver, unutterable by any voice, not to be seen by any eye. But we, being unable to apprehend His essence, use the help of sounds and names and picture, of beaten gold and ivory and silver, of plants and rivers, mountain-peaks and torrents, yearning for the knowledge of Him, and in our weakness naming all that is beautiful in this world after His nature—just as happens to earthly lovers. . . . Why should I further examine and pass judgment upon Images? Let men know what is divine, let them know: that is all. If a Greek is stirred to the remembrance of God by the art of Phidias, an Egyptian by paying worship to animals, another man by a river, another by fire—I have no anger for their divergences; only let them know, let them love, let them recall.[41]

This unknowability is the abyss-like source of divine desire, the paradoxical interplay between intimacy and mystery, between desire and abyss. Learning to tolerate this absence, this refraction away from every thought or experience or authority, is the path of the contemplative. But for the contemplative this comes to be not only a discipline of detachment but also sweetness of longing and of tasting in which one ceases to praise and becomes pure praise, an unending chant to the divine goodness. For this we are made.

# 3

# *Awakening to Beauty*

"God loves all them feelings. That's some of the best stuff God did. And when you know God loves 'em you enjoys 'em a lot more You can just relax, go with everything that's going, and praise God by liking what you like . . . God made it. Listen, God love everything you love—and a mess of stuff you don't like . . . just wanting to share a good thing. I think it pisses God off if you walk by the color purple in a field somewhere and don't notice it."[1]

"Beauty does not linger, it only visits. Yet beauty's visitation affects us and invites us into its rhythm, it calls us to feel, think and act beautifully in the world: to create and live a life that awakens the Beautiful."[2]

### HEAVEN'S FAIREST FACE

If we are accustomed to thinking of divine reality primarily in moralistic terms, inspiring social justice, or condemning behavior society deems immoral, beauty may not spring to mind as an attribute of Mother Wisdom. Our times have disenchanted beauty. Protestant Reformers were suspicious of beauty and stripped it out of churches and of faith. This denuding of the world of beauty dovetails with a capitalist preoccupation with profitability and efficiency. John O'Donohue argues that the crisis we are enduring can be understood in relationship to this indifference to beauty. He lists the "relentless images of mediocrity and ugliness in talk-shows . . .

> and these shows tend to enshrine the ugly as the normal standard . . . property development creates rooms, buildings and suburbs which lack grace and mystery. Socially, this influences the atmosphere in the workplace, the schoolroom, the boardroom and the community. It also results in the degradation of the environment that we are turning more and more of our beautiful earth into a wasteland. Much of the stress and emptiness that haunts us can be traced back to our lack of attention to beauty. Internally, the mind becomes course and dull if it remains unvisited by images and thoughts which hold the radiance of beauty.[3]

Decades earlier the French Jewish-Christian philosopher Simone Weil also bemoaned the assault on beauty by contemporary forces: "Today one might think that the white races had almost lost all feeling for the beauty of the world, and that they had taken upon them the task of making it disappear from all the continents where they have penetrated with their armies, their trade and their religion."[4]

In contemporary Christianity, the beauty of the world and of the Beloved are preserved primarily in old hymns such as "Fairest Lord Jesus," "Joyful, Joyful, We Adore You," or "All Creatures of Our God and King." But divine beauty is well attested in Scripture and in ancient philosophy and theology. Scripture celebrates the divine creativity, that "stretch out the heavens like a tent" and sends the wind like messengers. It makes "springs gush forth in the valleys . . . giving drink to every beast of the field." Trees are watered and birds build their nests. There is bread to strengthen us and "wine to gladden the human heart." The ocean teams with innumerable things, small and great, including Leviathan "that you formed to sport in it" (Ps. 104:10–11, 15, 26). The beauty and grandeur of creation caused the morning stars to sing together, and the heavenly beings shouted for joy (Job 38:7). The resilience and beauty of the natural world is a sign of hope, even when things are difficult:

> "For there is hope for a tree,
>     if it is cut down, that it will sprout again,
>     and that its shoots will not cease.
> Though its root grow old in the earth,
>     and its stump die in the ground,
> yet at the scent of water it will bud
>     and put forth branches like a young plant."
>                                     (Job 14:7–9)

The beauty of the earth is endlessly diverse and unfathomably complex. Billions of species weave their energies together into an interdependent whole, each necessary to the others. Beyond us, the endless explosion of the stars, galaxies, nebula, suns, moons, planets, black holes, and hints of things we have little inkling of dance across the vast expanse of living and vital darkness.[5] Diversity is the fundamental quality of creation and of all beauty. No single note makes a song. No single sound captures the chant of a moving creek. No flower exhausts the possibilities of color and fragrance. We humans like to keep things small and limited—two genders, one race, one religion, one nation. But the divine creativity is infinitely expansive, playful, dangerous, and exuberant.

Plato believed beauty was the aspect of eternal Goodness that provided the easiest route to the divine because it spoke to us of something deeply desirable. Gregory of Nyssa believed that we are made for beauty because this is part of the divine nature.[6] Pseudo-Dionysius insisted that beauty was a primary name of God. God, the ultimate beauty, was so "charmed" by beauty, She spun entire galaxies into existence to delight in the embodiment of beauty in created things.

> For beauty is the cause of harmony, sympathy, of community. Beauty unites all things and is the source of all things. It is the great creating cause which bestirs the world and holds all things in existence by the longing inside them to have beauty. And there it is ahead of all as [the Beloved] toward which all things move, since it is [the Beloved's] longing for beauty which actually brings them into being.

Beauty "entices" the Good from Its transcendent dwelling place to abide within all things.[7] God is beguiled into the work of creation by the beauty of the world. Imagining this beauty, our divine Beloved sings it into existence. At the same time, the beauty of the Good draws humanity and all creation back to its divine source.

In our love of beautiful things, we are already falling in love with the infinite beauty of the Beloved. A more recent lover of divine beauty insists that faith is not doctrine, belief, or moralism as much as "a response to Divine Beauty . . . a primal attraction, the deepest resonance of the self drawn to the elegance of its ancient origin . . . Such a profound attraction turns the body into a force-field of divine quickening. The whole self is taken up in an embrace of the divine tenderness."[8] As our heart is pierced and wounded by the delicate loveliness and vulnerability of beauty, we fall into the divine embrace, wounded by a tenderness that is perilous and unbearable and yet infinitely sweet. "Naked have I seen thee, O Beauty of Beauty."[9]

This devotion to divine beauty captures something of beauty's paradoxical quality. It is the most vivid and immediate expression of the Good. It enchants us with delightful scents, the nobility of trees, the fragility of trilliums, the poignancy of music, the sweetness of an infant's flesh, the dignity of an ancient face, the inspiration of a noble act. At the same time, what makes any of these things so heart-stirring

is something that is both fully present and yet something more, something that does not appear.

This is the mysterious allure of beauty. It is utterly present to
us—and yet absent. It is the utterly real and also the evanescence of a
divine presence, wafting in and through creation. Through it we taste
the Beloved, and in our tasting awaken to the beauty and tragedy of
creation.

## FALLING IN LOVE WITH THE WORLD

What alchemy allows us to awaken more deeply to the beauty of beings:
the beauty of the earth and the cosmos, moral and spiritual courage,
music and poetry, the precision of drum corps, the grace of athletes
and dancers? There is no answer to this, as there is no answer to any of
the great mysteries of human existence. But I believe becoming alive to
beauty's protean appearances helps us to fall ever more deeply in love
with the world. Divine beauty shimmers and shimmies throughout
the universe and in every barrio where someone is singing or weeping.
Because of beauty, our spirits are enlivened. We can again be enchanted
by the world, lament its neglect and abuse, and feel encouraged to fight
for the well-being of every living thing.

We may feel that so much has burned down that our eyes would be
wrong to occupy themselves with anything but survival or resistance.
Perhaps we are exhausted by empathy for this tragic world. "I must
confess there seems to be way more darkness than light."[10] Anguish or
anger makes beauty seem irrelevant or even a selfish distraction. We
may have become blind to the shards of light we call birds as they
move like music through the sky. Beauty may be nothing but aestheti-
cism or a reprieve offered only to the privileged. I am not opposed to
momentary reprieves, but beauty is more than a respite for a worn-out
or self-indulgent soul. It is our recognition that something exists other
than the projections and passions of our ego minds.

When the world disrobes itself and shows itself naked in its shattering beauty it is almost too much too bear. We have to practice simply
to endure the sheer force of the beauty of the world. For our hearts to
open, like a petal, to beauty requires spiritual energy, and this energy
must be cultivated. Beauty is not for something else, a dose of sugar to
help the medicine of responsibility go down a bit easier. It is the sacred
vitality of beings and of creativity. It is the unique and unrepeatable

wonder of each existing thing and the infinitely complex webs of relationship in which we are all embedded. But beauty has a twin sister from whom she is never parted. Delight in the beauty of beings walks with compassion for suffering. It is not that suffering is primordial, and so compassion and justice are the first spiritual fruits. Suffering is present wherever feeling, living beings exist. But it is not first. Sacred worth, vibrant zest, interconnecting patterns—beauty—is first. When we encounter the suffering or wanton destruction of sacred, beautiful beings, our heart naturally opens in sadness, dismay, lament, compassion, protection, resistance, and healing. Beauty opens the door to the significance of beings, and having seen and recognized this, we can no longer be unmoved or indifferent.

## BEAUTY IS NOT A LUXURY

Many beautiful things seem to be the reserve of the well-to-do: beachfront summer homes, a trip to the opera, or season tickets to Lakers games. Living some place where one has easy access to nature can also be associated with a degree of financial privilege. Buying a bouquet of flowers on the way home from work requires extra money. That some people have easier access to beautiful things reflects the stratification of a society that makes access to good things—food, medical care, good schools, respect—a function of one's tax bracket. To be defrauded of beauty is like being deprived of education or medicine.

We can also think of places more or less deliberately designed to exclude beauty: prisons, many public schools, hospital rooms, desolate urban wastelands, meeting rooms. The absence of beauty is part and parcel of the indignities people suffer in these places—either by design or by default. Poverty is being deprived of basic goods that human bodies and minds need to thrive. Lacking a beach front house may not be a form of oppression, but the absence of beauty is a socially produced impoverishment of the spirit.

Beauty is not a luxury, any more than food is.[11] "Give us bread, but give us roses, too" as the women strikers demanded.[12] Without food, our bodies die. Without beauty, our spirits die. Wealthier people may have more access to attractive things that calm and restore an agitated breast. But they may not have greater access to beauty. Beauty is entirely different from the urge to possess—the vase, the landscape, the winsome body. A wealthy person might collect paintings or wives but remain inert to beauty. Collecting and possessing may be little more than a version of the impulse to impress and dominate. Someone might own an amazing, heartbreaking painting by Rembrandt or Kara Walker and get no more pleasure from it than a miser fingering their gold.

At the same time, people who lack financial resources need not be assumed to lack sensitivity to beauty. The relentless assaults of hunger, ugliness, humiliation, lack of resources, random violence, and loss can gnaw away at the human spirit, leaving it dull and resigned. But the haunting beauty of spirituals emerge from lives of utter degradation. The Harlem Renaissance did not arise out of privilege. In the midst of violent assaults, people living in a South African township collected musical recordings.[13] A thirteen-year-old Syrian refugee writes an award winning poem.[14] Florence Reece, a miner's wife in Harlan County, Kentucky, penned the great labor song "Which Side Are You On" the same night thugs broke into her cabin to terrorize her and her children. Rachel Carson wrote her luminous books about the sea while supporting her mother and nieces on a small salary. A sharecropper sets a glass filled with wild flowers on her dinner table. A student one step ahead of food stamps enlivens their small room with prints, shawls, and music. A fisherman on the margins of survival listens to the arias of Miliza Korjus as he scrapes barnacles off his weather-beaten boat.[15] Gay activists, like thousands of anonymous people before them, gather to piece together a quilt.

Pretty things may be more available to those with financial resource. But beauty is a spiritual matter, and as such it is no respecter of social status. Beauty opens onto the world beyond our private concerns. It is our capacity to delight in something that exists for itself, beyond the reach of our possessiveness. Beauty endures the impossible painfulness of loving what must die. Beauty's weeping sister is compassion. The realm of beauty opens when eros and agape are joined, delight and terror twine together, beyond prettiness or possession.

## OPENING THE WINDOWS

We humans are made for the world. Our bodies and emotions and minds are designed so we can see, hear, smell, touch, think, feel the world around us. This embodied existence gives us access to the world, but only from our private point of view. What we are most aware of is how the world feels to us. The segment of a room or landscape we perceive is determined by where our body is in space. That point of view seems to us the "real" one. The meaning we give our perceptions has a great deal to do not only with the data by which we encounter them but also how we feel about them. Perhaps we walk into a room and get a whiff of musk similar to one we experienced when we were suffering harm. This new room has nothing to do with that event, and yet it takes on some of its horror. Or we hear a fragment of music evoking a sweet memory and the room seems full of happy possibility. For all its infinite vastness and complexity, the world remains centered in our bodily and emotional experience of it. In this sense we are all intrinsically and overwhelmingly egocentric. The world is quite literally centered in us.

This self-centeredness invites us to be good caretakers of our physical and emotional well-being. But this attention to ourselves carries with it the subtle illusion that we are the center of reality. Obviously, this is not true, and yet it is almost impossible to avoid so privileging our own bodily and psychological experiences that other things are real or important only in relation to ourselves. Things matter to us as they come into proximity to us. This makes most of reality invisible and irrelevant. Things of the world are categorized in terms of their capacity to please or threaten our personal perceived well-being. Even the beauty of beings is drawn into my *ego*logical center, serving to ease or please me, forced to translate themselves into objects of my aesthetic enjoyment. This natural egotism is not "sin"—it is just the way we are made. From this centeredness in our own experience, we experience pain and pleasure. We find ourselves entangled in ways of life that do not always serve our deepest joy. We experience privilege, oppression, enjoyment, and diminishment that we do nothing to deserve. We make mistakes, fall in love, behave bravely or kindly, vote, work—we live.

I do not know if this natural egoism ever is extinguished. Liberation from the ego-mind is the dream and promise of Buddhist arhats and bodhisattvas. It is the witness of Christian contemplatives, martyrs, and heroes: John of the Cross, Marguerite Porete, Priscilla and Felicity, Rosa Parks and Fannie Lou Hamer. We see a glimmer of it in the tired mother at the airport, whose endless patience with fussy children reminds us of the ordinary goodness that surrounds us every day. But however lively our natural egoism remains, we still are able to awaken to a beauty that constantly expands our reach, bit by bit, beyond the horizon of what matters to my private ego.

This natural egoism is not like a switch that goes on or off, completely liberated or hopelessly stuck. Awakening to beauty is like noticing a window and drawing back the curtains, then opening the glass, then seeing that the window (unlike ordinary windows) keeps getting larger the more we look out. Sometimes we climb through the window and roam around for a while, less encumbered by the preoccupations of our weary, petulant soul. We feel dewy grass under our toes, notice the chortle of a distant brook. We weep at the lament of a deer whose fawn was taken by a predator. Even when we return to the smaller confines of our little room, the window remains open and the world is more real to us.

## BEAUTY OF CREATIVITY

*National Geographic* produced a series on genius for its magazine and television channel on great geniuses: Einstein, Picasso, Leonardo da Vinci. It is fascinating to explore great minds who have imagined art and ideas that continue to unfold in our understanding. Great works move us as they bear witness to saints, lovers, natural beauty, and historical disasters—the dignity and catastrophe of life. "Geniuses" have the power to unlock what we have faintly perceived but have no words for. Their music, dance movements, artistry opens chambers in our hearts we never knew existed. In cultivating a sense of beauty, exposing oneself to these "geniuses" is very fruitful: museums, concerts, literature, the art of the Tang Dynasty, Bach's cello suites, Billie Holiday's songs, Alvin Ailey's choreography. We witness and participate in the great expanse and brilliance of the human spirit.

Theologian Paul Tillich understood creativity to be an evocation of the divine: "Gazing up at it, I felt a state approaching ecstasy. In the beauty of the painting there was Beauty itself. It shone through the colors of the paint as the light of day shines through the stained-glass windows of a medieval church. As I stood there bathed in the beauty its painter had envisioned so long ago, something of the divine source of all things came through to me. I turned away shaken."[16] African American poet Elizabeth Alexander defends the power of poetry to connect us to one another and to our true selves. It is idiosyncratic because it gives voice to our unique selves—"and are we not of interest to each other?"[17] Artistic creation moves and inspires us by revealing worlds that are ordinarily invisible in such a way that we feel empathy rather than disdain. It expresses our passionate interest in one another. We are able to enter into lives that are alien to ourselves. Films and novels expand our sympathy by taking us to colonial Africa, villages in Syria, slave plantations, dystopic or beautiful worlds glimpsed in an imagined future. Creative expression allow us to feel empathy for someone we might have dismissed. Dickens allows us to empathize with children raised in debtor's prisons or cast onto the street to be recruited by petty criminals. Jericho Brown opens us to the world of black gay men in his poetry. Robert Burns invites us into the poignancy of the story of a broken-down, alcoholic prostitute drinking in a pub that expands our sympathy for those ship-wrecked by life.

> Now I have lived for I know not how long
> And still I can join in a cup or a song
> And while with both hands I can hold the glass steady,
> Here's to you, my love, my young soldier laddie.[18]

Hearing these stories sung so tenderly and poignantly, we recognize the fragile humanity of people we might otherwise ignore or disdain. Art and creativity are happening all the time. In another poem, Elizabeth Alexander describes a series of common actions: sewing, repairing things, making music out of whatever is handy.[19] This common, everyday creativity is everywhere around us. An Appalachian woman is perfecting her biscuit recipe. A cabinet maker is carving perfect dovetails. Someone is dancing in the street or singing with their hands dipped into soapy dish water. A single dad is figuring out how to respond to a confusing moment in his child's life. A young mathematician is unraveling the secrets of Srinivasa Ramanujan's inspired formulas. We can recognize how important creativity is when we notice how energetically totalitarian governments repress it. The failure to support and defend creativity as a cultural value is yet another assault on the spirit of beauty and on the human spirit itself.

Art and creativity remind us of stories we have lost. "Where no monuments exist to heroes but in common words and deeds."[20] Folk songs keep alive stories our texts books have excised from memory. Fairy tales curate a moral world in which the lost and downtrodden become heroines. Work songs remind us why protection of children and fair wages are so important. A song of a massacre or wrongful imprisonment honors lives that have been lost and allows us to lament past injustices.

Whether humorous, playful, celebrating, or lamenting, creativity allows a depth of meaning to infuse ordinary life. In contrast to more consumer-dominated entertainment, it does not distract but inspires. The common or prescribed narrative of a social world is deepened or challenged. A whole genre of ballad offers a tacit criticism of a society whose moralistic patriarchy conspires in the tragedy of a pregnant girl cast off by her lover or murdered by a cruel father. Another celebrates the adventures of a cross-dressing young woman or "fallen" girls who end up happily-ever-after. Creativity is crucial in a troubled world because it looks at the world "slant," as Imogen Lycett Green insists: "Poets are in the fringes of society, they're not in the establishment," she says. "They look at events, at lives, at love and at themselves from a sideways position. And in glancing from the side, the truth can sneak in. If adult poets are seeking the truth, I think children who are burgeoning writers are even closer to the truth."[21]

Creativity allows us to mourn. We are so often invited to pass quickly over private grief or tune out heartbreaking public grief: passing quickly over news of children held in cages at the U.S. southern border or orca whales decimated by the collapse of their environment in Puget Sound. Music and art crack open our hearts and let us dwell in lament. Górecki's haunting Symphony No. 3 uses two Polish folk songs together with writing scrawled on a Gestapo prison wall to mourn not only the Holocaust and battle-fields but the relentless ache of mothers and children lost to one another by war. That a Sirius XM host played this symphony in honor of the families at our border in June of 2018 is an example of the power of lament to stretch over time and generations.[22] Paintings such as Picasso's *Guerinca* or Goya's *Disasters of War* series evoke not just the facts but the spiritual catastrophe of warfare. Dorothea Lang's photograph of a "Migrant Mother," conveys the raw-boned destitution brought on by the Great Depression. The recently installed National Memorial of Peace and Justice opens a jagged wound of pain for our nation's history of lynching. The Irish Famine Memorial testifies to a humanly orchestrated disaster. The Holocaust Museum instills a longing to say "never again." We stop and grieve for these lives cast aside like so many dry tumbleweeds. In helping us to lament the past, art opens us to grieve for lives in our own times that have been given over to mistreatment and despair.

Monuments, literature, rap songs "call forth tears, the aroma of holy work."[23] For Rainer Maria Rilke, the capacity to praise the goodness of life is bound up with our capacity to weep:

> Ah, the earth, who knows her losses?
> Only one who yet praising aloud,
> Sings the heart born into the All.[24]

For poet laureate Natasha Trethewey the recovery of personal and historical tragedies are "monuments" to what has been lost.[25] She uses poetry to tell forgotten stories about domestics, black civil war battalions, race, and the murder of her mother. For her, writing about grief honors the fallen but also provides a back-lighting of hope. "I will say this: as dark as some of my themes are, as painful as they are, the book is about resilience and hope. The writing of a poem is one of the most hopeful acts that one can engage in."[26] It is not the nature of creativity to end in cynicism or despair. The very act of creation is a refusal to accept tragedy as final. Creativity, perhaps paradoxically, allows us to grieve and lament even as it testifies—by its very existence—to the remnant that survives.

Art and creativity open underground rivers in our soul. They give us enormous pleasure. They open us to rich layers of meaning, symbol, and myth. They help us criticize what is wrong with society and celebrate what is right. Imagination allows us to enter worlds we knew nothing about with curiosity and empathy. People's lives come to matter to us more when we have glimpsed the human heart in an unfamiliar setting. Even if we do not especially care for Jane Austin or hip hop, shape note singing, or Dada paintings, they make our minds bigger— our imagination for the human adventure becomes more textured.

It is the power of the artist to do this for humanity. And it is the gift given to every human being to be able to exercise this power. Our consumer culture tempts us to think of creativity as a profession—artists whose paintings hang in a museum or whose songs we hear on the radio. But whoever we are, we can sing our off-tune melodies to children, draw silly pictures, design beautiful gardens, or arrange a handful of daisies in a jar. We can write poetry in a secret journal or sing out LGBTQ+ freedom in the Common Women's Chorus. Cynicism or tedium give way—if only for a moment—and we remember that

> for us existence can still enchant . . .
> words tenderly give way before the unutterable
> and music, always new, from the trembling stones
> builds in useless space her home fit for gods.[27]

## INTEGRITY OF BEINGS

Creativity functions in many ways. I have highlighted some of the ways it can open the heart. But because beautiful things are pleasurable, they might simply revert us to a preoccupation with our private satisfactions. One wants not only to look at the landscape but also to own it—to pick the flower, buy the painting—to somehow halt the ever-changing flow of life and beauty. But beauty is not simply attractiveness. It offers liberation from the prison of egoism. Our capacity for beauty is born when we begin to grasp that other things—people, animals, ecosystems, works of art—have a reality that has nothing to do with us. "The beautiful is that which we desire without wishing to eat it. We desire that it should be."[28]

Each thing exists according to its own integrity. Its desires, enjoyments, sorrows, fears, relationships are almost entirely unknown to me. "One lesson from affiliating with a tree—perhaps the greatest moral lesson anyhow from earth, rocks, animals, is that same lesson of inherency, of *what is*, without the least regard to what the looker on (the critic) supposes or says, or whether he likes or dislikes."[29] What appears to us is only the smallest sliver of what a thing is for itself. This is true even with those we know and love the best. Loving beauty is loving this quality in others: their persistent opacity to my understanding. In appearing to me, something captures my imagination and yet remains infinitely remote from me. This is not isolation or disconnection. It is the way beings retain a mysteriousness, a secret life, that no amount of knowledge or understanding can eliminate. This mysteriousness is not the opposite of intimacy but an element of it. The impulse to dominate and control others is the opposite of this—from ideology's pretense at total explanation, to the battering and belittling of domestic violence, to the degradations of oppression, to war and ecological ruin. Domination is a kind of abhorrence of the secret lives of others, a blindness to or hatred of the way beings escape its total power. The capacity for beauty requires that we *adore* the mystery of others and recognize it as sacred and deserving of protection.

When we taste the spaciousness within beings we encounter something that is both "instantaneous and eternal."[30] They are present as whatever they are but they are also apertures to the sacred. In simply being what they are, they are also news of divine beauty. We

> see a World in a Grain of Sand
> And a Heaven in a Wild Flower
> Hold Infinity in the palm of your hand
> And Eternity in an hour.[31]

Clothed in the wonder of its existence, the "something" of our encounter remains supremely mysterious. Falling in love with the world is loving the mere fact that beings exist whether they have anything to do with us or not. It is enjoyment and delight in the sheer beingness of what is. Randall Jarrell describes this in the chaste love a young woman experienced for an older man: "She felt again the pleasure she always felt at any reminder that he existed: she saved for him St. Augustine's best sentence: I want you to be."[32] What this fictional character felt for a much admired music professor, we can feel for the creatures of the world: I want you to be. In loving the ravaged beauty of a stranger's face, I encounter the sacredness of someone I know nothing about. In loving the half dozen species of moss cozied together in the shade, I admire the gentle interlocking greens, but I also love that these mysterious beings are weaving their complex relationships onto the forest floor in ways entirely unbeknownst to me.

Falling in love with beauty is delighting in the "self" of each thing that is singing out its existence according to its own inner vitality. It exists for itself and not as a fantasy of my thoughts or needs.

> As kingfishers catch fire, dragonflies draw flame . . .
>     Each mortal thing does one thing and the same:
>         Deals out that being indoors each one dwells;
>     Selves—goes itself; *myself* it speaks and spells,
>         Crying *Whát I dó is me: for that I came.*[33]

As Gerard Manley Hopkins puts it, "Each mortal thing does one thing and the same"—it cries out its name. This livingness, this "selving" is like a flame. Each thing is alive and burning with its unique and precious being. This point is obvious and simple. A muskrat swimming across a pond, a child crossing the street does not know or care one whit what I think about it. Its emotional life and bodily pleasures and pains belong to it. Its sense of self is a flame of consciousness burning in the very fact of its existence.

Each thing is its own spark of ego-consciousness, singing out the truth of its being. "What I do *is me*: for that I came." Whether I know or care anything about it is utterly irrelevant to the "*myself* it speaks and spells." I mean less than nothing to the billions and billions of entities that exist in the world. But this most obvious of facts is not at all obvious to our feelings about the world. It is beauty that pierces our natural egoism and allows us to experience the raw existence of a person or dragonfly or the world itself as something beautiful and good. Some glimpse of something as its own center of meaning and feeling penetrates my awareness. In a certain frame of mind, this awareness, as brief and intense as a lightning bolt, is horrifying. The security of my ordinary sense of being at the world's center is challenged. For an instant I become conscious of myself as simply one among trillions of others—no more or less real or important than anything else. To be aware that others exist for themselves effects a strange and disorienting shift in consciousness, perhaps intolerable to maintain too long—others experience the world as if I were nothing but part of their furniture, if they are aware of me at all. The flow of their experience derives from their own pleasures, avoidance of harm, seeking things that enable them to live and live well. Or inanimate things simply exist in the mysterious manner of rocks and breezes, the changing shapes of mountains, the movement of water. We can know almost nothing about the inner lives of created realities, although the pain and pleasure of those most like us can be easier to recognize. If we can get over the horror of dislocation, this stumbling into a fairy world, which has always existed without me, is utterly delightful. How good that all this goes on without me and will continue going on long after I have disappeared.

As aesthetic pleasure expands toward the apprehension of beauty, the integrity of beings dislocates our natural centeredness in our own experience. It is as if cataracts were removed from our eyes or we were restored to a sense of hearing or smell. Something appears to us in its own being, not as it experiences itself—something we can know only very little about—but in the knowledge that it does experience its own life for itself. Some inner stillness deep within our heart allows us to recognize this. Of course, we might already know this. A foraging bear, a fern groping for nutrients in the soil have an existence other than mine. Presumably they are operating out of whatever necessities drive them to seek life and avoid death. But beauty is more than this theoretical acknowledgment that we are not entirely imprisoned in a solipsistic or narcissistic nightmare. We are shocked in the experience of a world that is not centered in our own experience. We are decentered and recentered by a disorienting visceral awareness of the integrity and vulnerability of beings. Wordsworth captures something of this quieting of self-preoccupation so that we are able to "see into the life of things":

> Until, the breath of this corporeal frame
> And even the motion of our human blood
> Almost suspended, we are laid asleep
> In body, and become a living soul:
> While with an eye made quiet by the power
> Of harmony, and the deep power of joy,
> We see into the life of things.[34]

It is glorious that human beings can experience this—that we are able to be aware of something in its nonutilitarian goodness. The tree or forest is not merely resource, but it is a delight to eyes, ears, scent, touch. We awaken to the awareness that our "getting and spending" may be necessary, but it is not total.[35] Maintaining the means of life is not for itself; it is to make life in its fullest sense possible. Food, water, shelter, and community make survival possible, but survival is not the larger point of life (our neo-Darwinist friends notwithstanding). Life loves to live. We know so little about other forms of life, but perhaps the delight in life is why flowers clothe themselves in a bright array of infinitely diverse colors. It is why birds sit on tree limbs and warble out their joy. Song may procure a mate or alert other birds to the sun's daily sojourn, but it is also just plain pleasant to sing. Perhaps female birds are attracted to mates that are most joyful in their song.[36] From a theological point of view, when we say Divine Goodness was charmed or beguiled by the beauty of the earth, we are not saying God was invested, like a good banker, in the increase on his investment, but that life enchants by its own created radiance.

The beauty of nature and of all beautiful things lets us experience the world without a why. It has no reason other than itself. "Let the heavens be glad, and let the earth rejoice . . . . Let the sea roar, and all that fills it; let the field exult, and everything in it! Then shall the trees of the wood sing for joy. . . ." (1 Chr. 16:31–33). This joyfulness is not for something else; it is the purpose of life. Tuning into the raw delight in the world is an opening onto the truth of beings: in brooks, blades of grass, the patterns of clouds, the freshness of rain on a city street, the last dangling leaf, whose radiant red concentrates its entire existence before it falls to the ground.

Beauty decenters our ego by helping us realize that life is its own jus-tification. "For that I came." As our self-centeredness diminishes, the world appears in ever more intense colors, sounds, scents, movements, shapes, interactions, and changes. There is nothing static in beauty. It is ever changing, moment by moment. Nothing is the same as itself even for an instant. Moving through time and ever-changing relationships, beauty is always in motion. We can cling to nothing because there is nothing that lasts beyond its existence at that instant—before it moves onto the next instant, taking forward its past into a novel and zestful future. Beauty is not the security of possession because it is not possess-able. As soon as we try to grasp it, it flies away. The peaceful beauty of one instant may be immediately transformed as you stumble upon a half rotted corpse of a mouse or witness a crow tearing away at the flesh of a tiny bird. These transformations are not, perhaps, aesthetically pleasing, but they are part of the adventure of beauty—the living interdependence of what is, in complex and ever-changing relationships.

## MORNING HAS BROKEN

The way the dull yellow feather lies against the black stripe and white stripe seem a miracle of sprightly loveliness. The chirp, screech, cry, peep, and tap conspire to salute a new day. The faint chant of an almost dry creek bed cherishes the promise of water in this parched place. Trace of juniper or eucalyptus enthrall the senses. One is immobilized by the shocking beauty of scent. Walking down the street, the brilliance of a yellow poppy arrests you in your tracks. Time halts and the world arises simply as an intolerably vivid yellow-orange traces the shape we call "flower." The small lake, hidden in the mountains, "in the middle of nowhere," abounds with entities that mingle, compete, and cohabit: mitochondria, algae, fungi, spiders, otters, bluegills, osprey, wrens, rocks, pebbles, spray of water, scent of decay, and millions more. And all of these constellations of sensation and vitality pass away into the darkness gently governed by Grandfather Death. These intertwining lives belong to themselves and each other: their spring thriving and winter sleep. Whether I or any human mind know anything at all about these lives, they arise, flourish, and pass on the possibilities of existence to other lives, rocks, breezes with which they are entangled. How did I sleep through this? Where have I been wandering?

Perhaps I rolled over in my sleep to notice a pretty flower, a charm of goldfinch. But alert only to my aesthetic experience of another, I failed to register the beauty of things that exist independent of my preferences. But all this beauty—of feather, breeze, or stream—is not aesthetic. Its purpose or meaning is not subtly bound to my need for a psycho-spiritual reprieve as I walk by ocean, garden, or pond. That we can feel pleasure in beauty is good: in this difficult world, we need relief. We need the momentary ease of being in the presence of something that exists simply for itself. But the relief we feel in beauty is already opening us to something beyond ourselves. Beauty reminds us of a world that exists beyond our concerns. And this is the beginning of an awakening to beauty—but not the end.

The adventure of the spirit is not only reprieve. It is also awakening to the reality of others as existing for themselves, in the integrity of their own being and communities of being. Creatures inhabiting different kingdoms (fungi and algae) marry and become lichen. The roots of trees form an extended family of support and—perhaps, who knows?—mutual affection, in some tree-form we will never know anything about. We are all bound together in the great dance of existence, nothing apart and separate. We are in the lineage of the star dust billions of years old. We are aunts and uncles to whatever unimaginable life forms might dwell somewhere in a galaxy a billion years hence.

Awakening to this "without a why" of creation has no purpose other than itself. It is to recognize and participate in what is—not to change it, interpret it, care for it, or adjust it. Being awake is to participate in the flow of what is as it exists for itself. As Sug says to Celie, "God must be pissed off if we pass the color purple in a field without noticing it."[37] Being alive to what is alive is the glory of the human fully alive. This aspect of beauty is important because it emphasizes that other beings in their particularity and in their interconnections exist for themselves, with their own inner life, desires, and relationships. "Useless" beauty frees us from the tyranny of self-centeredness and utilitarian greed—not absolutely, but in glimpses. We wake up to reality in its loveliness, fragility, conflicts, and vitality and realize this is the sacred and holy truth of everything that exists. It matters, not because it matters to me, but because it shimmers with sacred worth.

## FROM BEAUTY TO COMPASSION AND JUSTICE

This singing out the integrity of life is not, of course, fairy land. It is a world in which beings are constantly threatened, in which their integrity is betrayed and assaulted. Poet Lucille Clifton describes this more hard-won song of the self as it emerges against the odds of those who would destroy her. Born already in exile, in a land that makes her—"nonwhite and woman"—a foreigner in her own country. She finds a way to be herself in a landscape that provides little appreciation for the song of herself. This is the defiant fierceness of a woman, mother, poet who "speaks and spells" herself in a context where "everyday something has tried to kill me and failed."[38] Here is the raw beauty not only of "kingfishers catching fire" but also of a spirit celebrating the strength that was not destroyed.

The beauty of her poetry opens us to the power of Lucille Clifton's resilience and thence to awareness of the terrifying vulnerability of creatures. It is as if beauty tricks us. First, courageous delight in the integrity of beings inaugurates a profound liberation that arises, phoenix-like, from the renunciation of the desire to possess or control. The eroticism of wonder displaces the urge to dominate and opens up a pool of ecstasy. Falling in love with the beauty of beings lets us "stand outside of ourselves" (the literal meaning of ecstasy). And, contrary to the calculating advice of the ego, this displacement of self-centered awareness is a kind of bliss. But by letting us feel that others are really real, we become more alert to the brutality of their pain. "Beauty captivates the flesh in order to gain permission to pass directly to the soul."[39] And it is this mysterious inner organ that houses beauty's sisters: compassion, lament, and justice.

When we realize something other than ourselves is really real, that it suffers like we do and sings out its name like we do, compassion and justice naturally arise. "The poet produces beauty by fixing his [sic] attention on something real. The act of love is produced in the same way. To know that this man, who is cold and hungry, really exists as much as I do myself, and is really cold and hungry—that is enough. The rest follows of itself."[40]

Each of us will be more alive to some kinds of suffering than others. We will be called into consolation and resistance in ways appropriate to our abilities and circumstances. As one of the mystical fathers of the civil rights movement, Howard Thurman, put it, "Don't ask what the world needs. Ask what makes you come alive, and go do it. Because what the world needs is people who have come alive."[41] Courageous beauty will awaken us to the world's needs, but our unique vitality will guide us to the work best fitting to us.

Whatever our vocation turns out to be, conveying to one another how beautiful we are, how important and special each of us is, is a special work of compassionate resistance. Rosemarie Freeney Harding identifies beauty and joyfulness as essential to her civil rights work. This capacity for beauty was imbued in her from her childhood:

> As I think about my family I ask myself, "What helped them survive? What was it that gave them the capacity to navigate their way through so many obstacles?" It had something to do, I'm sure, with knowing they were of great value. No matter what messages we got from the outside world, someone at home was always telling us how beautiful we were, how intelligent, how talented.[42]

This awareness of one another's beauty in its erotic, purposeless joy is the seedling for the birth of compassion and justice. The celebration of this beauty of beings, their communities and ecosystems, cannot exist without mourning assaults on them. Death comes to all things, but wanton destruction and greedy exploitation are painful interruptions of the dignity and grandeur of life.

Beauty does not remain in the rapture of presence, but in this rapture the journey toward others is animated. Emptying ourselves for beauty we become instruments of the Good. Eros weds kenosis.[43] Because of our delight in beings we join the drum corps of bodhisattvas and lovers of the gospel by embracing their commitment to relieve suffering and seek justice for all.

# 4

## *Practice*

"If you desire to pray as you ought, do not sadden anyone. Otherwise you run in vain."[1]

"One of my first tasks as a young organizer in the Southern Freedom Movement was developing an interracial social service project and community center called Mennonite House in Atlanta, Georgia, in the early 1960s. . . . Because of my mother's example, I understood very clearly how important it was to have spaces of refuge in the midst of struggle. Spaces of joy and laughter, good food and kind words. In fact, this kind of compassionate care is a transformative force in itself. As the Cape Breton novelist Alistair MacLeod writes, 'We are all better when we're loved.'"[2]

A contemplative way of life concerns what we think and do. But it is more fundamentally how we are disposed toward reality. I have argued that we are made for the Beloved and created with a capacity to recognize the profound beauty of all of creation. This is our essential nature, our inheritance and destiny. But the great paradox of human life is how alienated we are from this nature and how difficult it is to recover living intimacy with the Beloved. It is difficult to love creation with abandoned joy and searing compassion. Modern Christianity often emphasizes that one is a Christian by believing certain things. But for two thousand years Christians have also affirmed that it is possible not only to believe but also to live the path of transformation. This path is a kenosis that empties us of obstacles to our love. It is an eros that recognizes the beauty of beings. It is agapic love, cherishing the well-being of others—all others—as one's deepest desire. A contemplative way of life is one that is disposed to deepen these capacities, even as it embraces with gentleness and patience all of the experiences of life that seem alien to these desires.

Every person, community, and historical epoch will understand the path of transformation differently. I am proposing in these next chapters not a single style of contemplative practice but some examples that might nourish your own thinking. This chapter describes some basic principles about how and why practice is necessary. Chapters 5, 6, and 7 describe ways to work with mental habits and chapter 8 describes ways to dedicate periods of time to meditation and contemplative prayer.

## PRAYER AND THE SUBTLE BODY

As we will see in the next chapter, the mind is like an iceberg; much of it is hidden from us and out of the reach of immediate control or even awareness. Contemplative practice addresses all of the dimensions of our existence, those parts of ourselves we are aware of and those that we are at best only indirectly aware of. It affects our thoughts, our emotions, our habitual mental patterns, breath, body, and non-dual or nonconceptual awareness. But contemplative prayer itself operates at a more subtle level: it *uses* thoughts, breath, images, concentration, and open awareness, but it is itself not any of these things.

In addition to those parts of ourselves we are most aware of, we are made also of something for which I have no good word for—spirit, chi, prana, energy, subtle body—different traditions evoke it with different terms.[3] Ancient languages had words to evoke this subtle, inner life energy: *ruach, nephesh, psychē, pneuma, anima*; *prana*, chi, subtle body. It is neither mind nor body but is spirit, incarnate within us and yet also unconfined by flesh. It is activated in prayer and activates prayer. It opens eros and agape not only in our mind or actions but in the subtle spirit which infuses every part of us. It is the unnamable nearness of the divine Beloved within us.

The Hesychasts utilized a number of methods for working with "energies," including breath, visualization, mantra recitation, certain body postures, meditation, and ascetical practices.[4] More recently, Cynthia Bourgeault evokes a sense of this energetic aspect of prayer. In an early work, she describes chanting the psalms as a kind of Christian yoga.[5] Her book on the Trinity also describes the energetic level of contemplation. In a much more sophisticated argument than I am portraying here, she depicts the non-dual divinity expressing itself in the materiality of creation, bathing and circulating through reality. The unmanifest eternity becomes manifest. "'Let there be light.' And photons, galaxies, suns, trees, time, history, waves, tumbled into existence."[6] The Holy Substantiality of the divine is "the *cause* of created being, it is in fact its innermost nature—the root vibration of being itself."[7] This ongoing creativity inflects not only the materiality of the cosmos but also actualizes "more subtle qualities and aspects of the divine being that can be expressed in no other way. Examples of these qualities include equanimity, gentleness, joy, forgiveness, forbearance, generosity, compassion, dignity, boundless creativity."[8]

It is this holy vibration that circulates throughout the entire cosmos and illuminates the sacredness of all that is. Our spirit vibrates with Holy Sophia and the "gate of heaven" opens to us everywhere:

> Within the breadth and depth of Christ's "pneumatic corporeity" . . . the physical world now contains a world within a world: a world where the husk has cracked open to reveal the grain, where what sparkles in everything is the quality of its aliveness. The Kingdom of Heaven is the enlightened radiance of the eye that looks straight into being and sees that it is the Body of Christ—each bird, leaf, tree . . . totally transparent to the love that is its source and its destiny . . . our human lives are set ablaze to release the root energy of love, and we discover to our amazement just how much love can be borne in human flesh.[9]

Prayer is both periods of contemplative practice separated from the demands of life and also the interweaving of the practice of the presence of God into everyday life. Through prayer, we integrate the spirit or subtle body with unconscious and conscious experience. A raw and difficult insight might break through. A feeling of deeper calm and of heart-opening may arise. Or in mostly unconscious ways, our spirit begins to vibrate with divine harmonies.

## WHY PRACTICE IS NECESSARY

Early Christians thought that participation in the Jesus movement involved repatterning one's way of life. Before Christianity emerged as a distinct religion, people simply said they followed the Way or "the way of life." It was an intentional commitment that reorganized their entire lives. Christians from different parts of the empire and from different backgrounds understood this Way differently, but the heart of it was quite simple. The writer of the Didache described it in this way:

> There are two ways: one of life and one of death! And there is a great difference between the two. On the one hand, then, the way of life is this: first: you will love the God who made you; second: you will love your neighbor as yourself. On the other hand, the way of life is this: as many things as you might wish not to happen to you, likewise, do not do to another.[10]

Then and now, people have discovered that this simple "way" is actually very difficult to put into practice. Early followers of Christ understood these commandments as descriptions of a fully human life that they were called to live with all seriousness. To do this, they emphasized the role of concrete practices that would help alter the heart. So the simple description that opens the Didache is immediately followed by a series of trainings that will make love of God and neighbor the most intimate and spontaneous constitution of personhood.

> And for an assimilation of these words, the training is this: speak well of the ones speaking badly of you, and pray for your enemies, and fast for the ones persecuting you; for what merit is there if you love the ones loving you? Do not even the gentiles do the same thing? You on the other hand, love the ones hating you, and you will not have an enemy.[11]

The first training turns out to be even more difficult than the description of the way. But it was intended with all seriousness. This idea of loving one's enemies is one of the most radical of Jesus' teachings. There are few things that require a more complete transformation of the heart than the capacity to experience agape for those who are violent, harmful, cruel, and destructive. The first training places the death of the ego-mind and its way of navigating the world at the forefront of trainings in Christianity. It is the essential *metanoia* (turning around, transformation of the mind) that opens the door to the kingdom of God. Through this training, we encounter others, even dangerous and difficult others, not through the ego-mind's fears and hostilities, but as beings of sacred worth. To live this way required constant and dedicated practice.

Ancient Christians believed that practice was necessary because the way of life was quite difficult. It was not simply a matter of believing certain things. When they thought of practice, they had in mind chanting the psalms, bodily asceticism, prayer, and Eucharist. But, as the first training indicates, they also meant psycho-spiritual transformation of the mind. It was not enough to go through the motions of worship. The mindset one brings to prayer is as important as the prayer itself. Origen, like the author of the Didache, insisted that one must approach prayer with a pure mind, stretching "out 'holy hands' by thoroughly purging the passion of 'anger' from his soul and harboring no rage against anyone and by forgiving each the sins he has committed against him."[12] Marguerite Porete describes a similar kind of radical love as a precondition of contemplative prayer: "We neither do, nor think, nor speak toward our neighbors anything we would not wish they do toward us. These commands are of necessity for salvation for all: nobody can have grace with a lesser way."[13] For many of us, loving and forgiving everyone while putting aside our needs, anxieties, and desires is more the long-awaited fruit of prayer than its precondition. But we understand how seriously earlier Christians took the Christian path when we hear how insistent they were that inner transformation for love and mercy was both the path and the fruit of contemplative prayer.

Even if we are not prepared to wait until our anxieties and hostilities are completely pacified before beginning a period of prayer, we can undertake spiritual practice with the desire for radical compassion. We can make this intention concrete by dedicating our prayer to the flourishing of others, perhaps particularly those most vulnerable or those most tormented by hatred and selfishness. We can continually kindle a wish for the state of inner freedom that enables us to pray for persecutors and desire the well-being of all creatures. Setting this kind of intention allows us to lean into transformation, even if these ideals forever elude us.

## PRAY UNCEASINGLY

I have no way of knowing what Paul meant in his letter to the Thessalonians when he included in his list of recommendations that they pray without ceasing (1 Thess. 5:17). I would be surprised if he intended the little band of would-be Christ followers to stop everything they were doing and sit in a continuous state of prayer. But this phrase has been incorporated into contemplative Christianity and invited serious reflection. Interpreting it as a demand for unwavering attention to God may not be very helpful. But it does remind us that prayer can mean many things.

In the following chapters I am going to describe two general types of contemplative prayer. The last chapter describes a variety of practices that require the ability to carve out a few minutes from ordinary time to turn toward a period of concentration and attention. These practices include different kinds of body prayer (breath, yoga, chant) as well as forms of Christian meditation (centering prayer, *lectio divina*). It is not always possible during some periods of life, but when it is possible, finding time for dedicated practice is very useful and powerful.

To sanctify ten minutes for mindful yoga or ten days for silent retreat allows us to consciously weave our awareness into moments of intimacy with the Beloved. Over time, this dedicated practice is deeply nourishing and can be surprisingly transformative.

Another kind of practice is to weave contemplative intentions into everyday life, so life itself becomes the practice. The distinction between prayer and ordinary life blurs a bit. There are a number of ways to think about this. Because so much of our mind is hidden from us and because our mental habits are so engrained, noticing what our mind is doing and finding ways to understand it better is not a practice limited to sitting in meditation. It is a practice we can do all the time, gently weaving it into daily life. These two kinds of prayer nourish and inform each other, inviting our love for the world into the different moments of life.

## MAKING FRIENDS WITH OUR MENTAL HABITS

Before we consciously think or act, we *feel* the world in ways that are mostly unconscious. It is as if we all look through colored glasses at the world and see the world as already interpreted as rosy or dull-gray or sickly green. This feeling-tone will determine our thoughts and actions. If we are disposed to be suspicious, then the stranger will be thought of as a potential threat, and we will act accordingly. If we are disposed to be cheerful, a frustrating experience will not disturb us too much.

Many contemporary texts about meditation and contemplation focus primarily on methods. These are extremely helpful and full of wisdom acquired from deep practice. But methods of prayer or techniques of meditation do not necessarily by themselves effect the transformations of the heart that contribute to inner freedom. Our minds have habits and structures that fundamentally shape how we experience, how we feel, the world. Our habitual mental patterns determine what enters the foreground of awareness and what remains background noise. They determine what we deem important and what is irrelevant. They shape the preconscious attitudes that determine how we will interpret a new experience or a stranger's face or the news we hear. They create the background mood of experience—a general sense of depression or enthusiasm, shyness, arrogance, adventure, unease—that colors our encounters with the world. Meditation and contemplative practices certainly shape these habits. But it is also important to address the inner working of our minds directly.

## HABITS OF THE HEART  *reason*

The dispositions of our heart dictate what we experience, what comes easily to us and what is difficult or seemingly impossible. They frame how we encounter others, what we notice and what never rises to our attention. Our mental conditioning may make an employee at the airport or restaurant invisible to us. We do not spare them a glance. It might make us suspicious of persons of a different race, gender performance, ethnicity, or religious expression. Our conditioning might provoke contemptuous thoughts to anyone we see driving an SUV or using a plastic bottle. But none of these attitudes have anything to do with what we are encountering. They tell us about how our mind works but do not tell us anything about the SUV driver, the airport employee, or the trans man at work. In this sense, what we encounter is not the world but our own mental habits. In order to fall more deeply in love with the world, we must address our habitual ways of knowing and feeling.

The heart is so central to our experience of the world, it is odd that English lacks a good word for spiritual knowledge and awareness, a transformative way of knowing that combines head and heart, wisdom and compassion, intuition and insight, spirit, feeling, understanding.[14] But heart is an ancient word for this. The "heart" is not emotion. It evokes spiritual awareness as central (the heart of the matter) and as genuine and sincere (heart-felt). It also suggests a kind of awareness that integrates all the parts of oneself—intellect, emotion, action.

There is a story that when neuroscientists first went to study the brains of advanced Tibetan meditators, the meditators laughed when the scientists put all sorts of wires on their heads. The scientists thought the meditators were laughing at the strangeness of their machinery. But the meditators were amused that the scientists thought that meditation was a matter of the head when in fact spiritual awareness is located in the heart. However we understand the relationship between brain and heart, for our purposes I will use both "mind" and "heart" to evoke this mysterious intellectual-heart-feeling form of awareness. Mind and heart are not two different organs of awareness. They are simply different aspects of the practice of paying attention to the way our mind/heart works. Chapters 5, 6, and 7 propose ways of thinking about this habitual but nearly invisible kind of awareness.


## PSYCHOLOGY OF THE SPIRIT

We are usually only barely aware of our mental patterns and have little idea how deeply they affect what we see, feel, know, and desire. They are often at odds with our conscious values and self-image. Someone might seem very charismatic and self-assured. But in the hidden closet-under-the-stairs of their mind, they remain an unloved child, constantly in need of affirmation and terrified of loneliness or failure. Until that unloved child is raised to consciousness and tended, it will manifest in overwork, sabotage relationships, and inflict a mysterious anxiety. Someone else might be a dedicated activist, passionately working to alleviate injustice and bring about a better world. But they are eaten up with unconscious hostility or arrogance. They despise not only "oppressors" but also people who remain outside the struggle, and, eventually, their comrades-in-arms who have a slightly different opinion about strategy or priorities. The ideal of justice and compassion crashes against an attitude of contempt.

Earlier Christians were preoccupied with this aspect of contemplation. They provide relatively little specific information about techniques of meditation. They may have taught this orally, but only a small amount of that was passed down in writing. Early monastics were aware that the most difficult obstacles to freedom and agape are inside our mind. These are mental patterns we have acquired from our parents and home life, our religion and society, our personality, and our experiences. In order to live into a more open and welcoming awareness of the world, it may not be enough to spend time in verbal prayers or meditation. We must also decolonize the mind.

Christian contemplatives believe that it is necessary to pay attention to the way the mind and heart work in order to unearth the heart's secrets and to tend to patterns that inhibit our freedom and love for the world. In our own time, we may be more likely to see a psychotherapist to help us explore our psyche—which is often a very good idea. Contemplatives thought that everyone suffered from problematic mental habits. A "normal" mental state required sustained attention in order to discern how to tend to positive and negative habits. They thought of this attention as a kind of prayer. They believed that this prayerful attention was only possible when it was sustained by faith and love. Without confidence in the nearness of our Beloved, the interrogation of our mental habits can be too painful.

One of the great scientists of the mind was Evagrius Ponticus, a desert ascetic in Egypt who lived in the last part of the fourth century. He advised contemplatives to constantly observe the mind, noticing what thoughts arose, how frequently, and what seemed to provoke them. He called for a very close analysis of how one's own mind worked in its minute and obscure or invisible machinations.

> It is the approach of dynamic psychoanalysis with its emphasis on careful observations upon one's most interior and spontaneous thoughts in their risings and fallings, in their associations and relations to one another. . . . For Evagrius such observation was a form of searching for God. He simply assumes that Christ would have an interest in assisting such a monk to interpret his findings, for it would obviously be an aid to spiritual growth.[15]

For Evagrius, this attention to the workings of one's mind, together with meditation and other practices, were the essential building blocks of transformation. He opens his text on practice by insisting that faith, combined with attitudes of attention and patience give rise to inner peacefulness (*apatheia*) no longer governed by negative mental patterns. "This *apatheia* has a child called *agape* who keeps the door to deep knowledge of the created universe. Finally, to this knowledge succeed theology and the supreme beatitude."[16] For Evagrius, there is a sequence to the contemplative life. One is motivated to practice by love of God and of humanity, but one must train this desire by carefully watching the mind. As the mind is gradually pacified, one's desire to love others deepens into a felt experience of genuine compassion for others and happiness in their well-being. This sincere love for other beings is the necessary condition for a joyful awareness of divine reality.

Centuries later, Symeon the New Theologian and other Byzantine monastics continued to develop this style of contemplation. In a famous text attributed to him (though perhaps written by someone else in his monastery), he emphasized the danger of exotic or ecstatic forms of prayer. Instead, he insists that the most important contemplative prayer is to "guard the heart." His understanding of this was bound up with the ascetic monasticism of the Hesychasts.[17] But there is much wisdom in his writings that can be transposed to our contemporary context. For me, the most interesting idea is that contemplation is not ecstatic or supernatural experiences but is most primordially a way to guard our heart. A focus on "experience" can be distracting from the main purpose of contemplation. Turning attention to our heart/mind does not mean we protect it from suffering. It means that we pay attention to those thoughts and habits that interfere with our capacities for love, courage, and true freedom.

Symeon points out that negative thoughts and actions are not self-generated; they flow from habits of the heart that remain mostly invisible. In order to alter thoughts and actions, it is essential to unearth these habits. It is only by getting to know our heart more intimately and working with these negative habits that we will become freer of destructive thoughts.

> Hence they abandoned all other forms of spiritual labour and concentrated wholly on this one task of guarding the heart, convinced that through this practice they would also possess every other virtue, whereas without it no virtue could be firmly established. Some of the fathers have called this practice stillness of the heart, others attentiveness, others the guarding of the heart, others watchfulness. . . . But all alike worked the earth of their own heart, and in this way they were fed on the divine manna.[18]

More recently, Thomas Keating, Cynthia Bourgeault, and James Finley are among those who turn attention to how the mind works, how it is affected by meditation, noticing mental patterns and the painful resistance to changing them. In their different ways, they emphasize both the centrality of relinquishing our overattachment to our ego-identity as well as the painfulness of this gradual transformation.[19] With characteristic gentleness, James Finley likens this process to a small child who is crying because she is afraid to start kindergarten. Her parents, like our divine Beloved, feel compassion for her suffering but also gently encourage her to move past her tears and fears and enter the new place. "When we sit in meditation, we take the little child of our ego self off to school, where we must learn to die to our illusions."[20]

## DISPOSITIONS, WATCHING THE MIND, GUARDING THE HEART

By paying attention to the habits of mind that nourish or disturb us, the entire self is brought into contemplation: thoughts, emotions, dispositions, breath, body, relationships, action, and nondiscursive awareness. Contemplative practices provide a synergy that affects all of the dimensions of our existence. Monastic settings, which were the primary loci of contemplative practices in Christianity, practiced disciplines around food, sex, sleep, manual labor, chant, liturgy, prayer, meditation, hospitality, holy reading, and contemplation—each element supporting the others. Laypeople need not imitate monks, but we can explore how our mind, action, heart, and body conspire to support or thwart our contemplative desires. How do our habits around what we eat, watch, read, listen to, buy, clean with, vote for, wear, and think make us more alive to beauty? What unconscious dispositions open and close the world to us? This kind of attention helps integrate our whole self, seen and unseen, into a contemplative path. Nothing is separated from the Beloved and nothing is separated from a contemplative way of life.

One reason this is such a harrowing practice is that many difficult realizations arise that we have previously managed to conceal and repress. We cannot bear to see those ugly parts of ourselves unearthed, so alien to our intention and self-image. We cannot bear to feel so naked and exposed in our intransigent imperfections. Our ego mind has been hard at work to preserve us from those aspect of ourselves that are too painful to acknowledge—a bad memory, a feeling of guilt, a disturbing habit we can neither abandon nor ignore. These inner thoughts and patterns have been repressed in part because they are too painful to acknowledge. But we often add to this inherent discomfort the addition mental pattern of condemnation, disgust, or self-loathing. When this extra layer of afflictive thought patterns is activated, the difficulty of guarding the heart is doubled. This may be why Evagrius affirms that this process is prayer. It is done with the help, guidance, and care of Christ. Unless we understand that the investigation of our mind is done in the context of the Beloved Mother who cherishes us, it will be even more painful or impossible.

As James Finley points out, these feelings of shame and unworthiness are themselves afflictive habits that must be transformed for the fullness of freedom and life to live. This is even more difficult if we cling to the idea that God condemns us for our imperfections. The fear that God is condemning us makes it even easier to become stuck in the paralyzing horror of our inner thoughts. Paradoxically, "we do not want to give up the illusion that our weaknesses are obstacles to God's love for us. The perception that our weaknesses are real in God's eyes is bound up with our egocentric perception of ourselves outside God's sustaining love."[21] The difficulty of watching our mind can be exaggerated when we imagine God is our enemy in this process, rather than our tender guide and sustenance. There is a

> subtle violence inherent in our impatience with ourselves. . . . Compassion is the love that recognizes and goes forth to identify with the preciousness of all that is lost and broken within ourselves and others. At first it seems as if compassionate love originates with our free decision to be as compassionate as we can be toward ourselves. . . . As our practice deepens, we come to realize that in choosing to be compassionate, we are yielding to the compassionate nature of God flowing through us, in and as our compassion toward our self as precious in our frailty.[22]

Guarding our heart is a kind of religious psychotherapy. It is prayer. It allows us to ease into the awareness that the Beloved is intimately present with us throughout this process, cherishing and loving us in all we do, in all we are.


## RELIGIOUS EXPERIENCE

The religions of the world are aware that the human mind is subject to a wide variety of experiences, often occurring in the context of prayer, fasting, meditation, retreat, and so on. People sometimes experience visual images, auditory sounds, an insight or command. There are several things that might produce these experiences, and Christian contemplatives tended to be cautious in interpreting them. Premodern language notes that these experiences might just as easily be from the devil as from God. Or put in modern contemporary terms, we may experience something arising from the subconscious, a bad dream, wishful thinking, fatigue, or mental habits. Some experiences may be wholesome and encouraging. Some are problematic. Christian contemplatives considered the art of discernment to be a crucial element of their practice, a discernment ideally undertaken with the guidance of a wise companion. The fact that an image or idea arose in prayer does not necessarily mean it has any particular significance or value. It might even lead us astray.

Christian contemplatives went further, however, in their caution against religious experience. Though they acknowledged and sometimes described interesting ecstatic or visionary experiences, they also recognized that these experiences are at best something that might arise in early stages of practice. Even an experience that is wholesome and helpful can be destructive if we attach too much importance to it or believe it gives us some special authority. Anything that generates a feeling of arrogance or superiority is to be met with extreme suspicion. This is true also when we are looking for good teachers. Someone who talks a great deal about their experiences and realizations but does not necessarily display humility, kindness, and wisdom may be very charismatic but not trustworthy.

Rather than desire experiences or grant them significance, Christian contemplatives advise us to focus instead on the interior progress we make. On this long path, whatever contributes to our compassion and equanimity are to the good. Experiences, good or bad, are simply phenomena and should not distract us from the joy and discipline of a contemplative way of life.

## DISCIPLINE OF REGULAR PRACTICE

In addition to the attention to mental patterns, contemplation also invites us to identify periods of daily or almost daily focused prayer or meditation. Establishing some pattern of regular prayer is somewhat like jazz improvisation—it has a structure and derives from tradition, and yet it is undertaken somewhat improvisationally, especially if one is a layperson, making one's way in the absence of a tradition or community. Meditation practices offer lyrics, chords, and melodies that we may learn about from various traditions, in and beyond Christianity. We learn a great deal from those who are learned in meditation and contemplative practice. It is beneficial to subject oneself to a teacher, a small group or community, or spiritual director and to learn from their accumulated wisdom. We do not have the experience to know how to interpret what is happening without some external support. The practices, teachers, and communities we learn from can sustain and delight us. But it is also necessary to pay attention to our own inner wisdom. Christianity emphasizes the unique movement of the Spirit in each of us, according to our distinctive gifts and needs, according to the distinctiveness of the present moment we are in. We are each irreplaceable refractions of the divine life. The contemplative path is not imitation of someone else but the discovery of our own innate and unique beauty, vulnerabilities, and pathway. A community or spiritual director can help guide us in this process.

As in all things, this dance between community, direction, and inner wisdom requires *discernment.* When is following one's own intuition an act of handing oneself over to inner demons and destructive mental habits? When does obedience or emulation violate the wisdom of one's inner being? How does one work with advice that is good but impracticable? In one book, a wise and experienced monk blithely advises parents of young children to take an hour out of each day for meditation and contemplation—apparently ignorant of lives in which taking five minutes out of the day is a herculean or even impossible goal. Some teachers insist that it is necessary to tough it out and continue the practice even in the midst of increasingly severe depression or PTSD symptoms. Is this wisdom, or is it reinjury? Practices of discernment are an essential element of the spiritual path, because it can be difficult to identify bad advice or distorted intuitions.[23]

Because we are always in the middle of uncertainty, and our understanding remains constantly inadequate to our desires, it is necessary to draw on the spirit of generosity, gentleness, and compassion as we experiment with periods of meditation. The assumption that meditation or other spiritual practices "should" be a certain way can sabotage one's experiments. In training the heart to experience the beauty of beings, it is crucial that we love our own fragile little egos, our wounded hearts, our distracted minds. It may be that the greatest benefit of spiritual practices comes from this practice of compassion exercised toward oneself. In this way we can cajole the heart to open like a flower, so the spirit of gentleness radiates to those we meet.


## ESTABLISHING A PRACTICE

In our busy world, as laypeople who work and have families, establishing a contemplative practice can present major difficulties. There are no patterns to follow, only your own life and the mysterious blowing of the Spirit. There are many books providing helpful advice about this. My own suggestion is to place the bar very low. If three minutes is what you can get in, then three minutes is your practice. I am not disputing the benefit of longer periods, ideally twice a day at least, dedicated to contemplative practices and meditation. I am simply observing that there are many situations that make this ideal unobtainable. But it is possible to lay claim to contemplative desire, even if the only "practice" is to remind yourself of this desire in the midst of overwhelming obstacles.

It is wonderful to find a special space that helps you carve out time: an altar, a corner of a room, images of sacred and calm. But Catherine of Genoa had to snatch moments here and there to pray in a closet in her busy hospital. Giving even one or two minutes a day to contemplation is actually a powerful practice. It may be too little to effect the brain in ways scientists and advanced meditators describe. But it does feed the desire for silence and prayer when life circumstances are conspiring against you. It is a tiny rivulet, which may seem too small to count, too small to be worth the attention. But even the tiniest stream, the most minute turning of the mind toward the divine, dwells in eternity. In a mysterious way, clinging to this desire, this thirty-second prayer, can open the next door.

Catherine of Genoa notwithstanding, when it is possible, finding time and place for focused practice is a selfless act of devotion to your romance with the Beloved. Silence and solitude are like fresh water for a parched soul. The Beloved dwells in silence, and in quieting the internal and external noise to which we are always subject, faint stirrings of awareness are allowed to tenderly peep up. There are no names adequate to Unmanifest Goodness, no teaching, no word, no thought, no experience, no symbol. Silence is communion with this wordless depth. At a superficial level, it is simply calming external noise. More profoundly, it is the language of the spirit. "The divine school is held with mouth closed."[24]

Silence is not the language of our society. Every square inch of space is crammed with noise. Airports blast the news, elevators provide Muzak, new cars turn on the radio along with the engine, televisions stay turned on as background noise. It is as if the idea of quiet is so threatening that every opportunity must be maximized to make sure there is no scrap of mental quiet in which someone might reflect, pause, consider, stare for a moment into space and the empty beyond.

One must be deliberate about carving out moments of quiet, where background noise has been minimized. It might entail finding a place where sounds are more natural—a walk in the park, a stroll by water. Sometimes creating some sort of white noise can help drown out the cacophony. But if possible, refrain from always filling up silence with soothing music or other meditative sounds. Let the air calm down.

Silence also means quieting the mind, reducing the chatter and ruminations of the mind. This is difficult and one should not feel discouraged if the pitter-patter of thoughts continue, even if on tiptoe. Even a great contemplative like Teresa of Avila invited patience when our mind keeps on clacking away like a flour mill. Meditation is in part working with practices that contribute to inner silence, a gradual calming if not elimination of mental noise. This quiet, however imperfectly achieved, is deeply nourishing. It facilitates an interior calm but also connects us with the divine silence, the ambrosia of the spirit.

To the extent possible, nourishing silence supports a contemplative way of life. For some, this might mean periods of silent retreat or solitary camping trips. In one's home, it might be possible to dedicate a room or small corner as a place for meditation—an altar, a candle, a comfortable way to sit, a book of readings, the accumulating good energy of hours of prayers. Lovely! Structure a pattern of prayer that might include a few minutes of yoga or stretching, chant or mantra, a sacred reading of Scripture or poetry or Al-Anon's daily text. Set an intention. Time a period of some form of quiet or meditation. Conclude with prayers for others, dedicating your time to the good of the world.

For others, silence and solitude may have to be stolen by lingering in the bath just a few moments longer than absolutely necessary or leaving the noisy house to take the trash outside as the sun sinks down, enrobing the sky with color. It might be relishing the still moment before the house awakens, as brief as listening to the dawn chorus while sipping tea or nursing a baby. What is possible varies a good deal from person to person, and from one period of life to another. It is important to be realistic about the conditions one creates for inner prayer and silence. However infinitesimal, every second of conscious quiet feeds the soul and plants seeds that will grow in unexpected ways.

A friend described an encounter with James Finley at a retreat. A mother of a young child complained of her frustration that everything she was learning during the retreat would be impossible once she returned home. It seemed that her child had a magical ability to tell when she was trying to meditate and would wake up just as she began. James Finley, in his delightful way, suggested that she might think of God gently prodding the baby awake in order to share the feeling of tenderness between mother and child. The mother wanted a period of prayer but the baby was making it impossible. This sense of the divine Goodness incarnate in the infant joy in mother's lap may not be what she thought of as "meditation." We can certainly sympathize with her desire for a few moments to herself. We can appreciate how nourishing periods of meditation are. But weaving life with the Beloved with our real life is the core of contemplative practice—not second best but the flaming beauty and intensity of prayer itself.

Be a jazz musician, an improvisational dancer, working with whatever possibilities present themselves at different periods of your life. What is most important is the intention, the desire to fall in love with the world. Do not be discouraged by the things that interfere with your intention. They are all also part of the practice.

# 5

## Contemplative Dispositions

"Our task must be to free ourselves by widening the circle of compassion to embrace all living creatures and all of nature and its beauty."[1]

"Then the day came when the risk to remain tight in a bud was more painful than the risk it took to blossom."[2]

"There is but one thing needful—to possess God. All our senses, all our powers of mind and soul, all our external resources, are so many ways of approaching the divinity, so many modes of tasting and adoring God."[3]

### QUALITIES OF PRACTICE

A contemplative way of life seeks to enhance love and compassion for the fragile beauty of all beings—the white daisy whose fleeting beauty graces a walkway, the gnarled grandeur of an ancient tree or human face, the endless madrigal of the stars. Such a person opens the "ears of her heart" to the stories of strangers whose plight moves her heart and to the flow of life in her dearest friends. The courage to fall in love with the tragedy and loveliness of beings arises from the dark-bright abyss beyond being in which our thoughts dissolve as we adore our divine Beloved. A contemplative way of life deepens a sense of empathetic connection with friends and strangers

The mystery of what opens the heart to this relationship with reality is unsolvable. Why do some feel the world so intensely—so aware of its beauty and suffering—while others are inert to it? A contemplative wishes for this disposition to be enflamed in them, but it is not as if they can simply purchase a jar of Delight and Compassion at the pharmacy. Contemplative practices are meant to cultivate a deeper attention to reality, but they cannot directly produce this attention. The liberation of this capacity for empathy, appreciation, delight, and compassion is not like hitting a billiard ball correctly so it will predictably plop into the pocket. A contemplative way of life involves particular disciplines, but it also involves the moods and dispositions that provide the constant background to our thoughts and actions. It may be that attending to these mental patterns is more important than the practices themselves. By paying attention to our habitual dispositions, we can reshape our mental habits in gradual but substantive ways.

A contemplative way of life is in it for the long haul. It is not a six-week class that jostles with all the rest of life and is easily forgotten. It represents a sustained commitment to intensify desire for a joyful, compassionate relationship to the divine and to creation. A thousand obstacles present themselves to this desire. As one pacifies one obstacle ten more leap up in its place. Our fantasy of becoming one with God, being motivated by unconditional compassion and feeling more peaceful, is constantly thwarted by the reality of our ordinary life. The commitment to a meditation practice gives way to distraction. Our enthusiasm for a volunteer project wanes. Our work for social justice flags or degenerates into irascibility and contempt. Our destructive emotional patterns prove incorrigible. All of this can seem discouraging, as if all of our efforts are pointless. But it may be that we have simply misunderstood the way a contemplative way of life works.

Like the happiness of married life, contemplation does not consist only of moments of ecstasy or graceful peace. Married life is the dailiness of life together—negotiating housework, relaxing together for a moment or two at the end of a long day, slumbering through each other's snores, doing things together and doing things apart. If we expect marriage to be a fifty-year extenuation of that moment at the end of a romantic film when lovers fall into each other's arms, we will be disappointed. When conflicts arise or aridity sets in, it is necessary to realize that change demands a deeper examination of the relationship. What once was is no longer true. And so the partners courageously imagine a different future for themselves. The sweetness of youth and beginnings gives way to a ripeness and depth that young love can hardly imagine. The deepening of relationship is only possible if it finds ways of working with the starkly ordinary periods as well as with the unpredictable hard times.

One must expect conflict and aridity, just as an athlete anticipates a difficult maneuver. Where for ordinary people, intense physical challenge may be overwhelming, it is the delight of the athlete to call out their best physical and psychological resources. For this they have trained, and this allows them to master their art more perfectly. A contemplative way of life will be difficult, and whatever we thought was going to happen is the least likely to actually occur. A familiar practice suddenly becomes impossible. A traumatic event derails everything. In the trash heap of a hopeless situation, the stars suddenly blaze forth. Moments of defeat or utter confusion suddenly blow open the confines of imagination, and there is so much more than one ever expected.

A contemplative way of life is perhaps most of all the nurture of attitudes that undergird the changing landscape of belief and practice so that, whatever is happening, whatever one believes, there remains a fiery determination to continue the journey. A contemplative way of life burns with an urgency nothing can deter. It rests in a faith—not a belief or even hope—against which no darkness can prevail. Even if everything is in tatters and one's heart is pulverized, if all the dreams have failed and one's suffering is unbearable, "Until my fire goes out, I will praise you."[4]

## THE MIND IS AN ICEBERG

In thinking about the issue of attitude and disposition, we begin to recognize the multidimensional, multilayered qualities of mind. Mind is like an iceberg, which reveals only the tip of itself. Almost all of the action is undersea, difficult to see, and easy to crash into. Attention to our own mind is a powerful spiritual practice because normally we are so habituated to our patterns of thought we are hardly aware of them. This means that most of what we do and think is automatic, unreflective. Our natural, spontaneous way of experiencing the world is second nature. We do not give it a thought. The way we experience the world is shaped by the accidents of our embodiment, home life, and broader culture and society. Paying attention to our mind means raising up these preconscious, naturalized ways of experiencing ourselves and the world for analysis and reflection.

Meditation itself may do little to dislodge negative mental patterns. Someone might meditate with great discipline, enjoying many seemingly supernatural experiences. But if their underlying disposition is arrogance or scorn for others, it is not an effective contemplative practice.[5] The attitude of prayerful attention can help us become more aware of some of these personal and social habits.

In any moment of experience, we encounter some content—we see, hear, think, feel. But the conscious experience is shaped by desires and intentions of which we have little awareness. These give a general shape and valence to what is happening. The perceived content is given more density by the attitudes we take up about it. "This is frustrating." "That is ugly." "It is too cold." "I hate that color." "I adore my children." "I need some pie." That is, we experience whatever we are experiencing through the shading of our attitudes and emotions. If we are learning a piece of music, we are aware of the notes we see on the sheet, the fingering, the sound. But our attitude toward it is as important as what we see, hear, do. If we feel frustration, it will color everything about how we experience our practice. If we like to practice or love the piece of music, then the difficulty of a piece will be a pleasant challenge instead of an irritating obstacle. If we are tired or agitated, our concentration flags and our fingers make mistakes, making it seem as if the piece is harder than it is. The experience of learning the piece comprises many layers, some of which we recognize, some of which are in the background or invisible altogether.

Beneath our attitude toward learning this piece of music is a general disposition that shapes how we dispose ourselves toward the world. Perhaps a generalized anxiety remains in the background of awareness but shapes how the world presents itself. The world seems to be difficult, and minor obstacles are overwhelming. They prove we are incompetent, as we already knew. For someone else, a sense of adventure makes even severe obstacles seem more like high mountains that we *enjoy* climbing.

These dispositions are partly conscious and partly subconscious. We may typically respond to something with the idea that it will be great! A new adventure! Let's try it! Or we might typically respond with hesitation and want to analyze it a bit more. For one person the world is an endless parade of fear and anger. For another it is calm and relaxed. For others it is an endless round of humiliation or a constantly evolving set of responsibilities that must be accepted. The world may be colored in grays or in pastel colors or in vibrant primary colors. Events take their meaning against general feeling tones that pre-shape our experiences. In thinking about the general attitudes with which we practice, we are bringing to consciousness some of these patterns through which we have preloaded our interpretation of the things we encounter. We engage not only the discipline or activity at hand, but we also work with the layers of consciousness that predetermine our psychological and spiritual landscape.

Contemplation, more than most other ways of thinking about how the mind works, focuses not only on what is presented to awareness but also—and perhaps most of all—to what is buried in our unconscious and yet active in determining what we see, think, feel, do. Practicing with dispositions is indirect and subtle because we are only dimly aware of them. Because dispositions and mental patterns are it on the border-land of consciousness, we have to approach them more indirectly.

We all have particular and unique personalities. That is to be celebrated. We should not wish to replace our actual self with a fantasy or ideal of what we think we should be like. Some aspects of our personality might not serve us. Working with dispositions gives us an opportunity to tend to habitual anger, fearfulness, cynicism, discouragement, and so on. Other aspects are important to who we are, and learning to ride them well rather than repress them is important. In *A Wrinkle in Time*, Meg is characterized as flawed and temperamental. By contrast, her younger brother, Charles Wallace—whom she greatly admires—is described as spiritually mature and wise. And yet it is Charles Wallace who quickly succumbs to the enticements of the evil Black Thing. When Meg is sent to save her father and Charles Wallace, the angelic beings bless her only with "her faults." Needless to say, Meg is not thrilled by this. A burning sword might have been more welcome. But it was her spiky, loving anger that gave her the wisdom and fierceness to succeed. Her anger was not rage, not hatred, not belittlement. But it was her righteous energy that saw clearly through evil's deceptions and gave her the courage—the heart—to penetrate the Black Thing's defenses and rescue her father and brother. Our faults may not serve us. Or they might be what we most need, especially when we direct them toward the Good.

Ancient Christianity, like other religious traditions, was very interested in analyzing and reshaping mental habits. It left relatively little information about techniques of meditation, though Christians certainly did a lot of meditating. By contrast, in our own time, we focus a good deal on techniques but little is said about the underlying patterns that control our experience and response to the world. This may be because technique is easy to teach and easy for scientists to study while mood, disposition, and mental habits are much more difficult to work with. But without attention to mental patterns, technique does not go very far. It is like learning to correctly plunk out notes on a piano while not having a clear sense of what the music should sound like.

There are several layers of thinking about the mind that are at work in these chapters. One is attention to the way our own mind actually works. What habits, what patterns, what dispositions and emotions color our way of experiencing the world? Because these are deeply embedded in our fundamental way of being in the world, we may not be very aware of them. But contemplation allows us to begin to explore mental patterns that shape us deeply but unconsciously. Another layer is the mood we bring to our life and work, a general kind of response to things. It may be that we have a habit of harsh or sarcastic judgment, or we are very controlling of our environment and of other people. We may constantly belittle others or whisper an endless tale of our incompetence in our ear. Perhaps we operate out of a general mood of warmth and graciousness. A third layer is conscious practices that we can deliberately undertake to affect how we feel the world.

This chapter describes examples of positive attitudes and dispositions that texture our experience of life: gentleness, nonjudgment, relinquishing control, wonder, and adventure. I emphasize that these are examples. You will discern for yourself what attitudes and dispositions shape your experience and how you want to work with your mental habits.

An important caveat is needed as we begin this reflection: Dispositions are not like a water faucet—on or off. They become weaker and stronger, they morph into something else. We are unlikely to wake up one morning and find that the mental habit of unworthiness or of bad temper has disappeared with the morning dew. But we can *practice* to enhance mental patterns that are life-giving and disempower habits that do not serve us. We decolonize our mind a small scrap of land at a time. Or perhaps working with our mind has a spiral structure to it. It keeps circling around the same framework, and so it can appear as if nothing changes, and yet it does progress. Difficult habits weaken. Positive feelings root a little more deeply. The contemplative habit of working with the mind is a dance in which steps go forward and backward and yet continue to whirl in beautiful motion. It is important to remember that the cultivation of positive dispositions is always a work in progress.

## GENTLENESS

We live in a time obsessed with achievement—and the shadows this produces: paralysis and laxity. The attitude of gentleness can be a powerful antidote to gnawing perfectionism as well as to the expectation of a quick fix. Naturally, we will "fail" innumerable times in our efforts and intentions. Habits of condemnation and frustration promise that we will have a stormy time of it. A story told of Thomas Keating, one of the people who developed centering prayer, describes his response to a nun at his workshop. After a period of centering prayer, she complained that her mind had wandered away ten thousand times during the twenty minutes. Father Keating smiled and said, "How wonderful. You were called back to Christ ten-thousand times."

The spirit of gentleness can be honored as a general attitude that guides us as we practice. This spirit orients us to *the way* we practice more than to *what* we practice. Bringing gentleness into our practice softens the spirit of judgment and self-condemnation so we can focus more on the practices themselves. It can become a general attitude that shapes how we encounter the events of our day.

For example, we may have an image in our head of what meditation should be like, and when we fail to approximate that, we get frustrated: "I'm no good at this!" As we sit quietly on our pillow, an incessant cloud of worries, regrets, and trivialities bite at us like a swarm of mosquitoes. In addition to all of these importunities, we invite in the biggest bug of them all—we condemn ourselves. Distractions that preoccupy us are themselves shouted down by the voice that loudly points out what failures we are. Or as we review the past few months, we may be frustrated to discover that we seem to be just as tormented by memories or tyrannized by temper or paralyzed by indecision as ever. We harshly judge our "failure" to make spiritual "progress."

These are occasions to invite in the spirit of gentleness. Our mind is like a kindergarten room filled with unruly children: It is easy to be impatient with a room full of rambunctious children. But it is lovely to be able to be patient with them. Naturally children are active—it is their job. And naturally minds and emotions are busy. It is, if not exactly their job, at least their predisposition. We cannot expect our minds to be something other than what they are. It is the nature of the mind to occupy itself. It is the nature of the emotions to struggle with the complexities and difficulties of life. That they do this even when we are desiring a calmer mental state is natural. We simply work with what we have at the moment. In fact, working with the present moment *is* the practice. It is this work with mental states that makes the practice, not a fantasized state we are trying to obtain.

This gentleness is an ally in all of the aspects of a contemplative way of life. However imperfectly we respond to things and whatever mistakes we make, we can remember that imperfection and mistakes are an inevitable aspect of life. We need not despise ourselves or others for this truth. As Julian of Norwich insists, our Beloved Mother God does not condemn what she has made— and neither should we.[6] Approaching frustration and mistakes in the spirit of gentleness removes a layer of distraction from the practice. When we cultivate a spirit of gentleness, we can pay attention to whatever is happening and not add the mental noise of judgment, impatience, and condemnation.

The practice of gentleness extends beyond the attitude we take up about our own practices and patterns. As we practice gentleness with ourselves, we are more likely to be gentle with others. As we become habituated to the spirit of gentleness toward our perceived shortcomings, the shortcomings (real or imagined) of others provoke us less. And, of course, as we continually fail to experience this gentleness with either ourselves or anyone else, we can gently smile and remind ourselves that calm in the face of frustration may be a long-term project.

## NONJUDGMENT

Related to the spirit of gentleness is the practice of nonjudgment. Nonjudgment does not mean we have no opinions or that we cannot tell the difference between cruelty and justice. There is a kind of cynicism in the pretense at ethical neutrality, as if nothing mattered. But the governing energy of a contemplative way of life is a devotion to the good of creation. This is not an ethically neutral stance. Nonjudgment is something different from ethical indifference. Contemplation can contribute to a practical wisdom that helps us discern more clearly what is ethically called for. But this ethical wisdom is different from the habit of judgment and condemnation. Elie Wiesel attributes this attitude to the Baal Shem Tov: "Not to judge others was one of the Baal Shem's principles; his function was to help, not to condemn."[7]

Nonjudgment is primarily a stance of openness toward what one encounters. When we encounter someone or something, what we experience is dominated by our preestablished categories and emotional valences. This is most pronounced in our encounter with people through racial, gendered, class, and ethnic categories. When we meet someone, we typically do not see them as a whole person. We see them as an example of a black man, a trans woman, a Jew, or a sorority girl. Too often, the actual content of our experience is of our own categories rather than other people or situations. This is true of all of our experiences. "I hate malls." "The countryside is boring." "This kind of music is stupid." "Rural Americans are ignorant." "New Yorkers are arrogant." Nonjudgment is a pause that opens a small gap between one's prefabricated assumptions and the world.

Nonjudgment invites us to observe what is happening without rushing in to say "how wonderful" or "how horrible." We can appreciate something we have accomplished without attaching too much importance to it. We can acknowledge a confusion or shortcoming without rushing in to condemn it. Nonjudgment can create a zone, if only temporarily, in which we pause in the rush to judgment. This pause invites space for deeper truths to peep out and show themselves. We may discern elements of a situation that the rush to judgment had obscured. Perhaps the student always late for class turns out to be a newly single mother with four young children. Perhaps another is struggling with grief and insomnia. For them to show up to class at all is dedicated accomplishment. Did my condemnation serve anyone? Perhaps my irritating indecisiveness is leading to a more nuanced perception. Perhaps the mistake opens a path that would have otherwise been unexplored. Or maybe noticing our own mistakes without judgment helps us to be patient when others make mistakes. Or being patient with others when they become confused or misbehave may bleed over into a nonjudgment for ourselves.

By creating temporary nonjudgment zones, we create a small amount of space where beings can simply be what they are, and we do not have to try to control the situation by springing to judgment. For example, a difficult memory might spring up. Ordinarily, we might feel overcome. Or the painfulness of it makes us immediately distract ourselves. Or we fall into a familiar pattern of blame, guilt, anxiety, despair, fear. In the nonjudgment zone, we create a tiny space where this memory can simply exist. It is neither good nor bad. It is a memory. We are in the nonjudgment zone—it cannot hurt us. It might come bearing tidings. Because this is difficult, it may not be reasonable to expect it to endure for long. But every second in which we can forestall judgment creates just a bit more space for things to be simply what they are.

This nonjudgment zone can help us in unexpected moments of experience. Before we rush in to impose our assumptions about what is happening, we pause and simply pay attention, with curiosity and openness. Some time ago, two neat and proper church women of my acquaintance were headed toward a retreat house in rural Georgia. They had car trouble on a Sunday afternoon in a tiny southern town. A very large man on a very large Harley, sporting a motorcycle helmet from which sprung two large Viking horns appeared on the scene. In the inimitable accent of rural Georgia he offered to help. This was not the kind of help they were looking for. In the end, he directed them to a garage in town that would fix their car on a Sunday afternoon. He drove across town to pick up a part, and when that was not enough, the next day he drove to Macon to pick up the required part. It turned out that he had a friend a few houses down from the retreat center where they were headed. The women began their retreat with a wonderful practice of nonjudgment. Whatever category of white, Harley-driving, horn-wearing, Georgia-drawl-talking southern man they had placed him in eroded, and their world expanded.

It is good to keep a good "weather eye out" when traveling in unfamiliar places. People can be dangerous, and it is good to have healthy instincts of self-preservation. But it is also good to fall into the nonjudgment zone and allow our habitual responses to pause. Dimensions of a story we had been ignoring may appear. Our immediate emotional triggers may be pacified. Judgment can be slowed down when we observe (as irritating as it is to admit it) that we sometimes do similar things. "Such was the man who saw his brother doing wrong and groaned, 'Woe is me; him today—me tomorrow.'"[8]

Nonjudgment can accompany, though not necessarily replace, a discernment that a person is dangerous or a situation unjust and destructive. That is, one can passionately resist injustice or the harm someone is causing. A zeal for compassion moves us to protect the vulnerable and to disempower destructive persons and policies. Nonjudgment means that even in this situation, one withholds a blanket condemnation of a person or group of people. Even if they are acting with malice and have been extremely destructive, they remain beings worthy of concern. When we imagine the violence of their interior life we may taste a bit of compassion for what it would be like to exist as such a hell-being. Even as we do whatever is possible to defeat their actions, we can pray for them and wish for their healing and ultimate well-being. Dorotheos of Gaza wisely points out the links between criticizing someone, condemning them unjustly, and despising them. He notes how easy it is to move from a criticism of an action to contempt. Even if we are correct that an action is wrong, contempt for others is very damaging to the spirit.[9]

This point was emphasized by a number of the heroines of the civil rights movement. Rosemarie Freeney Harding describes a practice of keeping a picture of a Klansmen in her room and praying for him every morning and evening, insisting that even if he never knew it directly, it would affect him.[10] She argues that struggle can generate enormous compassion. Struggle "gives me something I need to share. It gives me an understanding of what it is to go through some of the world's worst trauma—to know that people *can* and *do* go through these things and *survive*. To know that we can bring magnificent light out of shrouded places."[11] Fannie Lou Hamer describes this kind of compassion for racist hatred: "I feel sorry for anyone who lets hatred wrap them up. No way I can hate anyone and hope to see God's face."[12] In these examples, nonjudgment did not mean that Harding or Hamer had no opinions about racism or racial violence. But their resistance to violence did not require them to utterly condemn those enslaved to destructive ideologies.

A caveat to this is to say that violence and injustice can be so soul-destroying that nonjudgment may not be the first attitude that it is healthy to take up. There may be a period when anger is more healthy. We need to feel our genuine feelings, especially when we have been harmed or witness to harm. Nonjudgment is a practice that may come later. It experiments with the capacity to recognize harm or wrongdoing but not despise wrongdoers as if they were no longer human, no longer deserving of membership in the family of beings. In some cases, this may take a long time or never feel authentic at all.

When we are able to enter the nonjudgment zone, we can pick up an experience like an interesting rock and turn it this way and that. There is new space around it so the usual patterns of response are deactivated. This requires courage and practice. It is good to start on easier experiences than the most difficult ones. Nonjudgment is perhaps simply spaciousness: it creates space that allows things to appear without being immediately colored by our assumptions and moralism. We need not be so immediately reactive. We can allow things to be seen that were invisible to us. Our sympathetic systems expand, and we allow more beings to enter into the zone of lives that matter. We become more tolerant or resilient when we face the inevitability of limitation and error.

## PEACEFULNESS AND RELINQUISHING CONTROL

It is both natural and important that we human beings enjoy some agency over what we do, think, feel, and the effects we have on the world. When we consciously choose good, we seek to employ our agency in ways that will benefit ourselves and others. When we take up a contemplative way of life we make choices, undertake disciplines, and exert effort that we believe will enhance our relationship to the divine

Goodness and to the good creation. And yet we do not control the outcome of our actions. We may have intended some good that backfired.
We may have said a word to a stranger that, unbeknownst to us, gave
them the precise help they needed at that moment.

This absence of control can be frustrating. If we are going to undertake various actions, we want some assurance that we will end up accom-
plishing what we are striving for. But this does not seem to be how the
world works. We affect things, but we do not control the outcome of
our efforts and intentions. In our own time, the fantasy for complete
control is very strong. Many people become anxious or angry when
they feel out of control. But the very fact that we are interdependent
with other beings means that there are many other forces influencing
us that have nothing to with our intention. Our subconscious habits
may derail us in ways that are invisible to us. We may strongly intend to
overcome an addiction or an abusive relationship and put great energy
into recovery. But we may be up against neural networks or social forces
that undermine our efforts. We may work very hard on a campaign on
behalf of women's rights, and yet our work comes to nothing. Generations of women marched and struggled; they were starved, beaten, and
imprisoned. But they never saw any indication that women would ever
receive the right to vote. A commitment to veganism is impossible without the luxury of time to cook and access to high quality ingredients. A
desire for a more contemplative life might be thwarted by the constant
demands of young children or the need to work three jobs. "In the final
analysis, we are not the masters of everything we do."[13]

In the midst of an out-of-control world, religions offer a picture of
equanimity that does not depend on controlling outcomes. It is not
that people do not act in the world with intentions, but they are able to
generate a feeling of inner peace even if they cannot control what happens. In the closing passages of Jesus' "Farewell Discourse" in the Gospel of John, he promises his disciples peace: "Peace I leave with you; my
peace I give to you. I do not give to you as the world gives. Do not let
your hearts be troubled, and do not let them be afraid" (John 14:27).
Jesus is talking to his followers on the night he was arrested by Roman
soldiers and soon after tortured and executed. It is difficult to imagine
anything further from peace. And yet it was precisely in that moment
that Jesus introduced his followers to a dimension of peace that comes
when every effort has utterly failed.

The offer of peace is a frequent theme in the writings of ancient
Christianity. "The Letter of Peter to Philip" attempts to encourage

Christians who are (quite rightly) terrified of what will happen to them. It concludes with an appearance of the resurrected Christ. He tells them: "Peace to you . . . joy be to you and grace and power. And be not afraid; behold I am with you forever. Then the apostles parted from each other into four words in order to preach. And they went by a power of Jesus, in peace."[14] In The Gospel of Mary, it is Mary Magdalene who stands in the place of Jesus to encourage them. The Gospel opens with a scene of terrified and weeping disciples: "if they did not spare him how will they spare us?" they ask. Mary speaks words that not only advise them but imbue the power of holy equanimity to them: "'Do not weep and do not grieve nor be irresolute, for his grace will be entirely with you and will protect you. But rather let us praise his greatness, for he has prepared us and made us into human beings.' When Mary said this, she turned their hearts to the Good and they began to discuss the words of the Savior."[15]

In these passages, the followers are not promised that everything will be alright. They are not promised that their efforts will succeed or that they will not suffer. To the contrary, the authorities are arresting and brutally executing Christians. The words of Christ or Mary do not change this. But they are being offered the power to retain some element of inner equanimity no matter what is happening. When we pray or work we wish for a positive outcome. This is an excellent thing to work for. But it is not always what happens. We should not identify the presence of divine Goodness with a guarantee that we will achieve the desired results. There are many causes in this world and sometimes disaster triumphs and efforts fail. The mental discipline necessary to keep our balance when our good efforts are frustrated is an essential element of contemplative mind-training. This habit of courageous peace can underlie emotions that still stir the surface. Even if we are afraid, frustrated, or grieved, another layer of our mind can remain calm.

We are vulnerable to external and internal forces that thwart our intentions. In addition, there is a mysterious, unpredictable quality to the effectiveness of our efforts. One person may meditate for years and only reify their negative mental habits. Another person may have poor concentration and haphazard discipline but find that the mental patterns that troubled them give way fairly easily. Why is there so much variation when people are doing more or less the same things? This is an unanswerable question, but religions insist that acknowledging this is an important part of the contemplative path.

The religions are aware that there is a disconnection between what we aim at and what actually happens. There are interplays between ourselves and the world we may not see or control. There are also interplays between ourselves and the divine Goodness or karma that remain impenetrable to understanding. In the *Bhagavad Gita*, Krishna explains to Arjuna that being too attached to the results of his efforts creates anxiety and reinforces a kind of selfishness. This is not because the desired fruits are bad but because one's motivation was bound up with the assertion of the ego and its desires.

> "You have a right to your actions,
> But never to your actions' fruits.
> Act for the actions' sake."[16]

Krishna insists that action should be performed with one's heart fixed on the Beloved, the "Supreme Lord." This instills resolution in action and equanimity in results, whatever happens.

Contemplative life invites us to work with focus and passion—performing every action with our mind set on Mother Wisdom. At the same time we are released from the expectation that we control or even fully understand what happens. Relinquishing control even as we practice energetically is a difficult and yet fundamental practice. By loosening attachments to outcome, we begin to practice for the sake of the practice itself—we practice "without a why."[17] We do not engage in prayer in order to achieve something or earn something but because it is a good thing to do. We can relax into the practices that are important to us and release from the anxiety that we accomplish something—quickly, quickly—if it is no trouble!

There is therefore a deep paradox at the heart of contemplation. It does require energy, devotion, attention, and commitment. But it also requires that we forge ahead without attaching ourselves too strenuously to our idea of what should happen. This is a kind of renunciation that is subtle—because it is not the renunciation of effort or of a burning desire for the good of beings. When we see things go badly astray, regardless of our deep commitments, we are pained. But this renunciation of outcome creates a reservoir of peace even in the midst of turmoil.

In our own time we desperately need the spiritual resilience to encounter defeat and continue loving. We may well face the end of life on earth as we have known it. We need to work and pray in such a way that we never turn aside from our commitment to respond to crises of our time or the demands of our personal lives. We are required to live both actively and peacefully in order to nurture compassionate relationship with the tragedy and beauty of existence.

> And even though it all went wrong
> I'll stand before the Lord of Song
> With nothing on my tongue but Hallelujah.[18]

Practicing toward this inner quality of relinquishment of results allows one to accept positive experiences without inflating oneself and undergo disappointment while maintaining a sense of balance and peacefulness. Whatever happens, good or bad, we continue to lean into the mysterious and gracious presence of the divine Mother in all things.


## WONDER

Peacefulness that evolves from the ability to (at least partially) relinquish results is not an emotional null point. A contemplative commitment does not seek to pacify difficult emotions as an end itself. Negative mental patterns weaken in order to liberate joyfulness. As Angela of Foligno put it long ago: "And my soul in an excess of wonder cried out: 'This world is pregnant with God!'"[19] The cultivation of wonder is another example of a disposition that is itself a practice and also orients other practices.

Wonder is not so much an "experience"—that is, it is not a return to the preoccupations of the ego. It is a kind of erotic attention to whatever is at hand—to the sparkling eye of a stranger, the intoxicating warble of an unknown bird. Wonder is a subtle shift in which what becomes primary is the thing at hand rather than *my experience* of it. Ordinarily, the primary texture of awareness falls back on the ego's experiencing of the world. What appears is a bit shadowy compared to the way I feel about experience. I might encounter an elderly woman but be dominated by a range of responses: displeasure at her ugliness, fear of aging, casual dismissal of her as no longer relevant to me, happy to see her, appreciative of her good humor. Even if the object of attention is the woman, the primary quality of the experience is not her but my feeling about her.

Wonder shifts this preoccupation with my experience. The primary object of awareness becomes the thing itself. The preoccupations of the ego are not likely to disappear, but they fade into the background. One moves in the world with a wakeful enjoyment and alertness, a childlike curiosity and openness to what one encounters: an "open reception of these events and persons for what they are."[20] An adult taking a child to the park is focused on getting to the park and having fun there. A child on the way to the park is astonished at the amazing blades of grass along the way. The park and the blades of grass alike are part of the flow of curious and interesting phenomena that have not yet been categorized as "fun," "getting there," "ordinary," "irrelevant."

Wonder is a way of seeing, which might also be understood as attention. Simone Weil was one of the great artists of attention. She insists that attention is possible to the extent that egocentric attachment and prefabricated assumptions are diminished. One must get out of the way to pay attention to something else. In the face of suffering, attention is the ability to ask Parzival's question: "what ails thee?" and to see the other in and for themselves and not as a specimen from the category "unfortunate."[21] But it is also the capacity to allow the beauty of beings to appear in their very "is-ness," just as they are and not what they are for us. Contemplation in this sense is the effort, as Elizabeth Johnson puts it, "to cease looking in the mirror long enough to look out the window at what is really there."[22]

Elizabeth Johnson describes Charles Darwin as a man gifted with this attentive wonder. She writes: "With immense discipline and over a long period of time, he focused his keen, powerful intellect and astonishing energy on painstaking observation of nature, from the varieties of barnacles to the shape of pigeon's bills . . . [he] was a beholder. He observed the smallest details with interest, and recorded his scrutiny with affectionate care."[23] Though Darwin became an agnostic, Johnson identifies his attitude as deeply religious. "It is a Christian conviction that in seeing reality [one] will discover grace, the Love that undergirds all that exists."[24]

Wonder's dislocation of egoism is the opposite of self-sacrifice—it is rebirth. Wonder requires also rest and calm. It permits us to cease our relentless activity and accomplishments—secular and spiritual. "Quaker Douglas Steere says that activism and overwork are contemporary forms of violence. It is easy to lose one's balance."[25] Wonder allows us to simply be and to quiet ourselves and our activities enough to hear and see and feel the beauty within and around us.

Attentive wonder allows us to embrace life with courage and curiosity. "Confident alertness toward the unceasing waves of events that come rolling over us drives out a fearful and anxious reception of those events."[26] The dominant relation we have to the world is no longer insecurity and the relentless effort to cling to what we think might protect us. We are betrothed to amazement. We open to wonder—and a spirit of adventure.

## ADVENTURE

These dispositions are all somewhat counterintuitive—gentleness and nonjudgment rather than condemnation, peacefulness rather than anxiety. They do not contribute to the certainty and steadiness our fragile egos crave. They invite us into a spirit of adventure rather than security. Life is by its nature unpredictable, and whatever we thought will or should happen rarely actually happens. We often try to ease the blow of this by surrounding ourselves with real and imaginary structures to give us a sense of stability. Strong locks. A political view that makes the world make sense. A belief in how God works. When the waves of life blow us over, the sandy foundation on which our security was built is revealed. This is often when people reject religion—the beliefs they cherished crash against experience. Other people cling all the more irrationally to their ideology, impervious to facts. Certain truths or facts feel as if they would be too shattering to admit into our awareness.

If we go to contemplative practice for calm in the storm, we might be disappointed. It does not protect us from anything that happens. If it gives us a sense of peace, it is, as Jesus says, not as the world gives peace. Paradoxically, contemplative dispositions grant us peace by embracing the storm with eyes wide open. "If you are going to do any spiritual work you will have to live without eyelids. You won't be allowed to blink. You must look at everything. The spiritual life is not about escaping; it is about embracing."[27] Contemplation is not an escape from life, it is a deeper immersion into it—in all of its beauty and terror. By practicing attention to what is, contemplation perceives the beauty of other beings and the wonder of existence with unparalleled power. A raw beauty shimmers off experience—the liquid brilliance of the moon and stars, the gentle eyes in a homeless person's face, the magical power of music and poetry, the astonishing deliciousness of a friend's blueberry-lemon cake. But contemplative practices also unveil the truth of suffering without the softening veil of ignorance, ideology, or indifference.

The spirit of wonder and adventure forces us to acknowledge suffering, injustice, and the limitations of institutions on which we had relied without question. Our beliefs fail us. Our parents turn out to be imperfect (or worse). We are betrayed by lovers and friends. We experience suffering that seems to burn us alive from the inside out. We come to understand how implacable and destructive injustice is—the endless blasphemy of racism, the never-ending assaults on women's bodies and minds, the incredible indifference to hunger and poverty. We begin to understand the dire dangers of climate change. Contemplation requires that we renounce our addiction to consoling fictions and distraction. If this sounds unpleasant, well . . . it is.

A contemplative way of life does not leave us without resource. These dispositions intertwine with one another to reinforce courage to face reality in all of its dimensions. The spirit of adventure is nourished by the equanimity that blossoms when we detach from the outcome of our efforts or desires. This is an inward reservoir of peace that empowers a spirit of adventure. When the New Testament or Nag Hammadi Scriptures describe the peace that is bestowed on Jesus' followers, they emphasize that it is a power. The followers are not only consoled; they are given the courage to go out and share a story about a zealous, life affirming love. Their terror gives way to a capacity to go out into the world, offering a dangerous counternarrative to domination and violence. "Joy be to you and grace and power. . . . And they went by a power of Jesus, in peace."[28]

Adventure does not mean an appetite for extreme sports or foreign travel. It is an attitude that embraces life with zeal. This is the zeal that Pseudo-Dionysius attributes to the Good Beyond Being and invites us to participate in: "That is why those possessed of spiritual insight describe him [God] as 'zealous' because his good yearning for all things is so great and because he stirs in [human beings] a deep yearning desire for zeal . . . because zeal is always felt for what is desired and because he is zealous for the creatures for whom he provides."[29] This is a disposition to relish life in its outsized grandeur and beauty, its wild diversity, its painful losses. To open our heart to what is. Life does not pass us by. We notice it. We notice how intensely beautiful, amazing, and endlessly curious beings are. Encountering cultures different from our own is fascinating—how much bigger the human adventure is than we had imagined. We sink into moments of tenderness and suck the sweetness out of all the good things we experience.

When the storm clouds mount, we adjust our sails. When we have lost what we cannot bear to lose, we weep and mourn—and then reset our compass. Tasting the bitterness of guilt or shame, we refuse to remain stuck there, limping on defiantly. When our work on behalf of imprisoned immigrants is met with only more draconian laws, we tear our hair—and begin again. When we come to a part of our story where all the paths are blocked and there is no way forward, we wait until a door appears in the wall. The spirit of adventure allows us to encounter difficulty and uncertainty as part of the journey. We have a heart for the adventure of life and do not easily despair. We are like sailors out on the wild sea. A good sailor knows there will be storms and so is not disheartened when they appear; she braces for them and rides them out—salt air filling her lungs and her blood racing. And afterward, she dances the hornpipe with the survivors. She remembers to dance, to sing, to be enchanted by stories, and to drink deeply from the well of silence.

The spirit of adventure inspires the journey of faith as well. When our beliefs lie in rags at our feet and everything we thought we had to believe in order to live meaningfully is gone, we dig deeper—because the infinite mercy of the Beloved Mother is never exhausted. What may seem like a total loss ends up opening rooms in the interior castle we had no idea existed. We can allow our beliefs to shatter because whatever we think we know about the divine Goodness is immeasurably less than the truth. Doubt is not a catastrophe—it is an essential part of the spiritual path. It means that some other depth is opening up that we were unable to previously imagine. Gregory of Nyssa says that our desire for God is infinite because God is infinite. We go from glory to glory. Our desire for the divine Beloved will never outstrip the Holy One's infinite goodness. Contemplation is not attachment to this or that belief about divine reality. It is a bed-rock confidence that Goodness will never fail our desiring hearts.

I have suggested some of the dispositions that can be cultivated as we explore a contemplative way of life. On the one hand, our personality structure and the stamp of what has happened to us is not infinitely pliable. We must love who we are, regardless, and know that we exist in a glorious web of a beloved creation. And yet, without reorienting our dispositions, we will continue to relate to the world, to ourselves, and to the Beloved through our old mental and emotional habits, no matter what meditation or other disciplines we take up. When these inner qualities begin to shift, the way we "feel" the world shifts and we are better able to be grateful for its beauty, wise in our relationships, compassionate to the suffering of others and their environments, joyful in our dance with the Spirit of holiness—and gentle with the persistence of negative mental patterns.

The elliptical Dark Mother creates beauty from epic failures and makes dark matter river, zestful, through galaxies. The Beloved is a holy and wild dance—voracious, dangerous—an everlasting ode to joy.

# 6

# *Watching the Mind*

"But how do we find our ways home? Continually, regularly? . . . The birds still communicate without any help from us. In that deep quietude, doesn't the air, and the memory, feel more full of voices? If we slow down and intentionally practice listening, calming our own clatter, maybe we hear those voices better."[1]

"Let mystery have its place in you—do not always be turning your whole soil with the plowshare of self-examination but have a fallow corner in your heart ready for any seed the winds may bring and reserve a nook of shadow for a passing bird; keep a place in your heart for unexpected guests, an altar for the unknown god."[2]

The dispositions and attitudes we bring to a contemplative way of life are shaped by our characteristic mental patterns. As we work to cultivate positive dispositions, we will need to notice how our mind actually works. We watch the mind to cultivate habits to support our aspirations. These are not gigantic leaps into some other personality or supposedly ideal set of feelings and insights. It is simply working with ourselves, in our precious particularity, with all of our unique gifts and challenges—weaving our life into the life of the Beloved in a way no one else has ever done or will ever do. As the great Hasidic master, Rabbi Zusya, said before his death, "In the coming world, they will not ask me: 'Why were you not Moses?' They will ask me: 'Why were you not Zusya?'"[3]

Perhaps because the rediscovery of Christian contemplation has been so influenced by Buddhist, yogic, and Hindu forms of meditation, we may tend to think of contemplation primarily in terms of techniques and periods of meditation. But most Christian contemplatives prior to the twentieth century wrote relatively little about techniques of meditation. They wrote instead a good deal about attitudes and virtues that are necessary to a contemplative way of life. For them, simply paying close attention to the working of their own mind was the basic and essential contemplative practice. "At bottom there is but one subject of study: the forms and metamorphoses of mind. All other subjects may be reduced to that; all other studies bring us back to this study."[4] Perhaps this is an overstatement. But the ancient science of watching the mind opens onto an infinite horizon. Not all of the wisdom of early thinkers translates directly into contemporary experience. But their emphasis on attention to the way the mind is working remains important.

## WATCHING THE MIND, GUARDING THE HEART

One layer of watching the mind is simply being aware of thoughts as they arise.[5] One can do this in mediation practice, dedicating a period to observing the nature of thoughts as they come and go without trying to repress them. But it is perhaps even more useful as a continuous practice throughout the day. "I am afraid when the phone rings." "I am impatient with my client." "I am craving a salty snack." "I am mildly depressed and don't know why." "The faint smell of coffee coming from somewhere makes me smile even though I do not drink coffee." Virginia Woolf brilliantly captured these peregrinations of a person's thoughts. Reading *Mrs. Dalloway* gives an example of what this kind of watching the mind might look like, though it is the novelist's observation of another mind rather than watching one's own mind.

By observing the flow of thoughts and emotions, one gains a clearer sense of what mental structures govern one's experience of the world. One might think of oneself as a gentle and compassionate person and pray for the well-being of everyone every day. This is to the good, as it reflects a desire to be such a person. But when one watches one's mind, one begins to notice all of the tiny snags that are opposed to the desire to be compassionate. Noticing—"I am deeply irritated just passing the office of this coworker"—helps us to realize that whatever we *wished* our mental state to be, our *actual* mental state is to despise our coworker and harbor a deep-seated anger toward them. Perhaps the anger is justified. But the observation of mind is not in the business of justifying or condemning the anger. It simply allows us to register what is actually going on in our mind. Symeon warns that "to those who have no knowledge of this practice it appears extremely harsh and arduous."[6] Acknowledging the unwelcome thoughts that are hidden away in the recesses of our mind challenges our self-image. But it is only by becoming aware of our real mental state that we will begin to feel "the delight to be found in the depths of the heart."[7]

The point of this exercise is not to so focus on every tiny fault that we are constantly castigating ourselves for our imperfections or perceived failures. The point is to cultivate an inner freedom in which we recognize the thoughts and feelings roiling around in us with honesty and compassion. We become a bit freer from the habit of self-condemnation. It is not that I notice that I secretly despise a coworker and then hate myself for an emotion that I feel is unworthy of me. It is rather that I am more honest about my real feelings and can work with them more carefully. Perhaps that I despise this person provides me with important information that my feigned politeness concealed. Perhaps it points me to some other experience I was repressing that continues to haunt me. Perhaps it punctures a spiritual pride that I was taking in my supposed patience and universal love. Perhaps I realize that all three things are going on at the same time. As I become accustomed to watching my mind I gain a bit more understanding of myself. I am given the opportunity to work gently with my real feelings. This is only possible if I have access to what I am actually experiencing.

At the beginning—and maybe for the duration—this practice is difficult because I am so unaccustomed to noticing what I am really experiencing. Access to my inner experience might be blocked by my overactive and judgmental superego or by family patterns that made self-reflection dangerous—much safer to stay on the surface and not think about what was really happening. Or perhaps we have such deeply rooted feelings of shame that to acknowledge even the tiniest mistake seems completely overwhelming. Alternatively, we might feel a deep attachment to an image of ourselves that is more ideal than real. Recognizing the existence of unapproved thoughts or feelings risks the undoing of my entire sense of myself. The attitudes of gentleness and nonjudgment can be allies in this practice, allowing us to acknowledge our thoughts and feelings without despising ourselves.

As I continue in this practice, I notice the disjunctions between what I thought was happening and what is really going on. By watching my mind, I may begin to realize that a perceived virtue is concealing a vice—my patience is masking my paralyzing fear of standing up for myself. Or I might have to accept that I am not the unworthy, hopelessly stained person I held onto for so many years. Actually, I am insightful, caring, and surprisingly strong. "Maybe I'm not as stupid as I thought I was." No, probably no one in the world is that "stupid." Oddly, giving up our negative self-images can be as painful as having our spiritual pride challenged. To embrace holy self-respect we need first to clear away delusional spiritual pride and equally delusional self-abnegation. This can be a challenge.

Evagrius Ponticus was a master teacher of the practice of watching the mind.[8] He advises his reader to carefully notice the circumstances from which various negative thought patterns arise. What difficult emotions come most often? What assault us most vehemently? Which are dispatched fairly easily and which are deeply entrenched? What are the associations among thoughts?[9] He suggests that his readers pay attention not only to the flow of their thoughts but also carefully observe what the more general underlying patterns and connections are. Paying close attention to what triggers anger or frustration—how long it lasts, what its emotional comrades are—one might eventually unearth an ancient terror that was lurking deep below conscious memory. You may have been damaging a relationship with your angry outbursts, unresponsive to reason or connection. But attentive observation over a period of time—maybe a long time—can help you realize that your anger is a defense against a blow from a long-dead parent. Your anger had nothing to do with the relationship at all and yet it was at risk of destroying it. Unearthing this deeper pattern is necessary to begin to pacify the real wound so it no longer threatens the present.

I love that Evagrius asks that in this process of painstaking attention we "ask from Christ an explanation of the data we have observed." Watching the mind is an ability to stay with whatever arises in the mind without panicking or running away. This can be difficult. In the moment we are too absorbed with the experience to gain any distance from it, and afterward it is passed over as something trivial or misdiagnosed or suppressed as too painful to remember. Evagrius counsels us to turn to the very thing that causes us pain. Do not dismiss it. Hesitate to diagnose too quickly, as our mental defenses may obscure its meaning. Endure the pain of the memory. But do this in a contemplative spirit. Invite the Beloved or Mother Wisdom or the Blessed Virgin to assist. This work can be painful and we need to be supported. We should also find help from therapists or spiritual directors. Evagrius had received crucial spiritual guidance from others, including Melania the Elder, and he was himself a beloved spiritual director. Evagrius's point is that though the work of watching the mind is interior prayer, we do not do it alone. In fact, it can be deleterious to engage interior practices without spiritual guidance and wise, compassionate support. "Concerning those who make a report about what concerns their interior life and do everything with counsel, it says, 'there is safety in much council.'"[10] We do not need to feel too discouraged because both our Beloved and our spiritual friends are accompanying us to guide us and strengthen our hearts.

Watching the mind can take us into the hidden depths where destructive habits are lodged but out of sight. It can also be an almost playful daily practice, noticing the thoughts as they come and go. "Impatience—yes, there you are, my old companion." "Good morning heartache, have a seat—I think you may be here a while." "Snide thoughts about a stranger—hmm, is that entirely necessary?" Watching the mind can also suggest counternarratives or antidotes to a negative pattern of thought. David Foster Wallace provides a vivid picture of both our negative habits and the possibility of rewiring them in his profound and enchanting graduation speech at Kenyon College: We might be in the grocery store, tired and irritable after a long day. Traffic was appalling and everyone in the store seems to be put there on purpose to aggravate me—the unbelievably slow cashier, the rude man pushing in front of me, the mother with the noisy toddler reaching over me to grab what I wanted. But what if this were all re-narrated? Before I start ranting about stupid, gas-guzzling vehicular monstrosities, what if I remembered that

> some of these people in SUVs have been in horrible auto accidents in the past and now their driving is so traumatic that their therapist has all but ordered them to get a huge, heavy SUV so they can feel safe enough to drive; or that the Hummer that has just cut me off is maybe driven by a father whose little child is hurt or sick in the seat next to him and he is trying to rush to the hospital . . . it is actually *I* who am in *his* way. Or I can choose to force myself to consider the likelihood that everyone else in the supermarket's check-out line is probably just as bored and frustrated as I am, and that some of these people actually have much harder, more tedious, or painful lives than I do, overall.[11]

He goes on to argue that we have a choice about mental habits like these. "It will actually be within your power to experience a crowded, hot, slow, consumer-hell-type situation as not only meaningful, but sacred, on fire with the same force that lit the stars—compassion, love, the subsurface unity of all things."[12]

Evagrius offers a number of antidotes for negative thoughts. Psalm-singing and alms are antidotes for anger, limiting water intake promotes temperance, ministering to the sick overcomes nighttime terrors: "such afflictions are extinguished by no other remedy so well as by mercy."[13] He identifies concrete acts of love and charity as especially effective against the more destructive negative thoughts. Though not all of his suggestions resonate with us, we can experiment with antidotes that assist us in our own situation. Prayers for those who annoy you; imagining the difficult lives of those who interfere with you; turning attention to something simple and lovely—the shape of a tree; the good-humored kindness of a parent with their toddler; reciting a favorite psalm, poem, or mantra.

Watching the mind in simple and profound ways exposes our mind and its patterns to us. It also creates mental space so that the feeling does not have to take us over. We do not so identify with the thought or feeling that we *are* it. We gain just enough time or space that we can choose how to interpret what is happening and respond to it with a bit more grace.


## TRUTH

Another method for watching the mind is to recommit oneself to truth in a new way. Truth is not just avoiding obvious lies. It is actually a fairly subtle practice, because it requires discernment and courage. A contemplative path is committed to truth, not in the sense of clinging to dogmas or ideologies whatever the evidence against them. Truth is a living animal, spirit not letter. It is not something to be grasped in our hand as a static and unchallenged possession. But it is to be cherished and pursued. We desire truth but do not possess it. Contemplatives are lovers of wisdom.[14] Truth concerns the way reality works and is woven together with mystery and wonder. It is bound up with our desire for the living God, beyond all of our thoughts. It concerns the truth of other beings, a dawning awareness of their sacred beauty. The desire for truth allows us to abandon ideas when we recognize they are unworthy of us. The courage to say "I thought it was true, but now realize I was mistaken" is crucial to a contemplative life. Paradoxically, an eros for truth is comfortable with doubt. There is much we cannot know definitively and truthfulness allows us to desire truth that we never fully possess. It gives us courage to step into the uncertainty of unknowing and bear the pain of having to forfeit an idea that turns out to be wrong. It is a heroic quest whose nobility lies not at the end of the road but in the endurance for the journey. The contemplative is called to "live the meaning of truth in all the ways of being truthful. . . . This is the vision of a great and noble life: to endure ambiguity in the movement of truth and to make light shine through it; to stand fast in uncertainty; to prove capable of unlimited love and hope."[15]

A commitment to truth requires us to be alert to the moment of history we are living through. Reading the news with mindfulness and hard questions becomes its own kind of prayer. Hannah Arendt argued that "dark times" are not just periods when terrible things happen— wars, massacres, cruelty, injustice. Dark times are also characterized by the assault on truth. She describes the presence of calamity rendered invisible by deception: "for, until the very moment when catastrophe overtook everything and everybody, it was covered up not by realities but by the highly efficient double-talk of nearly all official representatives. . . . When we think of dark times . . . we have to take this camouflage . . . also into account."[16]

In loving the truth, the contemplative is called upon to investigate the way language and rhetoric work. In what ways are we shaped to accept or reject something by the way it is presented, by the language used to describe it. If a news story emphasizes the short skirt of the rape victim and the prestigious school attended by the accused, are we not prepared to sympathize with him while subtly casting the woman in the role of slut or temptress? Arendt notes this magic of language, not to keep people ignorant but to "prevent them from equating [events] with their old, 'normal' knowledge of murder and lies."[17]

Material lies make actions that assault our conscience seem normal. In our own time, a disdain for truth is invading our public discourse. Facts that are inconvenient to our worldview or economic agenda are simply dismissed. We have become so accustomed to material lies we are no longer shocked by them. Perhaps if they are repeated often enough we begin to believe them. Obvious nonfactual lies circulate with impunity. The great lie that some human beings are unworthy of respect—open misogyny and racism; caricatures of Jews, Muslims, refugees—has been elevated to a legitimate place in civil discourse. Erasing the difference between scientific findings and opinion eases the moral odiousness of ratcheting up the assault on the environment even as the devastation of climate change is already upon us. The attack on truth is so widespread that it is impossible to avoid internalizing it. It is like secondhand smoke we cannot avoid breathing. The omnipresence of lies distorts our inner compass. It is a spiritual attack.

The issue of truthfulness may seem like a political matter but it is in fact deeply spiritual. The desire for truth is central for spiritual well-being: ". . . know the truth and the truth will make you free" (John 8:32). This desire for truth is not the same as a pretense at certainty where none is possible or a dogmatism that organizes everything according to a revered set of beliefs. This desire has to do with an eros for what is real. It is curiosity about actual states of affairs. Is the science on climate change persuasive? Are electric cars better for the environment?

Is our justice system structured by racist assumptions? What sources are reliable and what are more prone to ideological spin? These questions are not political, they have to do with material truth. Questioning whether something is real or true is a matter of basic spiritual hygiene. If we accept lies as normal and let ideology displace investigation, then we have abandoned the satyagraha (truth-force) that is essential to spiritual well-being.[18] We are lost in a world where nothing matters but how we feel and become committed to shoring up those things that make us feel good. When our passion for truth in all its dimensions becomes tepid, it is easier to ignore those things that make us uncomfortable. It is then all the easier to tolerate the destruction that is done.

Factual lies produce a troubling fruit. Once factual lies are accepted, the world they intend to create comes into existence. If Jews are bacilli sickening society or a cabal conspiring to take over the world, it is natural to eliminate them. If immigrants and refugees are rapists, terrorists, and drug lords, then it is incumbent upon us to mercilessly imprison them. The first lie spawns a world in which death camps or prisons where children are separated from their families are necessary—even divinely mandated.

You may wonder what this has to do with a contemplative way of life. Contemplation has to do with living in the world as it is with relentless honesty and courage and responding to that world with wonder and compassion. Watching our mind as we navigate the social and political landscape is integral to these aspirations.

The discipline of figuring out what is true and what is false is a practice that helps "guard the heart" against delusion and spiritual lies.

It is easy to become discouraged when we see so many cruelties around us, so much destruction and indifference. It can feel suffocating to realize that truth itself seems to have been taken prisoner. But loving truth is its own kind of joy. The spirit is made for truth. We are created for reality, not for consoling or terrifying fictions. Even when truth is challenging, it is life-giving. We turn aside from sweet poison and seek out nourishing food.

## GRATITUDE

In Hans Christian Anderson's fairy tale "The Snow Queen," the demons have made a magical mirror that shows everything good as tiny and limp as boiled spinach and everything bad as huge and overwhelming.

When the little boy in the story gets a splinter of this mirror stuck in his eye, his heart-vision becomes distorted. His friend, Gerta, goes on a long quest to rescue him from the frozen land of the Snow Queen and from the inner disfigurement of his perception.[19] Like all good fairy tales, this communicates a spiritual truth in a fantastic way. It is easy for any of us to be tempted by this magic mirror, to exaggerate what is ugly or difficult and to fail to register what is beautiful and good. It is easy to inflate the significance of what discourages us. The practice of gratitude can be a helpful antidote. It is a simple way of shining light on what is good and integrating that awareness into the ebb and flow of the days.

Gratitude has become a popular spiritual practice. There are now a number of books describing the value of this practice as well as journals dedicated to recording daily gratitude. Perhaps one reason it is a powerful practice is that it is a way to "guard the heart" against gloom or despair. It also is a kind of subtle truth telling. Because it is easy to be frustrated or down-hearted, taking time to consider what is good—whether large or small—can counteract a habit of discouraged or pessimistic thinking. It revives the significance of the sweet moments we take for granted but get lost in the surges of aggravation. Through this practice, the fabric of our mind becomes more habituated to noticing and appreciating pleasure, companionship, health or health care, the tender green of spring, the wildness of storms. The simple practice of recording two or three good things that happened during the day weakens the power of the demons' magic mirror.

This practice can sound trite—a journal bedecked with rainbows and unicorns when our personal life or social reality is very far from the land of rainbow-flying-unicorns. Gratitude calls on the love of truth to anchor it. It can be a simple and straightforward practice with far-reaching effects and it can also be a challenging dance with difficult emotions. The wisdom of this practice is attributed to Meister Eckhart, who reportedly said: "If the only prayer you ever say in your entire life is thank you, it will be enough." This makes a nice quotation to put at the end of our emails. But it also invites sustained meditation to unearth layers of his meaning. Any practice that focuses us on the actual working of our mind will unearth unexpected layers. Like other exercises that appear simple, it requires attention to practice well.

Spiritual practices should not obscure our true feelings from us. One might be in a period of life when the idea of gratitude is not only foreign but deeply offensive. "I am not going to be grateful for my cancer diagnosis." "I refuse to practice gratitude when our world is in such catastrophic turmoil." "I don't need gratitude—I need ferocious cour-age and anger." It is a mistake to repress honest responses. It is also the case that over the course of each life, we focus on different practices. The practice of gratitude is not a repression of genuine emotion but does raise the question of how to remain alert to the good, the true, and the beautiful when feeling angry, sad, miserable, brokenhearted, betrayed.

Gratitude might be practiced in several ways. It might be an ordi-nary, daily practice of raising to consciousness any small happiness, beauty, kindness in an otherwise dull or uneventful day. This is possible even when experiencing a day or a period that is unpleasant. Gratitude can season even difficult moments with lightness or hope. In bed with the flu, the cool rag felt good. The ER staff were all so kind and helpful. Even though my heart is broken, the stars are bright and beautiful. This kind of practice can be helpful but should not be forced. It reorients our perspective so that neither ordinariness nor difficulty seem abso-lute. We are constantly surrounded by good things. Without denying other feelings, we can practice in a way that allows us to recognize the good, beautiful, playful, pleasurable, life-giving things that never cease.

Another kind of gratitude practice is to extend gratitude to others. Though the custom of thanking people (sometimes in writing!) for gifts, dinner parties, and other kindnesses may be less robust these days, showing appreciation is a small but eminently useful habit. This is a particularly useful practice in situations where someone is "just doing their job." It is easy to take for granted work that is done on your behalf that you are paying for or that is part of a professional or service rela-tionship. But it is often the case that people toil away doing their work with care and competence and never hear a word back. The delivery room nurses that went out of their way to sit with a lonely pregnant woman, the physical therapist that advised you over the phone, the kind competence of an IT advisor, the harried kindergarten teacher, the store employee who helped you find something, the cook in the back of the cafeteria, the maid emptying your trash and remaking the hotel bed—all are performing their jobs but also bringing their humanity with them into work. To show gratitude for what they are doing lifts you and them out of the dreariness of alienated labor. They may very rarely hear that their work is appreciated—that someone noticed their contribution and their humanity. Even if you disagreed with someone or were slightly irritated by something, you can also notice that they were trying to do the right thing or perform well under taxing circum-stances. Showing gratitude reminds you both that this was a human exchange. It reminds you that someone did something on your behalf and you can both enjoy the feeling of appreciation for that. It is a heart-opening practice that reveals the everyday goodness and interconnectedness that happens all the time in the most ordinary events.

In speaking to a group of college students about the rigors of radical compassion, Rosemarie Freeney Harding also recommended simple, ordinary practices of gratitude: "The main thing is to be grateful. Call your parents and tell them how much you appreciate what they've done for you. Or anybody else who has helped you to become the beautiful, loving and intelligent person you are. Thank someone. Thank your ancestors. That will make us rise to the occasion."[20]

Gratitude is more difficult when things are really difficult or when one is feeling painful emotions or in a situation that seems—or is—hopeless. I have wondered if Meister Eckhart is thinking about these times when he praises gratitude. It may be that gratitude is a terrible practice at some periods of life and one should not try to practice it. But *if* one feels drawn to considering gratitude even in the dark times, it may be a practice for dropping deeply into the truth of tragedy and suffering and discovering there is a light, a brightness, a cosmic compassion and tenderness, a beauty that is more robust than destruction. Gratitude in this sense is a fierce, gritty "yes" to life. This gratitude does not bypass grief or anger. You may be licking out every one of the pots in Sorrow's kitchen. But gratitude refuses despair. It refuses to stop loving. Somehow a "hell no" shatters one's quiescence to pain and despair. Somehow there is some good that will not accept that destruction and sadness are the final word. Gratitude is not "yes" to loss, affliction, violence, or the suffocating victories of hatred. It is "yes" to something that these things cannot completely conquer. One can witness traces of this resilience in the Soweto Gospel Choir or the Freedom Singers. It is there when a painting or poem honors unredeemed tragedy. It is there in the simple kindnesses people offer each other in the midst of disaster or personal sadness. Palestinian American poet Naomi Shihab Nye captures the deep goodness that may not be obvious when things are going smoothly but that one sometimes glimpses when all is lost:

> Before you know kindness as the deepest thing inside,
> you must know sorrow as the other deepest thing.[21]

Whatever that mystery is, good shines in the heart of darkness when it appears that all is lost. And—sometimes—our heart can open in gratitude for that.

## COMPASSIONATE ACTIONS AND SYMPATHETIC JOY

I have already said a good deal about the centrality of compassion to a contemplative life. There are many books about generating compassion, from religious and secular perspectives.[22] The entirety of a contemplative approach to life is intended to contribute to a deepening of compassion. But here I will suggest simple mental practices that are ways of watching the mind and guarding against indifference or hostility.

Perhaps the most important practice is to be aware of what limits compassion. Each of us will encounter different limitations on our compassion. How do we deal with our hostility to those who harm us or others? How do we overcome conscious or unconscious prejudices against this or that group? How do we disentangle from the tyranny of our fears and pleasures? How do we work with paralyzing shyness or over-weaning brashness? Each obstacle will require a somewhat different antidote.

In matters of the spirit, we should avoid the temptation to so valorize an ideal that the distance between our real and our desired experience is overlooked. After a glorious retreat we may want to be good all day long and live in a rosy glow of universal love and understanding—and seconds later find ourselves cursing at someone on the radio, a rude driver, or a remembered slight. Simply observing, with a kind of good-humored gentleness, those things that erode compassion is itself a good practice. Here I will provide some examples of some simple, daily practices that keep the desirability of compassion before our eyes.

One practice, especially when bored or irritated, is to look around and wish for good things for those around you. While standing at the checkout line, wish that the cashier might go home and get a good rest, the restless child gets a treat, the doddering older gentleman finds his way home in peace. Wish for general good things to anonymous people—may the people in my town experience peace, safety, release from suffering, joy. When one finds oneself triggered, especially over something trivial, see if there is a way to imagine the other person's perspective. If someone is deeply problematic and impossible to feel care for, see if it is possible to wish that whatever poisoned their minds or actions could be pacified—if not now, then in some unknown future. Pray back four generations to imaginatively restore the deep roots from which their dysfunction grows. Pray forward one hundred or one thousand years and see if you can imagine a future in which they find peace.

If you cannot pray for them at all, enlist someone else to pray for them in your stead. Or if this is not reasonable either, there are other ways to practice that might be more realistic for you.

Give something to someone who asks for it. Donate money. Weed out belongings and find groups who need them. Water plants. Feed the birds. Avoid pesticides, or, when possible, avoid food grown with pesticides. Be an informed voter. Write your congressperson or a friend who is sick or sad. Send a book to your nephew living in a new city. Listen to the sound of the breeze, of trees creaking.

Listen to someone not only with your ears but also with your heart, not waiting to express your opinion or relate a similar experience. Listen someone into speech; let your attention be an invitation for them to connect with feelings they did not realize they had. Read a novel or magazine article about lives entirely different from your own. Cultivate curiosity about other people and appreciation for their way of life, however distant from your own.

None of these sorts of small, daily actions change the world, but these kinds of actions or thoughts tie you to the lives of others. As this becomes a habit it will spontaneously express itself in large and small ways in your life—in ways that you do not even realize.

When Oscar Wilde was transported to prison for his homosexual relationship with Lord Alfred Douglas, he was a man utterly broken and humiliated. In his beautiful letter from prison, *De Profundis*, he describes the infinitely precious act of kindness offered to him by one of the few friends that remained true to him:

> When I was brought down from my prison to the Court of Bankruptcy, between two policemen, Robbie waited in the long dreary corridor that, before the whole the crowd, whom an action so sweet and simple hushed into silence, he might gravely raise his hat to me, as handcuffed and with bowed head, I passed him by. Men have gone to heaven for smaller things than that. . . . When wisdom has been profitless to me, philosophy barren . . . the memory of that little, lovely, silent act of love . . . brought me out of the bitterness of lonely exile into harmony with the wounded, broken, and great heart of the world.[23]

May we each be granted the grace to know how to give such a gift.

Compassion allows us to feel and respond to suffering. But equally important is the ability to delight in good that befalls someone else. When you hear about someone receiving an honor or award, imagine how happy they must feel, how proud their family must be. Reading about a friend's exciting vacation, imagine how lovely it must be for them to get a break, see beautiful things, have an adventure. If you see a tiny child delighting in some pleasure, as only tiny children can, delight with them. How fine to be in a world in which ice cream or a swing set can be so magical. Seeing teenagers pouring from school as summer begins, celebrate with them in your mind. That delicious freedom that comes with the end of a school year—it will never be yours again, but you can be glad for them. Be glad in the pleasure a dog takes in rolling in the grass or a deer in loping through the woods. How wonderful to have a body capable of such physical pleasure. When someone takes pleasure in something you think ridiculous—a game, a shopping spree, a book, a party—put aside your judgments and be glad for them. Be glad when you encounter someone whose courage you feel you could never emulate or whose activism you can only envy. Take pleasure in their goodness or kindness or determination. Be glad for someone who can sing or play tennis or climb mountains—they have talents and abilities that you do not. But how happy they must be in being able to do these wonderful things.

This practice may make you aware of how often you felt judgmental or jealous, how you have foreshortened your heart toward other people's pleasures and accomplishments. Both compassion and sympathetic joy dislocate our natural preoccupation with our own experience. It is not only my suffering and joy that matters. The suffering and joys of others begins to infiltrate my awareness and color my experience. It becomes more natural to attend to the experiences of others. Compassion and sympathetic joy may result in some action. But we are not able to respond to everything that happens—good and bad—in the world. These mental practices—whether they result in a particular action or not—soften egoism and make us more ready, more agile in responding when the need arises.

These practices guard the heart against negative emotions such as jealousy or envy and provide a key to open the prison of self-absorbed focus on one's own pain and pleasure. They also expand our capacity for enjoyment and delight. By attending to what makes someone else sorrowful or happy, we begin to feel the world in a different way and encounter sources of beauty that we had not recognized before.

The shadow side of compassion is emotional fatigue. Googling "empathy fatigue" produces countless websites. I am not sure that "pride" is the root of sin, as Augustine insisted. It may be that it is painful and exhausting to remain open to the suffering of others. To fully enter into one person's disaster is vulnerability to an ocean of pain. The depth and breadth of suffering we can encounter in an ordinary day is infinite. It is therefore not enough to simply be "more compassionate." It is essential to calibrate what is possible and not demand of oneself actions or emotions that eat away at one's resilience and health. It is also essential to nurture the spirit with joy, rest, and beauty. We cannot give what we do not have.

All of the positive dispositions and virtues are intertwined and interdependent. One cannot work out the compassion muscle while ignoring the whole family of positive practices and dispositions that tend toward good spiritual hygiene. If compassion seems overwhelming and depleting, it may be a good time to concentrate on other kinds of practices. If one is in a situation that demands by its very nature compassionate response, it is all the more important to seek out whatever is necessary to ease and strengthen your spirit. Maybe instead of worrying about compassion or sympathetic joy, you need to take up gardening or dance classes.

## GENEROSITY

Generosity is a practice that is related to compassion, sympathetic joy, and gratitude. We might think of generosity in terms of the "charitable giving" we engage in. "Charitable" is a common term for financial contributions to the causes that are important to us. But it can imply a kind of "noblesse oblige"—some kindness we are free to extend or not extend, depending on how we feel. There can even be considerable status that accrues from charitable giving. It becomes part of one's reputation, or the reputation of one's company. Sometimes the charity becomes more important than those that it is purporting to help. Or it can be delivered in ways that imply that recipients are inferior, passive, ignorant of how to serve their own interests. The practice of watching the mind can uncover some of the subtle distortions that creep into our charity.

In the story of the good Samaritan in Luke 25–37, we are told that when the Samaritan came across the Jew that had been beaten up and left for dead by robbers, he was moved by *splagchnizomai*: This word is usually translated as compassion, which means to "suffer with." But in Greek it means a feeling so intense it is felt in the very bowels of one's being. In Hebrew, *rachum* (compassion, mercy) is derived from the word for womb. In both languages, compassion is something so intense one can do nothing other than act. It is like the spontaneous and fervid desire for a child's well-being that a mother holding her infant feels. It is visceral and irresistible. This is the feeling the divine Goodness has for humanity. It is this womb-like, visceral connection to a stranger's plight that drove the Samaritan to help someone who was ethnically alien to him and socially estranged.

When we think of generosity as a spiritual practice, it is this irresistible quality of care for others—including strangers and those alienated from us by society—that we are talking about. Generosity does not concern how good I feel when I engage in charitable giving (although one might say—by whatever means necessary). Generosity is a degree of self-forgetfulness when another person's situation invades me in such a way that I feel compelled to respond in whatever way I can.

The paradox of a spirit of generosity is that as it increases in strength, it runs up against implacable limits. It is impossible to respond to everyone who suffers, every vulnerable group, every cause for social justice, every environmental need. Generosity requires a kind of intelligence and thoughtfulness. How can one respond well when there are so many needs? Generosity is bound up with the painfulness of the limitations on what one can do in the face of the enormity of human and ecological privation. Rather than resist this pain, one might instead acknowledge it and live in the tension between what one can do and the infinity of need. Acknowledging this blocks the tendency to harden one's heart against those things that one can do nothing about. Let the pain be felt, perhaps offer a prayer but resist also the impulse to so dwell in suffering that one feels overwhelmed.

A way to watch the mind in the practice of gratitude is to allow micro-actions to be sprinkled through one's ordinary life. Drop in a quarter for victims of natural disaster. Provide some token of support when asked for it. Buy the Girl Scout cookies (even if you give them away). Let the happy spirit of generosity circulate, knowing these micro-actions are not changing the world but they are sacraments of your care. They let you participate in the flow of good.

Generosity can also concern time. It may be that giving time to someone is more important than giving money. This might be volunteer work. It might also be as simple as giving someone your attention, taking a few seconds to really see them and respond to them humanly. Be generous toward the earth. Don't run water unnecessarily. Be mindful of your cleaning products. Recycle where you can. Find the sacraments of generosity that you can joyfully weave through your day.

Like all spiritual practices, generosity is without limit and so it is necessary to live the practice of it without succumbing to the "not enough" trap—that nothing you give, no project, no volunteerism, no amount of money relieves you of the feeling of obligation. Generosity is connected to the radical compassion that contemplation generates and there is a kind of painfulness in that. But the heart of spiritual practice is the joyfulness of connecting to others with a gracious attitude. Respond as well as you can, and that is enough.

## INTERCESSORY PRAYER

Intercessory prayer is a common practice in many religions and can be understood in a variety of ways. I include it in the chapter on watching the mind to emphasize that whatever else it might be, it is a form of heart-mind training. When we pray for others, we cannot know what the outcome will be, and yet it alters our mind simply by doing it. "He prayed as he breathed, forming no words and making no specific requests, only holding in his heart, like broken birds in cupped hands, all those people who were in stress or grief."[24]

We cannot have any clear idea of how the universe works and whether or how prayer might affect outcomes. We do not know the nature of the divine relationship to the world or the mechanics (so to speak) of the Beloved's participation in events. Hardly anything could be more clear than the fact that disastrous events occur even when a million or more people pray to be spared them. Millions of Africans were transported to the Americas. No one's prayers protected them from slavery. Millions of Jews, LGBTQ, and others were lost in the Shoah, and the millions of prayers that went up to avert disaster could not compete with the force of evil set against them. Young mothers die of cancer. Black men are shot without cause, and their killers are exonerated. Children remain at the mercy of their abusers. We cannot think of intercessory prayer as a magical charm that enables us to obtain a desired outcome. And yet the practice of it nourishes empathy and resilience.

The awareness that horrible things constantly happen does not stop amazing and unexplainable things from sometimes occurring. We may witness moments of deep presence of divine aid, succor, guidance, clarity, assistance. There are studies that suggest that people who are prayed for, even by strangers, have a greater statistical chance of surviving their hospitalizations. We need not dismiss the power of these experiences.

I have no theories about prayer, other than to observe these contradictory good and bad events. I do not think we need to understand how prayer works. I suspect clinging too hard to a particular theory of prayer may interfere with the actual practice of prayer. "Do not be over-anxious and strain yourself so as to gain an immediate hearing for your request. . . . For what greater thing is there than to converse intimately with God and to be preoccupied with his company?"[25] To pray is already to have prayer answered.

If we think of intercessory prayer as a practice of watching the mind and guarding the heart, we are freed from a concern about outcomes. We pray for ourselves or others because it is good to do so, regardless of the results. Perhaps prayer in some mysterious way draws down the Good. Maybe it helps to open a path for healing, justice, protection, wisdom to enter and perfume the world. There are infinitely complex causalities circulating in the world, most of which we know nothing about. Perhaps prayer is one.

When we pray for someone, we are in effect wishing them good things. We are lighting a candle of hope in the presence of the Holy ones: the Beloved, God, the Father, the Mother, the Blessed Virgin Mary, the saints, the Spirit of Goodness, Christ, White Tara. We are weaving our own desires for good into what we understand to be an ultimate power of goodness. This weaving together of our desires with ultimate goodness is itself a good thing. We may be mistaken in our prayers. We may pray for things that would actually be quite negative—we pray for a marriage that does only harm; we pray for a life that is over and needs to be released for whatever comes next. But even if we are mistaken in the content of our prayer, when we connect a desire for good to the divine Goodness we are dropped into a purity of good that is more than we ourselves can understand. Desiring good is always right, even though we make mistakes about what is right in a particular setting. Weaving our prayer into the divine light, we may be able to release a bit from our ideas about what should happen. We have set out our wishes for good and then we rest in the divine goodness, regardless of what happens.

This does not necessarily mean that we are confident that good will come. Our prayers that an innocent man escape execution may be thwarted by a diabolical death penalty system. We need not assume that the execution of innocent people is "God's will." But prayer unites a community and unites our heart to the Beloved. In the ebb and flow of life, in the kaleidoscope of good and evil, in the travails of suffering and the relentlessness of oppression we remain held by our divine Beloved.

Intercessory prayer, for ourselves and others, reminds us who we are. What Cheryl A. Kirk-Duggan writes about spirituals is true in the context of racism and slavery, but it has analogies beyond those: "spirituals proclaim that slaves knew who they were, despite the institutionalization of slavery. . . . These persons of color knew they were fully human in God. . . . The slaves used their musicking to affirm their own being and to survive their predicament. . . . These litanies of praise and protest reflect the real merciful justice alive in God, not as a Marxist opiate, but an ontology of the faithful."[26] Non-African Americans cannot experience this in the same way as the victims of slavery and racism do. But there remains a truth that can apply to people in different situations that Kirk-Duggan illuminates: prayer reminds us who we are. It holds us open to the mercy and justice alive in God even when the relief we crave is withheld.

To put this another way, we might think of two aspects of ourselves. There is a part that is deeply invested in what happens. We can hardly be indifferent when the innocent person is prosecuted or our children are in danger. We often pray for things with all of our might because the outcome is more important to us than our own life. When disaster strikes, we will be brokenhearted. But there is simultaneously another part of us that is not the same as our urgent desires for good to happen. The spirit in us vibrates with Spirit. It wishes for good but it tries to be peaceful with what happens. There is a dimension to us—to all reality—which is not absorbed by the immediate outcomes of events. This eternal part of us does not ebb and flow with good and bad outcomes.

Julian of Norwich offers an extended discussion of the relationship between our "sensuality" and our "substance," that is, our lived experience in the world and our eternal union with the divine. Mother Christ, Holy Wisdom "wishes us to be aware that humanity's dear-worthy soul was preciously knit to Him in the creation and this knot is subtle and so powerful that it is one-ed into God. In this one-ing it is made endlessly holy."[27] This precious one'ing does not mean we do not suffer. It does not stop the Hundred Years' War or the black death or the Inquisition. We are embodied and social beings and subject to a great deal of difficulty. But in all of this, we are never abandoned.

Julian is at pains to acknowledge the reality of the two dimensions that constitute our being—the part of us that is bodily, earthly, limited, suffering—and the part of us that is eternally one'ed with the Holy Trinity. "Notwithstanding all our feeling, woe or well, God wills that we understand and believe that we exist more truly in heaven than on earth."[28] We may suffer when things go badly but some part of us remains securely enclosed in the divine life.

Our prayers help us to resonate with Spirit and experience consolation even in difficult situations. These two dimensions do not cancel each other out, but they can modify each other. We can continue to feel terrified or broken-hearted even as some part of us is consoled and strengthened by the Spirit. If we make our trust in the Beloved contingent on good outcomes, this is less likely to happen. We will feel not only that something terrible has befallen us but that God has abandoned us, does not care, or does not exist. But prayer can run in the opposite direction. We cannot know the reasons for the terrible things that happen or how the divine agency intertwines with events. I do not believe that everything that happens is the will of God or that intercessory prayer forces God to act on our behalf. But I do believe that the Beloved Mother holds us and the world in ways I do not understand. Prayer can open us to this presence. One part of us can be terrified or grieving or angry or broken-hearted. But another part of us can experience a consolation that accompanies these feelings, not deactivating them but making them more bearable.

Intercessory prayer also has the effect of expanding our imagination for who is included in the relentless compassion of the Beloved. Churches often pray for generic suffering—people in refugee camps, people who are hungry or are endangered in their homes, people in a war-torn area, prisoners, the sick, the despairing, the addicted, the lonely and grieving, the ravaged earth. These prayers might be a dull pro forma murmur one has to get through before being released for a lovely afternoon brunch. But they can also be moments when heart and mind are carried beyond the world of private concerns toward situations we may not naturally bring to mind. The people of Syria?—*hmm*, . . . I guess God cares about them too. Perhaps a tiny dislocation occurs and the people of the world are for a moment more than our foreign policy. People endangered in their own homes? Suddenly the grinding terror of domestic violence pierces the heart in a way it had not before.

Intercessory prayer can be an imaginative exercise that reminds you of the sacredness of people you know almost nothing about. An article in a magazine alerts you to a neighborhood in Detroit or the Congo that is struggling for clean water or better schools—and so you pray for them. You cast your mind to some part of the world or social milieu strange to you, and you pray for the people of Tibet or an urban hip-hop artist.

Even when one is consumed with anxiety for a personal situation, intercessory prayer can include anonymous others in a similar situation. When I am especially concerned about someone and dedicating a period of prayer to them, I ask the Beloved to find someone else in a similar situation who has no one to pray for them and rain on them all of the protection and care I yearn for so urgently for the person I know. When I was driving down the interstate to take someone very dear to me who was suffering insulin shock to the ER I was nearly beside myself with fear and sadness. So I began to pray for all the other drivers sailing down the highway. I prayed for the people already in the hospital. I prayed for the nurses and doctors and janitors. I imaginatively clothed everything I could think of in the power of mercy and compassion. This might be semi-magical thinking. Why would God help someone I happen to pray for and ignore others, if God indeed has the power to intercede at all? I have no theory about this. But I do it anyway to spread my care beyond my immediate concern and remind me of the web of suffering and compassion in which I reside. I expose myself to the divine goodness without understanding anything at all about it, knowing that my prayers do not control what happened to my dear one or anyone else. I was held up by intercessory prayer whether it "works" or not.

Intercessory prayer becomes a small, subtle way of disorienting us from our usual patterns of seeing and categorizing the world. Even if we do not feel the depth of suffering of a stranger serving a life sentence in the same way we feel for our own children or neighbors, this practice is a tiny reminder that lives matter whether they touch us directly or not. The suffering of others matters even if my way of categorizing the world had rendered them enemies or people of no consequence.

There is a lovely prayer attributed to St. Augustine that captures some of the tenderness of intercessory prayer: "Keep watch, dear Lord, with those who work, or watch, or weep this night, and give your angels charge over those who sleep. Tend the sick, Lord Christ; give rest to the weary, bless the dying, soothe the suffering, pity the afflicted, shield the joyous; and all for thy love's sake."[29] I especially love the rare wisdom of the line "shield the joyous." Our intercessory prayers are usually directed to those in need. Aware of its vulnerability, many churches include the earth itself in their prayers of intercession. But Augustine's prayer reminds us that many beautiful things are also happening. Children are being born. Young couples are falling in love, and elderly ones are still aflame for each other. Friends are taking a long walk together. Seedlings are stretching toward the sun. A cardinal is warbling in the treetops. A prisoner is released. Enemies reconcile. The illness fades away. Celebrating joy and delighting in happiness expands our imagination and reminds us that there is much to be grateful for.

Dear One, Fragrant Flower of all good: pity the afflicted and shield the joyous, and help us to do the same.

# 7

# *Guarding the Heart*

"When faith survives and thrives to the point of being a source of heal-ing for others, it manifests itself in the form of courage. If all that is cre-ated comes for God, then courage must come from God. But how does one attain this courage in a world of violated relationships?"[1]

"God breathes through us so completely, so gently we hardly feel it yet it is our everything."[2]

Our mind shapes us even as it hides from us. As we familiarize ourselves with the working of our mind, we notice habitual ways we respond to things and can better discern patterns that have not served us. Because of this, contemplative practice is not simply the assertion of willpower. It is guarding the heart against those things that have determined our decisions and actions before we had a chance to choose or reflect on them. We pray and meditate. We watch our mind. We find ways to work with things that throw us off balance. This requires effort and attention. But the mystery of the contemplative life is that our efforts are only a part of what is happening.

The power of transformation is divine goodness. This is why atten-tion to mind and heart is itself a kind of prayer. Contemplation is a dance with the divine so the power of goodness can become more real and stable in our life. The yearning for divine goodness is the first and most basic contemplative practice. This desire allows one to drop more deeply into relationship with the Beloved. This relationship makes possible the modification of those dispositions that do not serve us or block us from deeper joy and compassion. It is by throwing ourselves into our love affair with the Beloved that we gain wisdom as we watch our mind and guard our heart.

This love affair enlivens a lived sense of connection to all things. Because relationships are so fraught and because extending con-nection ever more broadly can seem dangerous, inviting our Holy

Mother to help us is a foundational element as we learn the wisdom of guarding our heart.

## YEARNING FOR RELATIONSHIP

Notwithstanding the stereotype of a meditator as someone absorbed in their private experience, relationship is the heart of contemplative practice. Interdependence is a basic principle of Buddhism. Paul emphasized the absence of borders between one person's suffering and another, insisting that when one member suffers, all suffer with them; if one is honored all are honored also (1 Cor. 12:26). Platonism insists on the relationship of everything to everything else. Classics of Christian mysticism describe unconditional love (agape) as the primary fruit of devotion to and union with God. Activists understand that if anyone is harmed, we are all harmed. As Emma Lazarus succinctly put it, "until we are all free, we are none of us free."[3]

When we read the lives of saints and mystics—from Amma Syncletica to Howard Thurman, Rosemarie Freeney Harding, and James Finley—we discover that falling in love with the Beloved arouses contemplatives to a feeling of connection and tenderness for the world. John of the Cross was remembered not only for his remarkable mystical writings and poetry but for his enormous gentleness and warmth, and for his particular care for anyone who was sick or in need. He would take the brothers out into nature to relax and enjoy its beauty. He spent the night praying under the diamond-spangled sky. Teresa of Avila and Hildegard of Bingen both led the sisters in song and dance. The detachment from egocentrism enhanced their vibrant relationship to nature, music and song, and to people from every walk of life. Genuine love for the world and all of its creatures appears to be a fundamental disposition that we find in His Holiness the Dalai Lama, Desmond Tutu, Sister Chân Không.[4] These testimonies depict a spontaneous experience of being acutely connected to others. This is not an ethical choice as much as a vivid feeling of interdependence. Inner freedom gave them a great capacity for loving and enjoying the world. Cultivating this relational feeling is an essential component of a well-guarded heart.

It is the nature of goodness to love and seek relationship. There is no such thing as a self-contained or merely private good. There may be any number of pleasures or benefits that are private, but the good radiates goodness. Goodness is good only because it is involved with the well-being of something other than itself. Because contemplation is participation in Divine Goodness, it participates in this yearning for relationship with others. It seems to be on fire with a desire that the good circulate among all beings, so that every living thing can flourish. "I wanted life and I wanted the abundant life. I wanted it for others."[5]

The deep well of a contemplative way of life is a desire for a more vivid relationship with the divine Beloved, Mother Wisdom, Dancing Spirit. This desire is at the same time a desire to participate in the Spirit's love for creation so we also cherish all that is cherished by the Divine Goodness. Even if this desire for relationship starts out small and fitfully, something of which we are barely aware, it is the secret fire that fuels our search.

This desire is materialized in the kinds of relationships we nourish. But to nourish life-giving relationships, we have to attend not only to our actions but habits and patterns that may inhibit or enhance our capacity for relationship. Contemplation does not reject knowing and doing but it does pay particular attention to what underlies them. We have to be deep sea divers of consciousness to cultivate the qualities of relationship we desire.

When we consider this relational quality of contemplation, we are including concrete relationships with people—our ordinary circles of care and wider circles of contact. But this quality extends beyond these particular relations toward an intimacy with reality itself. It is a subtle sense of being woven into a fabric that moves far beyond immediate contacts with people and places of our everyday life. It is a kind of welcome and curiosity toward what exists. It is a posture of hospitality toward what presents itself, however unfamiliar or unexpected.

This quality of relationship acknowledges and celebrates the disconnections between our ideas about reality and reality itself. Contemplation cultivates a quality of relationship with the mystery and beauty of beings rather than relationship with our *ideas about* others. We will never perfectly apprehend a red-tailed hawk in flight or the way the forest trees communicate to one another.[6] We will never fully understand ourselves or our closest loved ones. We will never grasp the ultimate nature of the divine. Loving the world is bound up with a desire to understand it better but contemplation orients us to a different dimension of ourselves. It is concerned with that part of ourselves that is capable of intimate relationship with reality—not grasping for complete understanding but tasting the raw beauty of existence. It is an attitude or feeling for relationship that not only tolerates but also cherishes the mysterious depth of beings.

Of course we must categorize and name and locate things within the furniture of our mind. But these names do not capture the inner truth of other beings. The longing for relationship is an opening beyond names and categories to some "thusness," some quality of being, that I do not control or fully understand.

When we fall in love with a lover or with a new baby or walk through the portal into deep friendship, we may have some knowledge of the person's history and personality. But the relationship is not primarily that. It is the experience of nearness to another being, another heart. Relationship thrives in silence and touch as much as in words. Intimacy is a way of being together in which we come to understand one another more deeply, but it is not limited to the realm of knowledge. If we love a piece of land, we may want to know the names of the trees and bugs on it. We may come to a kind of wisdom about its rhythms, its flourishing and diminishments. But the love of the place is the flow of relationship with it—sitting on the rocks, listening to a birdsong. These relationships are not for something else. They do not achieve anything. Their sweetness lies simply in the relationship itself.

This contemplative intimacy is not only the familiarity that grows through years of long friendship. It is also a quality of contact that may be as fleeting as a darting lizard or the glance that passes between strangers on a street. We cannot be close friends with every person on the planet or have the same sympathy with every life form or habitat. It might be as brief as noticing the raw marvel of a patch of mushrooms or a skateboarding teenager. Relationship in this sense is a posture of intimacy and care with whatever we encounter, however ephemeral. The disposition toward relationship is not actual contact with everything that exists. This feeling of connection goes beyond awareness that all beings matter as part of the sacred fabric of creation. It is an active hospitality even in fleeting encounters and openness toward the unnumbered beings on the borderlands of one's awareness.

The stories of Jesus in the Gospels capture this quality. He pauses to adore the beauty of wildflowers in a field. He seems supremely disinterested in any kind of social standing, health (mental or otherwise), gender, ethnicity. He knows nothing about the strangers he encounters. But everyone he encounters seems to have a vividness to him. He is available to an intimacy that opens them to radical transformation. They are seen—and this itself is an enormous healing power. This capacity to pay attention to someone, to honor the sacred and unique beauty of their being is a rare and precious form of generosity. It is eros and kenosis—love and self-emptying. Giving and receiving in this sacred encounter is deeply healing.

Sometimes this sacred quality is hidden beneath many layers of distortion. It can be hard to accept that someone who does great damage in a family or in the world has sacred worth. We do not have to believe their actions or the horrifying distortions of their mind are sacred. We do not have to hope that their cruel endeavors succeed. Compassion for them and for others might require a fierce resistance to everything they are trying to do and protection for those they are harming, including ourselves. But there are no limitations to the scope of the good as it circulates throughout the cosmos and beyond. Somehow these cruel people are also held by the Divine Good, and we can hope that their ultimate destiny will be a liberation from the prison of anger and violence that has enslaved them.

Contemplation is the desire for this quality of intimate relationship with creation and with the Beloved. The wonder of what *is* arises in us and we begin to cherish beings more tenderly—in some faint reflection of the infinite delight the Beloved takes in all things. But as this yearning blooms for more untrammeled relationship with the divine Mother and Her creation, we may become aware of the limitation of our actual love of others—our reach exceeds our grasp. This awareness turns us toward our inner obstacles. What mental patterns thwart us? Where do we feel juicy and alive? This kind of attention is the work of guarding the heart.


## SUFFERING

We have spent some time considering the possible ways our heart-mind can continue to open to others. This is the beautiful dream of contemplation. But as we boldly dream this dream, our ordinary life continues just as before. Contemplation does not do one thing to protect us from the contingencies and tragedies of life. In fact, the more we open our heart, the more unprotected it is from the difficulties of life. We cannot fall back on angry ideologies that blame some despised category of people for what is happening. We cannot escape into a haze of alcohol or numb ourselves with hours of empty or violent entertainment. Because we have suffered and will suffer, it is necessary to consider suffering as an element of contemplative practice. Attention to suffering does not valorize suffering as if suffering were necessarily good for us. It does not suggest that we should try to suffer. It simply acknowledges that we do suffer and therefore paying heed to how we respond to suffering is integral to a contemplative way of life.

Suffering is not something that happens to other people, for whom we might feel pity or compassion. Suffering is woven into the fabric of life. No one escapes its cruel breath. We cannot think of contemplation as something that happens outside our real life of struggle and suffering. Suffering is the very meat and drink of contemplation. How we suffer deeply affects everything else and is therefore important to a contemplative way of life. Events can conspire to make us "despair of the world and oneself."[7] When this happens, contemplation seems like an absurd dream. As desperately as we may wish for the suffering to cease, it is crucial to discover what resources there are on the contemplative path to resist this kind of despair.

The view that suffering is caused by divine punishment can be spiritually destructive. The reasoning goes that since God is in complete control, and punishment is the way God restores order to the world, if there is suffering, then there must be punishment. The only explanation for suffering is that God has become angry and rejected us. This is a familiar but completely unhelpful way to interpret suffering. Or we may utterly reject this view as oppressive and spiritually violent—but because that was our only way of understanding God, we are left to negotiate our difficulties in a spiritual void. I may feel as if God is only interested in me when I am doing good things and feeling appropriately pious. We may meditate or do other spiritual practices, but we exclude "him" from the difficulties we face. My real life is banished from my life with God.

Everything suffers. Whatever capacity a creature has for feeling its environment will cause it pain as well as pleasure, because environments are not designed to always perfectly match a creature's needs and desires. Everything will be diminished and die and lose things precious to it. This is not a product of the fall or sin, it is inherent in life. Christ is for Christians an icon of innocent suffering, showing us that we are not vulnerable to suffering because of sin but because of how the world works. We, too, whatever our faults, are innocent sufferers in the sense that the terrible things that happen to us are unrelated to guilt and punishment. If the Buddha witnessed to the fruits of serene meditative practice, Jesus entered history to witness to its turmoil, poverty, and imperial violence. In Jesus, we see the story of humanity itself.

The Beloved enters history and suffers with us so that we will not be deserted or alone in whatever befalls us. In the passion of Christ, we are promised an ever-faithful companion in suffering and shown a glimpse of something beyond the seeming victories of suffering.

Human beings encounter suffering that is, in a literal sense, unbearable. The intensity or hopelessness or overwhelming quality of suffering is more than the human frame can accommodate. The spirit may be badly maimed, losing capacities for connection, enjoyment, hopefulness—descending into despair, depression, debilitating mental illness, rage, addiction, illness, paralysis, suicide. The heart may be distorted so that a capacity for evil and cruelty bights deeply into it. There is suffering that simply destroys: unjustified, unredeemed pain that, in this lifetime, finds neither release nor nobility.

If we do not acknowledge this, we will be unprepared for the suffering that befalls us. We will cruelly judge those who are undone by their tragedies. Our spiritual well-being requires us to accept awareness of the tragedy of human life and the destructive power of affliction and trauma. Otherwise, we will be surprised, perhaps ashamed or judgmental, when we or someone else faces afflictive suffering from which they cannot recover.

Without valorizing suffering, a contemplative can try to accept it for what it is. We can try to turn and face it rather than struggle to remove the Nessus tunic.[8] As my teacher describes it, contemplative posture toward suffering involves a "willingness to lean into the darkness of oneself and embrace what one finds there, all for the sake of wholeness. The shadow embraced yields the golden gift . . . Jesus and Judas kissed one another. I once heard an old Jesuit say that the prayer of Jesus, the Divine Healer, brought Judas to him. I hold the mystery of that in my heart. God does not waste anything. Everything in a person's life is valuable. Pain must not be wasted—it is a teacher to be honored."[9] This is not to say that God inflicts suffering, but that God encourages us not to waste it, not to let it defeat us. If we are able to make our pain a prayer, to weave awareness of divine presence into our suffering, we may find a bit of ease. We may be able to diffuse the destructive effects of suffering, even if the difficulty itself cannot be removed.

In considering suffering as an element of contemplation, we must remember that suffering is not itself a path to be sought out—we do not have to worry about finding it; it will find us. Periods of happiness and well-being are causes for celebration. But when suffering does befall us, it does not do any good to flee it.[10]

There is nothing intrinsically ennobling about suffering, nothing inherently redemptive about suffering. There are interpretations of suffering that romanticize it or defend its pedagogical value, and these may have some merit. But my point is not that suffering is somehow good for us. My point is that suffering is inevitable and that since it exists, we have to learn how to cope with it the best we can. Nothing pierces the veil of mystery to explain why we human beings suffer or why some find a way through suffering and others do not. Even without understanding, we can incorporate our own suffering into spiritual practice and learn from it what we can.

In considering suffering as a path to awakening, we must accept the raw experience of suffering as something opposed to our desire, will, effort, and hope. Suffering befalls us as an unsought opponent or enemy. The inherent quality of suffering is something that assaults us body and soul. It is a power opposed to our well-being; it seems intent on our defeat and destruction. Suffering is pain—of body, mind, soul, relationships, spirit. Suffering is like being trapped in a room with no escape. It is a burden laid upon us that we have no way to remove. Each kind of suffering has its own delicacy of anguish: terror, grief, loss of a capacity, illness, death, betrayal, disappointment, grinding oppression, the inability to protect children, physical pain and fear, imprisonment, addiction, abuse, violence, homelessness, exile, hunger, poverty, cold, frustrated creativity, abandoned hope. The shame of a victim of abuse will have a different character from the anguish of a returning veteran. The heart gnaws at a situation that cannot, in the moment or perhaps ever, be changed. The heart shatters like pottery thrown against a wall as it beats itself against an implacable foe. One twists and turns but there is no escape, no respite. And now the spirit must conform itself to this condition, which cannot be removed, and to the pain, which is now as intimate as dye moving through water.

In suffering, we glimpse the instability of our being. We taste the harsh truth of mortality. All humans are mortal. I am a human. Therefore I am mortal. But somehow we cannot accept this. This is ridiculous in one sense, but in another it is just how we all feel. Of course we know human beings are mortal and susceptible to every kind of loss; and yet when we experience our mortality it is as if the floor shook, as if a small earthquake jolted the appearance of stability.

In facing suffering, we take into account its implacable and destructive power over one's life. Suffering might be subtle yet persistent—marriage is a dull or caustic desert, work a daily assault of boredom and humiliation. It is as familiar as bread, a gray hopelessness that grinds away at bodily health and corrodes the spirit. Suffering may be horrifying, visible to all. We become repellant: "as one from whom others hide their faces" (Isa. 53:3). Desolation isolates the sufferer; no one can bear to glance at it. Or perhaps the sufferer conceals their affliction, moving about in the world with bright face and active hands, even as they are consumed with bitterness, and "wormwood and gall" (cf. Lam. 3:19). You smile at coworkers, read to the children—then weep bitter tears as the household sleeps—your spirit like a nursling child dying of thirst (cf. Lam. 4:4). What words can describe the intolerable, implacable intimacy of suffering that throws a bit in your mouth and leads you where you would not go?

When the world is unmade, the heart quails. This might cause what we now label trauma or PTSD. The psalms have a variety of visceral images for this pain, describing suffering as a "roiling pit" and "the thickest mire" (Ps. 40:2).[11] The psalmist calls upon the Beloved "from the depths" (Ps. 130:1).

> But I am a worm and no man. . . .
>
> Like water I spilled out,
> All my limbs fell apart.
> My heart was like wax,
> Melting within my chest
> My palate turned dry as a shard
> And my tongue was annealed to my jaw,
> And to death's dust did You Thrust me.
>                 (Ps. 22:7, 15–16)[12]

Trauma can activate in the ENS (enteric nervous system) a freeze response, which Philip Helsel describes both psychosomatically and spiritually:

> ENS activation honors the possibility that there may be long seasons of inactivity in a survivor's return from trauma and also honors these responses as part of the person's survival skills rather than as a pathology, since this activation can include a consolidation. Accompanied by the caregiver, the survivor can gradually welcome the outside world by including other experiences and expressing signs of safety.[13]

The significance of Helsel's description is that some of the seemingly pathological and disturbing symptoms of trauma are not only somatic responses out of a person's conscious control but also reflect a deep bodily wisdom that allows a person to be still or removed while they gradually heal from the inside out.

Trauma has particular symptoms and will shape contemplative practice in distinctive ways. Trauma resides deeply in the cellular memory and cannot heal without attention to the body.[14] It is social as well as bodily. Afflictive suffering is unattractive. People turn away from it. Friends and family abandon the sufferer. "True compassion for affliction is a more astounding miracle than walking on water, healing the sick or even raising the dead."[15] Meditation, mindfulness practice, yoga have been indicated as helpful in healing trauma. But one has to work carefully with these practices and determine what about them is useful at one time and not at another. Trauma may make it impossible to undertake any of the prayers or meditation. It may be that meditation feels like your mind is being rolled around in broken glass or leaves you with a vague sense of depression. Is this "good" for you, or is it reinforcing the mental patterning of trauma? Certain ways of doing yoga may feel too vulnerable. Perhaps your mind cannot hold in its memory three syllables of a chant long enough to repeat it. The no exit of moral injury may seem to block every escape. But a contemplative way of life is not certain practices. It is acknowledging our desire for the Beloved. Trauma may be its own contemplative practice when praying the way you thought you should pray is no longer available. Life is prayer. Every single thing that gives you sweetness is prayer. Anything that makes your body relax a bit or your sleep slightly easier. Every consoling thought. Every activity, however small, that brings you joy—standing in the shower, breathing in the air, remembering something good. Acupuncture. A veterans groups. A babysitter. Trauma takes so much away. Prayer becomes whatever begins to piece you back together again, however imperfectly; whatever gives you relief, however incomplete.

Trauma can instigate a disintegration of the moral universe. But as Michael Yandell argues, the absence of the good one had known produces a kind of negative revelation of the good. Although the good is present only in its tormenting absence, it is this very desire that can become a thread back. In the survival of this desire in a world that seems to have abandoned all that is good and decent, the good remains as lure and yearning.[16] This desire for good, even when our suffering has made us lose faith in the universe, in ourselves, in God—is itself good. This desire for good, which may have been ignited by the absence of good, is itself good—a silver thread that leads toward the good.

An Eskimo story explains the origin of light as follows: "In the eternal darkness, the crow, unable to find any food, longed for light, and the earth was illumined." If there is a real desire, if the thing desired is really light, the desire for light produces it. . . . It is really light that is desired if all other incentives are absent. Even if our efforts of attention seem for years to be producing no result, one day a light which is in exact proportion to them will flood the soul.[17]

As long as we desire the good, even in what seems like its utter absence, we are on a journey of healing. This desire is a presentiment of the good it desires. It produces the good because it already is rooted and grounded in the Good, however invisible that Good is at the time.

When an abyss opens at my feet, I seem to die. But in this perishing, a hope can gleam. The encounter of such radical fragility may so shatter my ego that, paradoxically, I begin to re-inhabit my spirit. I have seen the worst. I have taken it into me and yet I awake in wonder. I no longer see others only in their relation to me—attractive, fearsome, irrelevant. They are no longer objects external to me but, like me, part of the raw wonder of time and change, of arising and releasing. Each flaming moment, with its light rays, energies, yearnings is seen in the tenderness of pure being—the striving of cells, molecules, nerves, colors to exist. A small flock of birds darts across the sky—tiny bundles of desire, joy, fear. How fragile and lovely, how unbearably perfect. I glance at a dead leaf and notice a tiny, neon-pink gnomes' hat—some species of mold the size of a few grains of sugar—demanding to exist. We are stripped down to the glorious beauty of precarious, inessential existence, coming into being and passing away—sometimes in the grand, gentle movement of the seasons, sometimes with the shocking evil of violence. But we all exist. In our fragile, tender yearning to be, we participate with the whole interdependent cosmos, singing the eternal, ephemeral, "I am."

We cannot understand the human condition if we do not acknowledge the destructive sovereignty of pain in all of its infinitely diverse permutations. We must understand that suffering has the power to turn us to ash. We must also understand that for many there is no phoenix that rises from this desolation. Our fantasy of reliability and meaning is shattered. The theological bulwarks we cast up against disaster are washed away. This can be a moment of utter meaninglessness and hopelessness. It might also be a moment when we begin in earnest to explore what is left. When the fantasy of trustworthiness washes away, we can begin to seek what is real.

There is a mystery in the human spirit that is not exhausted by the power of suffering. We grant the kingdom of suffering too much if we fail to record the secret journeys that testify against its omnipotence. I have no theories about why some people experience terrible suffering and yet drop only deeper into the spirit of goodness—I can only observe that suffering can sometimes be transmuted into radical compassion that recognizes beauty everywhere. We have this testimony in slave narratives and civil rights memoirs. We see it in artists who transpose disaster into art. John of the Cross's great poetry was written while he was imprisoned by fellow Carmelite brothers who took him from his cell to ritually torture him every week. In the midst of his physical and spiritual agony, he wrote some of the finest religious poetry that exists in any language.

> Let us rejoice, O my Beloved!
> Let us go forth to see ourselves in Your beauty,
> To the mountain and the hill,
> Where the pure water flows,
> And further, deeper into the thicket.[18]

It was only when Israel had lost absolutely everything—when the Temple was destroyed and Jerusalem turned to rubble, when the royal family was killed or carried off in chains, when the people were dragged away as exiles in Babylon—it was only when they had lost everything that they discovered the compassion of God. It was during another period of terrible persecution and pogroms that the Baal Shev Tov emerged in eastern Europe with news of the intimacy and tenderness of the Lord. "He taught them to fight sadness with joy. 'The man who looks only at himself cannot but sink into despair, yet as soon as he opens his eyes to the creation around him, he will know joy.' And this joy leads to the absolute, to redemption, to God."[19]

In a different, but also horrifying and violent situation, Sojourner Truth gradually liberated herself from the religion of her sadistic master and sought out a God that, as her mother taught her, would hear her however cruel her master was. As she struggled against the internal and external oppressions to which she was subject, "she created a place away from everything to pray every day or more often . . . chosen by her for its beauty, its retirement and because she thought that there, in the noise of those waters, she could speak louder to God . . . To this place she resorted daily, and in pressing times much more frequently."[20] After her escape from slavery she became a famous advocate for the antislavery movement and for women's rights. Stories like this remind us that suffering is not sovereign and can, paradoxically, open to more beauty and compassion. But testimonies to the mercy that can arise, phoenix-like, from suffering are not limited to the great or famous. We recognize it in the courage of a parent or child, a neighbor, patient, or client.

There in the ash smolders a tiny spark. This spark is the luminosity that is our divine and eternal inheritance. It cannot be extinguished, unless divine reality itself can be extinguished—the Tao, the Buddha mind, the divine image—this does not perish. What was unmade by suffering is entirely real and yet not absolute. We begin to choose things that make us happy or bring consolation. We forget for minutes or hours or days at a time. Prayer, mediation, chant, dance, song, art, nature, friends, community can speak to that part of us that wishes to live again and be glad. Our heart has been cracked open and into and out of these fissures, the light shines. When we begin to awaken from the dream of despair, the flowers are brighter, the music more tender. Our hearts are softer with compassion for what others suffer.

There is no primer for incorporating suffering into the contemplative path, though there are any number of resources that can be helpful. The journey is long and has many stages. Sometimes it may simply be a prayer—today, Beloved, our prayer together with be terror or grief. Another day we may be able to work with our heart as its struggles with anger and confusion. It may be that the pain or diminishment never goes away but one learns to walk – and even dance—with a limp.

However one navigates this, the spirit of gentleness is a good guide. The journey may be long and difficult, but in life and death you are held by One who cherishes you completely and unconditionally. "I have seen what you want; it is there: a Beloved of Infinite tenderness."[21]

## FALLING IN LOVE WITH THE FEMININE DIVINE

People on a contemplative path will be drawn to the images of divine reality appropriate to them. But it is impossible not to bear a spiritual wound from the aggressive masculinity of the religious traditions. Awakening to the feminine divine can be a powerful dimension of a contemplative path. It guards the heart against toxic theology. In graduate school, I became familiar with feminist theology. I went to churches that sometimes tried to use inclusive language. But I was once at a meditation class during which we chanted names of the divine

Mother for twenty or thirty minutes. I realized that the feminine was in my head but not in my heart or my body. This absence estranged me from myself. I could read about divinization and putting on the mind of Christ—but the feminine in me could have no home there. This estrangement from myself was also an estrangement from the divine Beloved, Holy Mother Wisdom. My studies did not remove the white male god from my imagination. In separating myself from my spiritual life, I also separated the Beloved from a fuller depth of meaning. The wounding of the feminine in each of us and in our society and religions is a spiritual wound.[22] This is not only an issue for women. It is for all of us—male, female, trans, nonbinary. The feminine energy that is in everyone must be nurtured for a fully developed spiritual life. To disregard or despise this aspect of reality carries with it unfortunate spiritual, psychological, and social consequences.

This is certainly not to say that masculine images for the divine are out of place. But Christians have badly violated the second commandment, which forbids us from making images or likenesses of God from anything on the earth, under the earth, or in heaven (Exod. 20:4-6). In picturing divine reality exclusively as male, in some cases very literally, we have impoverished our relationship with the Good and with one another and with the earth. We have defrauded ourselves of the countless feminine images of divine reality that are in the Bible, in less familiar Christian writings, and in thousands of years of poetry, prayer, and theology.

This is an ethical issue, as this idolatry of maleness has upheld the right of men to possess, control, and violate female minds and bodies. This worship of the power of domination has caused great harm to both women and men. If women are disempowered by the worship of maleness, men become locked into a diminished experience of their humanity. The full spectrum of gender expression is reduced to a male-female binary and perceived to be a problem rather than an aspect of the beauty of the great dance of the Spirit. Patriarchal religion is not only an ethical problem but also a deeply spiritual one—for all people—men, women, nonbinary, trans, queer, heterosexual. Recovering the divine feminine is another way we guard the heart. It surfaces ways we have all been wounded by the denigration of the feminine. This integration of feminine and nongendered images for the divine is not a rejection of masculine images. Neither is it an affirmation that God is female or feminine. As the second commandment insists, there are *no* images that are adequate to divine Goodness. But by allowing a synergy among images to respirate our mind-heart, we both enrich our imagination and detach from the idolatry of any one image.

In the last few years of his life, Thomas Merton discovered the divine feminine and this seems to be part of the radical transformation that he experienced before he died. Some of what this meant to him is articulated in his prose-poem "Hagia Sophia" (Holy Wisdom). In it, he synthesized biblical images of Wisdom from the Gospels, Proverbs, and the Wisdom of Solomon with his own spiritual rebirth, reinvigorating a theology in which Holy Wisdom is the feminine principle of God, through whom we experience radical mercy and tenderness as well as union with the divine. He describes this as an invisible fecundity beyond all names that permeates all things. It is the Mother and Wisdom.

At a friend's house, he saw a picture of a woman placing a crown on a young man's head. When asked about the painting, the friend said he did not know what the painting represented. Merton replied, "I know her. I have always known her. She is Hagia Sophia."[23]

Merton's discovery of the divine feminine helped him heal from his inability to relate to real women or experience the divine tenderness. His mother was austere and died when he was six. He spent most of the rest of his youth in boarding schools. From 1941 until his death he was a monk and priest in a Trappist monastery. Neither actual women nor feminine sensibilities were part of his identity or spirituality. "Merton used the biblical figure of wisdom as a way to deal with his own ambivalence toward women and his self-perceived inability to give and receive love."[24] One of the great mystics of the twentieth century was healed, in part, from psychological and spiritual wounds by Lady Wisdom.

The divine feminine was for him an opening to a profound understanding of the depths of the Beloved's mercy and tenderness, an aspect of God that was underserved in his previous theology. It is also that aspect of the divine that makes union with God possible. As all great contemplatives learn, union with the divine is at the same time a visceral understanding of the unity of all humanity. In Her tenderness, her mercy, her unitive power, Holy Sophia is the relational and redemptive principle of God.

In raising up the theological and spiritual importance of Lady Wisdom, Merton hews closely to biblical texts. In Proverbs 4, the father pleads with his son to follow Wisdom. Like the painting Merton saw, the father promises his son that if he loves Her and never forsakes Her, "She will place on your head a fair garland, she will bestow on you a beautiful crown" (Prov. 4:9). The Wisdom of Solomon identifies Wisdom as the creative and redemptive manifestation of God:

> She is the breath of the power of God and a pure emanation of the glory of the Almighty; . . . She is a reflection of eternal light, a spotless mirror of the working of God, an image of his goodness. Although she is but one, she can do all things. . . . She reaches mightily from one end of the earth to the other, and she orders all things well. I loved her and sought her from my youth; and I desired to take her for my bride (Wis. 7:25–27, 8:1–2).[25]

Beginning in chapter 10, the Wisdom of Solomon details the redemptive work of Wisdom, beginning with her protection of Adam after his transgression and throughout the history of Israel. "Wisdom protected the first-formed father of the world when he alone had been created; she delivered him from his transgression and gave him strength to rule all things" (10:1–2). The litany of Wisdom's redemptive acts continues throughout Israel's history. "When a righteous man was sold, wisdom did not desert him, but delivered him from sin. She descended with him into the dungeon, and when he was in prison she did not leave him" (10:13–14). The New Testament authors identify Wisdom, an emanation of God, with Jesus: "Christ the power of God and the Wisdom of God" (1 Cor. 1:24). The Gospels also associate Jesus with Wisdom, even though few people recognized him as such. But "Wisdom is justified by all of her children" (Luke 7: 35).

A number of biblical texts associate the divine feminine not only with Wisdom but maternal fierceness and tenderness. She is like a bear defending her children (Hos. 13:8) or a woman in child birth and suckling her young (Isa. 42:14; 66:13; 49:15). She is like a mother eagle who protects her children and helps them fly (Deut. 32:10–11). She is like a bird protecting her children, guarding them under the shadow of her wings (Ps. 17:8, 57:1). Jesus likens himself to a mother hen trying to care for her chicks (Matt. 23:37; Luke 13:34). His parables often use the figure of a woman to evoke the kingdom of God (Matt. 13:33; Mark 12:41-44; Luke 15:8–10).

Poets, mystics, and theologians have continued to sing praises to the divine Mother. St. Anslem dedicated a poem to Her: "Jesus, like a mother you gather your people to you; you are gentle with us as a mother with her children." In this poem he extolls her gentleness, her comfort in affliction, her anguish that labors over our redemption and prepares us "for the beauty of heaven."[26]

Julian of Norwich (whom Merton identified as the best theologian in the English language) dedicates several chapters of her *Showings* to the development of a theology of divine motherhood. Jesus, the divine mother, is driven by His/Her/Their "dearworthy love" of humanity to feed us on herself, suckle us, give birth to us, allow us to fall, knowing that we will rise.

> This fair lovely word "mother" is so sweet and so kind in itself, that it cannot truly be said of anyone nor to anyone except of Him and to Him who is true Mother of life and of all. To the quality of motherhood belongs natural love, wisdom, and knowledge—and this is God . . . the kind, loving mother who is aware and knows the need of her child protects the child most tenderly as the nature and state of motherhood wills. And as the child increases in age, she changes her methods but not her love.[27]

But in all we suffer, in all our mistakes and sins, the Trinity, Father, Mother, Spirit never gives up or abandons us. "He shall never cease this sweet fair activity, nor pause, until all His dearworthy children are birthed and brought forth."[28]

For Meister Eckhart, divine motherhood is a point of connection between God and humanity. God is always giving birth to us: "What does God do all day long? God gives birth. From all eternity God lies on a maternity bed giving birth." And participating in the divine motherhood we give birth to God, because God is always longing to be born in the world through us:

> We are all meant to be mothers of God. What good is it to me if this eternal birth of the divine Son takes place unceasingly, but does not take place within myself? And, what good is it to me if Mary is full of grace if I am not also full of grace? What good is it to me for the Creator to give birth to his Son if I do not also give birth to him in my time and my culture? This, then, is the fullness of time: When the Son of Man is begotten in us.[29]

These (mostly male) writers who have been drawn to the divine feminine are joined by more contemporary men—John Philip Newell, Pierre de Chardin, Richard Rohr, and Marcus Borg. But women have also written a good deal about the feminine divine. The beguines often used Lady Love as a primary metaphor for God. Lady Love is not especially maternal, nor is she identified directly with Wisdom. She is a mediator between humanity and the Godhead, an intimate partner, a teacher and guide. She is also what makes God divine. Without Love, divine power is an empty and sterile abyss. There is no divinity without Love. Lady Love is not associated with one member of the Trinity, neither is She an additional divine being. Lady Love is what animates the divinity within the Godhead, within the Father, the Son, and the Spirit. Love is what makes God *God.*

In the Catholic tradition—ancient and modern—the divine feminine is embodied in Mary, whose characteristics are very similar to Merton's Hagia Sophia or Julian's Mother Jesus. A friend of my daughter did not identify his family's religion as Christian, which he identified with evangelicalism, but said simply: "we follow Mary." She is Theotokos: she who gives birth to the divine. As saint and intercessor, she can be more reliable than the distant and sometimes harsh Father. "Remember, O most gracious Virgin Mary, that never was it known that anyone who fled to thy protection, implored thy help or sought they intercession was left unaided. Inspired by this confidence, I fly to thee, O Virgin of virgins, my Mother; to thee I come; before thee I stand. . . . O Mother of the Word Incarnate, despise not my petitions, but in thy mercy hear and answer me."[30] Whatever her theological designation, she functions as the presence of the divine feminine, an embodied divine mother and Hagia Sophia available to nourish, inspire, and protect those who love her.

Clarissa Pinkola Estes reclaims the multifaceted power of the divine mother who saves and protects us, who unfreezes the frozen sea inside of us, "The Great Woman, Holy Mother, holding her close, no matter her name, garb, race, or face."[31] She is the inspiration for those who suffer, rising up from the bloodshed of the 'massacred, reminding them to "dream bold dreams." "'Rise up! Even after bloodshed . . . especially after bloodshed' says La Conquista, Our Lady of the Conquered."[32] She wears a "shirt of arrows," protecting the vulnerable. She remembers us in our desperation because "she cannot be harmed, for She and the Divine Child are eternal. . . . She ever and immediately moves through us to protect every child on earth."[33]

The Divine Mother stays with those in prison, on the street, who are drunk or in refugee camps, in villages in Mozambique where they dance at church, at the U.S. border where they wait and weep for their children, in Chinese house churches where they huddle in secret, because with Her, "there is no condemnation of any kind. . . . Only being sentenced to Life. . . . A long life of Love and more Love yet, with you forever, Holy Mother."[34]

The Holy Mother awakens that part of us that is also the divine child, born from the eternal Mother and bearing Her likeness and image. In remembering Hagia Sophia, Lady Love, the dark and bright Mother, we guard our heart against those forms of religion that justify us in our hostility to one another or fill us with shame and self-loathing. In the midst of disaster, She strengthens us, and in the midst of joy she whirls among us, leading us in the great dance.

Rebecca Cox Jackson, founder of the first African American community of Shakers, also received a revelation of Wisdom as Divine Mother:

> I received word of understanding how the Spirit of Wisdom was the Mother of children. I was in the spirit speaking these words to the glory of God: "I know Thee by revelation, Oh, Thou Mother, Thou Spirit of Wisdom, I was begotten in Thee and brought forth, though I knew Thee not. They that have revelation must live it, that they may see the Father, Son, and Holy Ghost. Oh, how I love thee, my Mother."[35]

Bright-dark Abyss, Holy Wisdom, Divine Mother—may the love of the divine, revealed as feminine, masculine, nonbinary, beyond-human guard our hearts against what harms us from within and from without. Help us to cultivate radical relationship, heal our suffering, and decolonize our mind-heart. May Your Holy Spirit delight in us and through us in the beauty of the world and respond with courageous compassion to the tragedies that assault it.

# 8

# *Contemplative Practices*

"We cannot practice meditation; all we can do is make the conditions right in body and mind so that meditation—the merging with our natural state—may spontaneously occur."[1]

"When you pray, go into your room, close the door and pray to the Beloved, who is in secret."

Matthew 6:6 (paraphrased)

We have explored the essential nature of humanity as created for the Beloved. We have also explored ways we can attend to the mental patterns that shape our way of being in the world. A third approach to a contemplative way of life is to carve out deliberate times to focus on practices that help train the heart and mind for openness to the world. This chapter will present examples of concrete practices of prayer that can be used together or separately. There are many books that describe these practices in great detail and with much learning and wisdom.[2] One can also follow teachers on YouTube. Rather than going into significant depth in describing these practices, I am providing little more than an overview. The reason for that is that I want readers to know that the contemplative life is richly fed by deliberate practices of meditation and prayer, but no single technique is required. In my experience, people find different forms of prayer and meditation suitable to their condition. Different practices are possible at different moments of life. If one type of prayer is merely frustrating or even impossible, then one need not abandon contemplation but explore other approaches. A second issue is that we humans are multidimensional and prayer affects different aspects of our being—body, voice, breath, mind, spirit, emotion, relation to nature, relation to justice, community, and non-dual awareness. No single practice infuses every one of these dimensions. One might think of meditation and prayer as a kind of cross-training in which different disciplines reinforce one another.

Sometimes our life situation makes moments of silence, solitude, and focused attention impossible. But when it is possible, turning aside, at least for a few moments, from the urgings of everyday life is a powerful practice. But in creating the sacred environment of prayer, more important than candles or a quiet corner is the intention to open the heart to the Beloved and to dedicate our practice toward the good of creation.

Periods of prayer root and ground the heart in the Beloved. Carving out time to nourish relationship with Holy Goodness means we are not without resource amid the confusions of daily life: "Mine, o lord of life, send my roots rain," as Gerard Manley Hopkins poignantly cried out.[3] Prayer waters our roots and opens up a spaciousness beyond immediate demands and frustrations. Contemplative prayer includes thought and voice and body—but it employs these not to reify dualistic or egological awareness. It employs them to activate the unity between our spirit and the divine Spirit. In prayer, we take seriously the possibility of "putting on the mind of Christ" (1 Cor. 2:16, Phil. 2:5). This "mind of Christ" is the transfiguration of our heart-mind-spirit by the indwelling of the divine. It occurs at the energetic level, as Symeon the New Theologian suggests, describing the perception of Symeon the Studite: "he possessed the whole Christ, he was the whole Christ himself, and all his members and the members of every other [person] he always saw one and all as Christ."[4] Periods of contemplative prayer participates in the energy of transformation of ourselves and our world.


## PREPARATION

Creating a sacred period of prayer begins when we turn our mind toward practice in a deliberate way. An initial preparation for whatever follows is to "put the mind in the heart," as meditation teachers often say. Rather than remaining in the cognitive and discursive dimension of our brain, it can be helpful to consciously relocate awareness into the heart, the center of spiritual awareness.

As the business of discursive thinking relaxes, the mind begins to quiet. But it is difficult to quiet the mind without quieting the body first. I am not sure how realistic it is for most of us to rush in from work or our daughter's soccer practice, plop down, and turn on the timer for twenty minutes of meditation. The first posture in yoga is simply to note: "now I am doing yoga." Delineating sacred time and space can help make a transition. Light a candle. Repeat a prayer, poem, or line from a psalm. Find a piece of music for contemplative listening. Take a breath. Some sort of bodily practice can help do this, even if it is as simple as rolling your shoulders and neck, stretching your hands, arms, feet, legs. Sometimes the primary practice may be body movements because the mind is just too scattered to relax. Dance is a beautiful practice in itself or for preparation for meditation.

To continue calming body and mind, find a comfortable sitting position—on the floor, on a cushion, in a chair. To the extent that you can, try to keep your spine straight or find a situation that will support your straight posture. Bodies vary, but a straight spine can assist in alert and relaxed attention. You do not want physical discomfort to distract you. Finding a relaxed, alert physical form can contribute to your attention to the moment. Imagine a tiny breath between each vertebrae, not stretching or straining, just creating a bit of space. Relax shoulders, mouth, jaw, arms. Balance your head on top of your spine. Your position should be both attentive and relaxed, in accord with what makes sense for your body. If your body is in pain, chronic or otherwise, experiment to see if there is any position that provides a bit more ease.

Close your eyes.

Take several calm breaths, noticing that without any effort your breath gradually becomes deeper and longer.

As you continue to breath mindfully, pause briefly at the top and bottom of each breath.

As your mind settles, you are prepared for whatever approach to prayer you are undertaking.

Or that may have been the whole session!

## PRAYING WITH THE BODY

Earlier Christians were aware of the ways the body is both an obstacle and an ally to prayer. Opening the whole self to divine love and experiencing the transformation of our entire being into that love includes praying with the body. As Gregory of Palamas puts it: "the grace of the Spirit, transmitted to the body through the soul, grants to the body also the experience of things divine, and allows it the same blessed experiences as the soul undergoes."[5]

Though our bodies are temples according to Paul, in our modern world, especially in many Protestant traditions, the body is checked at the door, reviled, or ignored. But the body is an essential dimension of our spiritual life. It holds our darkest memories and houses the divine Beloved. Looking to the wisdom of the Christian past and of other traditions, it is easier to reincorporate the body into contemplative prayer.

## Yoga and Stretching

Many Christians use yoga as a form of prayer.[6] Body prayers can be their own prayer or a preparation for other kinds of prayer. Especially in our stressful world, it is beneficial to cleanse the body of its agitation before beginning prayer. It is like tuning an instrument. Stress and anxiety are toxins that interfere with our capacity for worship. They make focus and attention more difficult. Living in such a stressful society, addressing the negative effects of stress is a part of contemplative life. If our body is a temple, then yoga, tai chi, qigong, or simple stretching are ways to tend the temple grounds and prepare it for the Bridegroom.

Even without engaging a particular discipline such as yoga, one can incorporate the body in prayer. One might take a deep breath and stretch your hands over your head and exhale as you bend over as far as your body can. Hang there for a breath or two. As you inhale, gently role your spine back to an erect posture. Take several breaths this way. There is no need to strain or press to the edge of flexibility. Moving within three-fourths of your natural range of movement rather than pressing all the way to the extreme can make sure the practice is gentle and without force.

You might sit on the floor or in a chair and inhale your arms open wide over your head, aware of the blessings that flow to you. Exhale and bring your arms down in a gentle twist, wringing out tension, activating a different kind of energy. Inhale back to your center and exhale the other direction.

Lie on your back. Bend your knees and raise your feet slowly toward the ceiling until you are shaped like an L. Point and flex your toes.

Lie on your back and let your knees drop to one side and then the other. Finish by taking a deep breath and bending forward from a sitting position.

You can incorporate the body into prayer in any number of ways. You can integrate yoga classes into your contemplative practice. You can use simple asanas as preparation for other kinds of meditation or as a form of contemplation in themselves. You can integrate chants or prayers with your yoga. You might, for example, chant the Irish prayer to the sun as you do the sun salutation.[7] You might recite a mantra to Mary as you do a twist. You might pray for peace as you do the warrior poses. If this kind of prayer speaks to you, you will find the combinations that suit you.

Your body is always available as a method of prayer. Compassionately praying with pain, gratefully savoring the sensuous joys of food or a hot bath, delighting in the way your body feels as you exercise or walk in the woods are all prayers. Gardening is prayer. Nursing is prayer. Chopping vegetables is prayer. Exhaustion is prayer. In this holy temple, the Beloved is always present, shedding divine light and love on the varied anguish, tedium, and joys of our incarnation.

## INTENTIONAL WANDERING: PRAYING WITH NATURE

The power of contemplating nature can hardly be exaggerated. Earlier Christians insisted that there were two revelations: the book of Scripture and the book of nature. For complicated reasons, many contemporary Christians limit "revelation" to Scripture and reduce revelation even further by conceiving of it primarily as the literal inspiration of individual words. But before this literalization of the Bible, Christians conceived of revelation as directed toward the whole human person in community with all of creation. It therefore included creation itself as an essential self-communication of the divine and proper object of contemplation.

In our own time as we experience the spiritual ravages caused by the amputation of nature from our lived experience, remembering the revelation of nature is more urgent than ever. It feeds a part of ourselves that is otherwise undernourished while reminding us of the sacred power and worth of creation. But because so many of us live far from natural environments, this kind of meditation may not be easy to nourish. But opening to the unpredictable mystery of nature remains a powerful contemplative practice when it is possible.

If one lives in a setting that makes meditation with nature seem impractical, it may be possible to become more aware of the way the natural world slips through the concrete cracks. The sky is an endlessly fascinating object of beauty, dynamism, and contemplation. Noticing where the moon is as she dances across the horizons, waxing and waning, a hunter's moon, a blood moon, a wolf moon can be its own contemplative focus. One can become aware of the bright stars that still pierce the light pollution—Vega, Arcturus, Sirius. It may still be possible to follow the journey of Orion, the Big Dipper, the Swan, or Cassiopeia. Honoring the solstice and the equinox tunes us into the holy rhythms of the heavens. The astonishing monuments to these movements at New Grange and elsewhere in Ireland and Scotland retain the memory of the sacredness of the movement of the sky, even though these people have been forgotten for thousands of years.

It may be possible to walk even in a city or suburb and feel the changing breeze, the blessing of sun and rain, the glories of a garden or park, the changing patterns of bird migration and leaf color. This requires a shift of awareness, a different way of walking. Using nature as a form of meditation, we allow ourselves to tune into what is already there, however obscured.

This kind of meditation can be available to someone confined to their room. An elderly person I know who does not walk well found a way to practice while others were wandering in the woods. She sat by a window and communed with a tree. This was not a familiar way of thinking to her, but she found she could do it quite easily and began to practice this way in her kitchen, looking out the window at the birds and passing seasons. Trained to think of prayer as words one says in church, this practice opened up a new world to her. The spirit of this kind of prayer is captured in this Celtic prayer:

> "I find it good just to let my gaze wander, without any concern for time and without any attempt to force concentration. Gradually one part of the woods catches my attention, and then one tree, and eventually one branch on the tree. My scattered thoughts come to focus on a single experience, and then dive deeper and deeper into that one reality (the universe in a blade of grass). Oftentimes the result is that my attention is absorbed by some small flower or leaf at my feet which I had not even noticed before—and I am at peace!"[8]

If one has access to larger swathes of the natural world, either on a regular basis or as a holiday, nature can become a potent object of meditation. Nature invites our wandering, not for exercise or to remember the names of species, but as a form of contemplative awareness. Let thoughts wander, but also allow yourself periods of attention to nature itself. Bring attention to the nose and become aware of countless scents. Bring attention to ears, then feet, then eyes, and let these organs provide objects of contemplation. Sit and observe. Be aware of the minutiae—a drop of water suspended on a spider's web hidden in a tree stump, the frolicking explosion of thousands of species of mushroom as fall rains begin, the endless variety of tree trunks twining in miracles of creativity and wonder. Walk with a question, and notice that nature responds. Lie on the moss, and let the earth receive your grief, your fatigue, your anxiety. Find a quiet place by the ocean, on a rock, in a glade to sit and practice Zen meditation or centering prayer.

## SILENT OR IMAGELESS MEDITATION:
## CENTERING PRAYER

Evagrius Ponticus extols the benefits of prayer without images, both as it contributes to beatitude and also because it allows one to "view the welfare and progress of men with as much joy as if it were his own."[9] Prayer that minimizes words and images is related to the apophatic approach that we discussed in chapter 1. Instead of relying on words, concepts, and familiar images, we allow ourselves to let go of images and rest in the divine abyss beyond thought. The Hesychasts integrate apophatic prayer into their other practices. Since divine reality is beyond every thought, image, concept, and experience, this kind of prayer speaks to a deep truth about the divine nature and also about the nonconceptual aspect of our own nature. But imagelessness is difficult to understand in even a superficial way and even more difficult to practice. We are very lucky that a form of silent prayer has been made widely available through the centering prayer movement.

In the 1970s, Trappist monks of St. Joseph's Abbey began noticing the popularity of Buddhist meditation among younger people and began to consider how to make Christian meditation more available outside the walls of the monastery. Drawing on ancient Christian texts and their own experiences, they developed a simple technique that would reintroduce Christian contemplation to laypeople. There are many wonderful books written about this practice.[10] If you are able to study this practice with an experienced teacher or read the descriptions of the practice offered by Bourgeault or Keating, it becomes clear that this simple practice is quite complex. It affects the basic structure of the psyche and raises up painful and difficult parts of our mind. It dwells in silence and moves beyond images, which our ordinary, dualistic mind finds challenging. It opens us to infinitely mysterious, surprising, and even dangerous intimacy with the Dark and Light Mother Wisdom, deeper than any words or thoughts. My very brief description here is more of a "trailer" than an adequate account of centering prayer.

The core of this practice is to orient one's desire or intention toward the sweet mystery of divine life. Any thought, even a holy and admirable thought, is still one's own thought. Every thought must be left "behind beneath a cloud of forgetting. . . . Allow no other ideas about God to enter your mind. Yet even this is too much. A naked intent toward God, the desire for him alone, is enough."[11]

This intention or desire constitutes the heart of the practice. The emphasis is on dropping the mind into the heart rather than meditating with the energy in the head. But to support this intention, one sets aside a period of time for meditative attention. This kind of prayer is imageless; it is the kind of prayer that strives to be free from concepts. But the mind will continue to do its job, generating a thousand thoughts. In order to pacify the relentlessness of thoughts and to release the mind from concepts, one uses a sacred word to dispel thoughts: peace, love, Beloved, calm—any word that you associate with the mood of this practice. An artist said she worked with images more easily than words. You, too, might use an image instead: a flame, a flower, or an icon. Focusing on the breath is another way of working with distraction. As your mind becomes caught up in the ten thousand things, simply return to the object or word of focus. Using the word to still the mind invites a deeper calm or silence to emerge from the depths of one's being. Even if you resort to the word every nanosecond or find yourself constantly distracted, simply returning to the intention, supported by your tender word, is all the practice requires. The only mistake is to imagine that the goal is no-thought and the frustration that this is not happening. There are no "bad" meditators. There is only the practice, that day, the way it is.

This quieting of the mind allows a pool of silence to grow and deepen so unitive consciousness expands. The habits, patterns, and bad memories that structure the mind become less firmly held by the hard work of the ego. Cynthia Bourgeault notes that the fruits of centering prayer do not occur during the prayer itself, but as it "gradually works its way into your system, most people will typically begin to notice a greater spaciousness and flexibility in their daily life, and along with this an improvement in their personal relationships."[12]

This form of prayer also facilitates a necessary but less pleasant consequence of purification and healing—the "unloading of the unconscious"—as Father Keating puts it. This may be gentle and gradual, or it might be very unpleasant. It may make one (temporarily) more irritable, more upset. It can—and in a sense, should—initiate a "dark night of the soul" in which belief patterns but also deeper structures of the unconscious are dismantled. Periods of spiritual difficulty are, unfortunately, simply part of contemplative practice and require support and care.[13]

Teachers of centering prayer recommend twenty minutes, twice a day. This is an excellent recommendation. For many, however, it is impossible. The day is too busy. The children or elderly parents too consuming. The three jobs necessary to make ends meet are too overwhelming. The mind too savaged. There are other ways to pray if this approach does not suit you. Improvise according to the possibilities of your mind and your day. Some people focus exclusively on this prayer. Others use it as a base. Centering prayer is an intention, a meditative technique, a form of imageless prayer, a path of transformation. It can be integrated into other kinds of contemplation, providing a technique that helps to still the mind and savor silence. One approach is to move back and forth between images and imagelessness. Hold an image in your mind and allow it to dissolve. When distraction displaces the clarity without image, return to the image. Vacillating between image and imagelessness can be another helpful way of working with the mind's relentless desire for images. But if this is not a prayer that suits you, experiment with other possibilities.

## PRAYERS OF THE IMAGINATION

Christian contemplatives emphasize the particular power of imageless contemplation, that is, prayer that has released concepts and images. Through this kind of prayer, we become less preoccupied with ideas about the divine and become more intimate with the great mystery of divine love itself. Imageless prayer gradually disenchants us from those things that distract us from the beauty of creation, the goodness of the Beloved, and our joy and compassion for others. But the mind tends to resist imagelessness, always wanting to find something to cling to, even in the deep silence of contemplation. Using images to disenchant images has been a common method of Christian prayer. Some people use an icon, holy image, or piece of art as their object of attention. Many contemplatives generate visual images. Visualize the Divine

Mother holding you or protecting you. Construct a scene from nature and explore it very carefully in your imagination. See in your mind's eye the cave-like space of your heart and allow your mind to wander there. The imagination opens recesses of the mind and accesses emotions and feelings to integrate into prayer.

## COMPASSION MEDITATION

Another way to employ the imagination is by exploring different kinds of compassion meditation.[14]

### Compassion as Radiance

After preparing yourself for prayer:

Visualize in your mind's eye an image of divine love: this might be the face of Mary or of Christ, it might be a flame or a scene from nature, it might be a scene from Scripture of a tree planted by a flowing river, Jesus embracing the beloved disciple to his chest, or Lady Wisdom protecting someone in trouble.

Hold this image in your mind, returning to this image as your mind wanders and becomes distracted.

Gradually notice that this image is dissolving into light. In your mind's eye see the divine love not only in concrete image but as pure light.

Visualize this light entering you through the crown of your head.

Be aware of this light gradually flowing through you:

through your brain and mind,

your eyes and ears,

your face and neck;

notice its flow through your chest, lungs, and heart.

It flows through your arms and fingers.

It flows through your torso, internal organs, hips, down your legs and toes.

Allow this light to fill your entire being, your body and breath, your heart and mind.

As you dwell in this silent radiance, be aware that this light radiates effortlessly from you. Without you doing anything, it radiates to those near you. It radiates to strangers you encounter at work, in a store; it shines in a quick smile that recognizes the humanity of strangers. It shines on those in prison, on the street, in the arms of their lover. It radiates to those who are difficult. It caresses the city where you live, and beyond, to every country, to the blades of grass, the flowers, the oceans, the creatures at the bottom of the ocean. Loving, compassionate, joyous light radiates through the darkness between the stars.

Dwell in this silent darkness, delighting in the Divine Emptiness from which such great and infinite love ceaselessly flows.

Slowly gather your mind back, take several breaths, relocate your awareness in your body, in the present moment.

Call yourself from prayer with a verbal prayer, a poem, a passage from Scripture, or some other way of enclosing your meditation.

Enjoy the rest of the day, whatever it may bring.

### Compassion for a Friend, a Stranger, a Difficult Person

Visualize some image of divine love before you: a light, the face of Christ or Mary, the sun.

To your right visualize a person dear to you; visualize the love and light of divinity pouring onto them, wish them well, wish them ease and peace, wish them happiness and freedom from what distresses or harms them.

Next, imagine someone before you who is a stranger or someone whom you do not care about one way or another: a waitress, the mail carrier, someone you pass in the halls at work. Imagine the divine love pouring on them; wish for them ease and peace, wish them happiness and freedom from what distresses or harms them.

Third, visualize someone on your left with whom you have difficulty. It is wise to choose someone easy at first. It can even be the person dear to you who you are currently angry with, which annoys you. It might be something about yourself that irritates you, so you are the person with whom you are having difficulty. As you practice this way you can introduce people you know or know of who have been harmful and explore the sense in which you might offer them compassion as well. Imagine the divine light and love pouring on them. Wish for them, to the extent that it is possible for you, ease and peace, happiness and freedom from what distresses or harms them. Conclude this prayer by allowing the divine light and love to fill you and dwell in that light, savoring silence.

There are other forms of compassion meditation. The common ground in this kind of meditation is that it creates a bodily experience of compassion. It grounds compassion in a visceral experience of the Beloved's compassion for you and then extends this compassion to others. Without this experiential grounding in awareness of yourself as cherished, beloved, and adored in your beauty and in your challenges, it will be difficult to convey compassion to others. Compassion may feel brittle or exhausting. But grounded in the divine compassion, you are aware that the source of your compassion is not your ego mind, not even your ethical commitments. You are accessing the divine power of compassion already within you and allowing it to radiate from you.

## LECTIO DIVINA

"Divine reading" is another ancient and modern method of prayer. It may be one of the most commonly described forms of meditation in medieval manuals of prayer.[15] There are many good books on this kind of prayer, ancient and contemporary. Again, I will give only a brief description. Traditionally, *lectio divina* is praying with Scripture. Some people find themselves alienated from Scripture or just needing to expand their holy reading. Praying with poetry is a good alternative. There are also many books that provide daily readings. Another modification of this practice is *visio divina*—praying with an image.

In earlier centuries, Scripture was not understood as a repository of correct information but rather as food for the soul. Just as the human person has a body, soul, and spirit, Scripture is multidimensional and has the power to address all the parts of the person. At the most external or straightforward level, it tells stories that address our thinking self. But it moves more deeply into us, engaging the less discursive and affective parts of us until it lifts us to communion with the Beloved. Scripture, as food for the whole self, nourishes this journey from stories and images to imageless communion. Praying with Scripture was and is a way to connect spirit to the Divine. This kind of prayer begins by reading or reciting or chanting a short passage from Scripture. As one drops away from the literal meaning, an image or word may stand out. One begins to sit with this image, feeding on it, letting it do its work without controlling its significance. As one continues to let the image or word rest in one's mind, the word itself fades away and there is left only quiet communion with the Beloved. Beginning with the passage, one ruminates on it in meditation (using words and thoughts) then passes into contemplation (dwelling in nonconceptual silence).

*Lectio divina* is not concerned about analyzing a passage or attending to historical criticism or fighting with its literal meaning. A brief passage serves as a pathway that connects one's own heart, at this moment, exactly as it is, with the heart of the divine. One allows the passage to work on one's heart, sitting with it, dwelling with it, letting it do its work without too much interference from one's reasoning powers. "The word is very near to you, it is in your mouth and in your heart" (Deut. 30:14).

There are texts that describe in more detail techniques for this prayer that are quite helpful. You can explore your own ways of working with short passages from Scripture and let the grace of the passage do its work. You might work with a lectionary or some other daily reading. You might have a spiritual director or online group that suggests a passage. You can also use poetry or sacred texts from other traditions.

Typically, you might read the passage over once, then twice, then a third time, drawn into different levels of its power. You might read the passage aloud or chant it slowly. You might find yourself drawn to a single word or phrase or image. You might enter the narrative, smelling the flowers, feeling the water flowing around your roots, holding the infant Jesus in the stable, or lurching from the tomb like Lazarus. The divine reading is not interested in the historical or theological meaning but what the passage is saying to or doing with you. It is you who is emerging from the tomb, half dead and dazed. It is you who is a tree, whose deep roots are spreading toward the flowing water.

Allow the images to fade away and allow the silence of the divine presence to fill you, simply dwelling with the Beloved. Or it may be that a passage opens onto a door of memory or emotion that needs tending. Allow the Holy One to circulate through your being, bringing consolation, understanding, healing, delight, or perhaps simply resting as a sympathetic presence. The inspiration of Scripture is its power to be ever-new, to breathe life into each of us in the immediacy of our present moment.

The purest parchment upon which Scripture is written is your own soul. It enters you as you enter it.

## PRAYING WITH THE BREATH

Many modern Christians associate praying with breath with other religious traditions, but the breath is the presence and symbol of the Holy Spirit. In the biblical languages, the word for spirit and breath is the same. It is a place where body, spirit, heart, and mind flow together, where inner and outer meet, and where the Holy Spirit and our spirit join. We have probably all had the experience of calming ourselves by simply taking a deep breath. Deep breathing activates a calming effect on the body and contributes to overall health.[16] This physical response to pneumatic prayer is good in itself. Whatever helps detoxify stress is to be celebrated. But breath also contributes to an increased ability to focus on prayer and meditation with less distraction. Praying with breath is a powerful method for quieting the mind and also deepening silent awareness of Lady Wisdom. There are many ways of understanding praying with the breath. I will mention only a few.

*Example 1*: Focus on the breath itself, without words. Place one's mind on the inhale and then on the exhale. This is similar to centering prayer but uses the breath instead of a word to draw the mind toward calm.

*Example 2*: A second way to pray with the breath is to experiment with different breath techniques. Because Christian practices with breath have mostly disappeared from our view, it is useful to turn to the wisdom of yogic practitioners who have significant insight into the use of pranayama in prayer. It is an excellent way to refresh and sharpen the mind. It is both a preparation for prayer and prayer itself. Examples of this kind of breath prayer include:

*Ratio breath*: inhaling and exhaling on a specific count. For example, inhale for six counts (or ten or whatever count is comfortable and not forced), and then exhale for six counts. One can also insert a brief pause between inhale and exhale: inhale six, pause three, exhale six, pause three; or inhale ten, pause five, exhale ten, pause five—and so on.

An alternative is to exhale more slowly than the inhale: inhale eight, exhale ten; or inhale eight and exhale sixteen. These ratios should be controlled but not uncomfortable. If you begin to feel breathless adjust the breath. The point is not to aggressively manipulate the breath but to use your natural cycle of breath in a more controlled way.

*Alternate nostril breath*: There are various modifications of this breath, but they all involve inhaling and exhaling through only one nostril. The simplest is to close the left nostril with the right ring finger, inhale through the right nostril; then use your thumb to close the right nostril, leaving the left nostril open for your exhale. Repeat this cycle for several minutes.

### Breath and Body

Another way to pray with the breath is to synchronize a body movement with your breath. Lie on the floor and slowly raise your arms over your head as you inhale and lower them as you exhale. Sit on the floor or in a chair and inhale as you raise your hands in the ancient posture of prayer, your arms in a slight V shape over your head, shoulders down and relaxed; exhale, drawing your hands toward your heart in the more modern prayer position.[17] Inhale and turn your head to one side, exhale to center; inhale and turn your head to the other side, exhale to center.

These prayers can focus your mind simply by being aware of the unity of movement and breath. It activates your sympathetic nervous system and creates a sense of calm. This release from stress is not only something that makes us feel good. When our bodies begin to release from the toxicity of tension and stress, we are more available to the movement of spirit. These simple body-breath prayers are invitations for Spirit to dwell within us—or rather, for us to become more aware of this indwelling.

One can use these (and other) breath practices as a prelude to contemplation, as a form of meditation, or even as a prayer one uses all through the day: mindful breathing as you sit at a traffic light or wait in a doctor's office.

## PRAYERS OF REPETITION

The practice of reciting a short prayer over and over is an ancient and modern way of prayer. This is a familiar practice to Catholics who pray the rosary or recite prayers to Mary such as the Hail Mary or Memorare. More recently, some Christians have borrowed the term "mantra" for this kind of prayer, but it is almost as old as Christianity itself.[18]

One of the most ancient prayers, dating to the fourth century, was one that yoked the Jesus prayer to the breath with the intention of so uniting breath with the heart that the heart opens and remains constantly in prayer. It was understood to be especially powerful for the awakening of the heart for love. A simple version of the Jesus prayer is "Jesus Christ, have mercy on us." But almost any short prayer or word can be used in this way.

Mantra recitation can constitute a period of prayer. You can set aside ten or twenty or thirty minutes to calmly recite a mantra. Mantras can also be recited while waiting in line at a store or listening to a boring lecture. You might begin a period of prayer with ten minutes of mantra and then drop into centering prayer.

For example:
Inhale—Beloved
Exhale—Jesus
Inhale—Mother
Exhale—Jesus
Or:
Inhale—Holy
Exhale—Wisdom
Or:
Inhale—Mary mother of God
Exhale—pray for us now
Inhale—and at the hour of our death
Exhale—that we may be mothers of God
Or:
Inhale—God who created the sun
Exhale—You are the sun of my soul
Inhale—And you make me glad
Exhale—Light of the sun be with us today
Or:
Inhale—In the ebb,
Exhale—In the flow
Inhale—Oh Thou
Exhale—Triune of grace
Or:
Inhale—Bright morning star is rising
Exhale—Day is breaking in my soul
Or:
Inhale—Lady Wisdom
Exhale—Heart of my desire
Or:
Inhale—Jesu
Exhale—Christe

Or:
Inhale—Sophia of God (or Beloved Jesus)
Exhale—Overshadow me with your love

## PRAYING WITH ENERGY

The body is not only flesh, organs, the flow of blood. It is also energy, and this energy can be incorporated into prayer. Some Indian and Tibetan traditions have developed sophisticated ways of using energy to facilitate contemplation. The examples here are very simple.

We can imagine sites in our body where energy is gathered or concentrated. One way to do this is to allow the body to mirror the holy Trinity. Imagine the base of your spine as the energy center related to divine Goodness manifest in the stability and beauty of creation. The heart vibrates with the energy of the divine Love in tenderness and compassion. The crown of the head concentrates the energy of divine Wisdom and holy peace.

After preparing for prayer, shift your attention to the energy centers of your body. Focusing on these three energy sites is a way of weaving consciousness of the Trinity into the body. The more you engage this practice, the more you will be aware of the opening of these energy centers to awareness of the divine presence.[19]

The simplest way to begin this practice is simply to be aware of each of these three locations in your body, breathing into each one. You can stay at each energy center for several breaths, or you can go up through the energy centers, one breath at a time, several times. You might visualize a bright light, like a brilliant star in each of these centers.

You can also add sound as you move through energy centers. Sound activates a different kind of vibration in your body and facilitates prayer. For example, focusing first on the base of the spine, as you inhale, be aware of being held in the divine Goodness and safety. As you exhale, release a small hmmmmmm, aware of your participation in this Goodness.

Next, bring your attention to your heart. Be aware of your heart as the site where the tenderness of divine compassion flows through you. Be aware of the caressing of your heart by this love, cherishing you, adoring you exactly as you are. Inhale awareness of the divine tenderness. Exhale awareness of your heart's opening to this tenderness. Hmmmmmm.

Bring you attention to your wisdom eye, aware of the immense beauty of the divine Wisdom: the calm, nondiscursive embrace of all reality. Consider awareness of divine wisdom, free of anxiety and calculation, lovingly aware of all creation throughout all of time and space, held in the love of the Divine Mother. Inhale calm awareness of divine Wisdom. Exhale the peace that arises from Holy Wisdom. Hmmmmmm.

As you conclude, take several additional breaths, guiding the breath, like a beautiful, golden light, up your spine from base to crown and exhaling your breath down the spine, from crown to base. In this way you imaginatively integrate the security and trustworthiness of the divine Goodness, the cherishing tenderness of the divine Love, and the calm insight of the divine Wisdom. Shift your attention to the radiance of your own heart. Be aware that the indwelling of the Holy Spirit radiates from you. Effortlessly, you participate ever more deeply in this love and are able to radiate goodness, compassion, joy, and wisdom throughout the day.

Sit in silence, dwelling in the tender presence of the Beloved.

## CHANT

It is also possible to do this kind of prayer but using chant instead of visual imagery or a gentle hmm. Chant is perhaps the most ancient form of religious practice and is present in all traditions. For early Christians, chanting the psalms was the most basic prayer. It has the virtue of combining breath and body, heart and mind. Chanting in community enhanced the vibrations that united those in prayer with one another and with their divine source. Cynthia Bourgeault insists that chant is a kind of Christian yoga, uniting body, breath, spirit, community. In this ancient practice, monks and nuns submit themselves to "a highly precise system of inner alchemy. Whether consciously articulated this way or not, the chanting was a kind of yoga, producing definite changes in the subtle energetic structure of their being according to a well-calibrated blueprint."[20] The popularity of Taizé chant suggests that this practice is being rediscovered by Protestant as well as Catholic communities. Some people turn to other religious traditions for simple chants. It is easy to find chants on YouTube. If you are not familiar with chanting, this is a good way to find someone to chant along with you. You can turn any of the prayers of repetition listed above into this kind of prayer.

## WATCHING THE MIND

In a previous chapter, we discussed watching the mind as an ongoing practice that is woven into daily life. There are also ways to mediate on the mind, using the mind itself as an object of attention. A few examples of this practice follow.

### Observing the Flow of Thoughts

After preparing for prayer, instead of working with techniques for banishing thoughts, allow thoughts and feelings to rise and fall. Watch them as they come and go. Instead of clinging to them, simply watch them, like clouds in the sky. Allow them to follow their own path of appearance, intensity, and dissipation. If you do not grasp at them, they retain relatively little stability. This kind of meditation allows us to gain awareness that the flow of thought and feeling, even disturbing ones, is not identical to our whole self. Likewise, good feelings absorb us and then pass away. They rise and fall. They change. We are not identified with our thoughts or feelings. We can create distance—not in the sense of repression or denial, but noticing that some part of our mind need not be helplessly absorbed in pain or in the constant flow of distractions. Following the rising and dissipating of thoughts in meditation can weaken the tyranny of difficult emotions and open more spaciousness in everyday life.

### Prayer with Difficult Thoughts

In many forms of silent prayer, we are instructed to release thoughts and not follow them. But sometimes allowing the thought to itself be an object of meditation can be useful. If some persistent or difficult thought or feeling arises, watch it, tend it, care for it, study it. If it is something unwelcome, rather than pushing it away use this circumscribed time, when you are explicitly in the presence of the Beloved, to sit with the difficulty and learn what it is, what its news to you is, what it needs. Watch and see if there are roots to this that you were not aware of; follow the thought or emotion and see if you can find its hidden lair. Allow it to be bathed in the divine love. You do not have to love this pain or difficulty, but you can allow it this moment to be seen and better understood or tended.

## BRIDGING MEDITATION AND EVERYDAY LIFE

From a contemplative point of view, there is no firm distinction between intentional periods of prayer or meditation and everyday life. These intentional periods can be deeply refreshing. Sometimes these practices can help heal old wounds or vivify our capacities for gratitude, joy, and compassion. But the real practice is life. How we treat other people, journaling, nature, art, music, erotic love, family life, work, addictions, anguish, hope, laughter—everything is practice.

We live in dark times and they are likely to become darker, especially as climate change begins to take its relentless toll, and terror paralyzes us or turns ordinary people against one another. As we struggle for justice and for courage, contemplative practice weaves heaven and earth, stitch by stitch, breath by breath, tragedy by tragedy, kindness by kindness. It is the joy and danger of falling in love with the world even in the darkest times. It is the practice of the present moment, discovering the Beloved in all things. We walk from holy ground to holy ground. Never forsake your desire and the demands it makes on your life.

Practice. Practice. Practice.

# Notes

## Introduction

1. There are a number of books that emphasize the unity of ordinary life and contemplation. Jon Kabat-Zinn has authored many. The book written with his wife is especially helpful, as it offers the point of view of a mother nursing a baby in the wee hours of the day and negotiating with a teenager: John Kabat-Zinn and Myla Kabat-Zinn, *Everyday Blessings: The Inner Work of Mindful Parenting*. Beverly Lanzetta offers deep insight of lay monasticism in *The Monk Within: Embracing a Sacred Way of Life*.

2. Brother Lawrence, *The Practice of the Presence of God with Spiritual Maxims*, 90. This little book is not actually written by Brother Lawrence but was put together primarily from conversations and letters by his admirer, M. Beaufort. Brother Lawrence was a seventeenth-century monk who worked in a monastery kitchen. His primary practice was simply to see God in whatever he was doing—cutting vegetables, sweeping the floor—nothing was excluded or alien to the presence of God.

3. Brother Lawrence, *The Practice of the Presence of God*, 105.

4. Rosemarie Freeny Harding and Rachel Elizabeth Harding, *Remnants*, 262.

5. Galway Kinnell, "Flying Home," Poetry Soup, https://www.poetrysoup.com/famous/poem/from_flying_home_444.

## Chapter 1: Contemplation on the Borderlands

1. Fyodor Dostoevsky, *The Brothers Karamazov*. The first part of this quotation is from the long speech of Father Zossima in part 2, book 6, chapter 3, p. 357. The second half of the quotation is a paraphrase of the rest of the chapter on the website "Monasteries of the Heart: on On-line Community Sharing Benedictine Spirituality with Contemporary Seekers," an outreach of the Benedictine Sisters of Erie, 2011, https://www.monasteriesoftheheart.org/daily-and-other-prayer/thursday-prayers-earth.

2. Karen Baker-Fletcher, *Dancing with God*, xii.

3. W. B. Yeats, "The Second Coming," in *The Collected Poems of W. B. Yeats*, 187.

4. Pope John XXIII in an address to bishops in October 1962, quoted in *All Saints: Daily Reflections on Saints, Prophets, and Witnesses for Our Time*, ed. Robert Ellsberg, 243.

5. Pope John XXIII, *All Saints,* 244.

6. Rosemarie Freeney Harding and Rachel Harding, *Remnants: A Memoir of Spirit, Activism, and Mothering,* 235.

7. Walker, *The Color Purple,* 195, 197, 198.

8. Meister Eckhart, Sermon 87, in *Meister Eckhart: A Modern Translation,* trans. Raymond B. Blakney.

9. Philip Sheldrake, *Julian of Norwich: In God's Sight,* 22.

10. "First, we must love Him with all our heart. . . . And our neighbors as ourselves: that is, that we neither do, nor think, nor speak toward our neighbors anything we would not wish they do toward us. These commands are of necessity for salvation for all: nobody can have grace in a lesser way." Marguerite Porete, *Mirror of Simple Souls,* 81.

11. This is a phrase from Gerard Manley Hopkins's "God's Grandeur," in *Gerard Manley Hopkins: Poems and Prose,* ed. W. Gardner, 27.

12. See, for example, Thomas Keating, "The Unloading of the Conscious," *Open Mind, Open Heart: The Contemplative Dimension of the Gospel,* ch. 9.

13. A classic expression of this is a from a twelfth-century monk, Guigo II, *The Ladder of Monks and Twelve Meditations.*

14. Bourgeault, *The Heart of Centering Prayer,* 17–18.

15. Stanford, Emory, Brown, and the University of San Diego are among those that offer research in the area of contemplative studies. Like these universities, the Mind and Life Institute is dedicated to research into meditation using both scientific studies and the insights of advanced practitioners. The University of Redlands offers a summary of some of this research on its website: https://www.redlands.edu/study/explore-academic-resources/meditation-room/contemplative-education/benefits-of-meditation/. Courage of Care provides both online and in-person trainings and workshops to deepen capacities for compassion and activism through contemplative practices.

16. David Shapiro, Forward, Anne Porter, *Living Things: Collected Poems,* xv.

17. Richard Rohr, October 9, 2019, Center for Action and Meditation daily email, "Richard Rohr's Meditation, Week Forty-one, Franciscan Way: Part Two."

18. Hopkins, "Hurrahing in the Harvest," *Gerard Manley Hopkins: Poems and Prose,* ed. W. Gardner 31.

19. Pseudo-Dionysius, "The Divine Names," 82.

20. Charles Darwin, in Elizabeth Johnson, *Ask the Beasts: Darwin and the God of Love,* 45.

## Chapter 2: We Are Made for the Beloved

1. Catherine of Siena, "Consumed in Grace," in Daniel Landinsky, ed., *Twelve Sacred Voices from East and West,* 183.

2. Plato, *Phaedrus,* trans. Alexander Nehamas and Paul Woodruff, 227A.

3. Teresa of Avila, *The Interior Castle*, trans. E. Allison Peers, Mansion 1, ch. 1, p. 28.

4. Teresa of Avila, *The Interior Castle*, Mansion 1, ch. 1, p. 39.

5. Guigo II, "Twelve Meditations," *The Ladder of Monks and Twelve Meditations: A Letter on the Contemplative Life and Twelve Meditations*, 91.

6. Guigo II, "Twelve Meditations," 111.

7. Philip Sheldrake, *Julian of Norwich: In God's Sight*, 7.

8. Julian of Norwich, *Showings*, 51. This is my own translation.

9. Julian of Norwich, *Showings*, 61. This is my own translation.

10. *Metanoia* is a Greek word that occurs in the New Testament, often translated as "repent." But this translation is a Reformed theology anachronism, imposing on the text a religious view that arose centuries later. The word means something more like a transformation of mind-spirit at a very deep level. "Transform your mind [repent] for the kingdom of God is at hand" (Matt. 4:17, my translation) is an invitation to a complete reconstitution of one's basic sense of reality. The kingdom of God is completely available, here, now—if you transform your mind, you will experience this.

11. Sinead O'Connor, "This Is to Mother You," on *Gospel Oak*.

12. Julian of Norwich, *Showings*, 51. My translation.

13. Aelred of Rievaulx, "Three-fold Meditation," in *Treatises and Pastoral Prayer*, 95.

14. Aelred of Rievaulx, "Three-fold Meditation," 102.

15. Mechthild of Magdeburg, *The Flowing Light of the Godhead*, trans. Frank Tobin.

16. Symeon the New Theologian, *Divine Eros: Hymns of Symeon the New Theologian*, Hymn 15, 130–50, 170, 225, trans. Daniel Griggs. Most of this passage is also translated by Stephen Mitchell more loosely (but perhaps more beautifully) in *The Enlighted Heart: An Anthology of Sacred Poetry*, 38.

17. Guigo II, "The Ladder of the Monks," 68. This brief summary of the steps of the ladder can be found on page 68 of this text but is expanded through the entire short essay.

18. Anne Porter, "Music," in *Living Things: Collected Poetry*, 54, https://www.writersalmanac.org/index.html%3Fp=9278.html.

19. Simone Weil, "Reflections on the Right Use of School Studies for the Love of God," *Waiting for God*, trans. Emma Craufurd, 59, 61. This beautiful essay is available on line at Hagia Sophia's website as well: http://www.hagiasophiaclassical.com/wp/wp-content/uploads/2012/10/Right-Use-of-School-Studies-Simone-Weil.pdf.

20. John of the Cross, *A Spiritual Canticle of the Soul and the Bridegroom of Christ*, trans. David Lewis, stanza 1: http://www.documentacatholicaomnia.eu/03d/1542-1591,_Ioannes_a_Cruce,_A_Spiritual_Canticle_Of_The_Soul,_EN.pdf. There are many good translations of John of the Cross's poetry, but this one is available online.

21. John of the Cross, *A Spiritual Canticle*, stanza 39.

22. See Rascal Flatts, "Bless the Broken Road," which is not about faith but is a lovely image for it.

23. Julian of Norwich, *Showings,* ch. 77. My translation.

24. Dorotheos of Gaza, "On the Fear of God," *Discourses and Sayings*, trans. Eric Wheeler, OSB, 109–10.

25. Julian of Norwich, *Showings*, ch. 75. My translation.

26. Mechthild of Magdeburg, *The Flowing Light of the Godhead*, 114–15.

27. Peter of Alcantara, *Treatise on Prayer and Meditation*, trans. Dominic Devas, OFM, 98.

28. Peter of Alcantara, *Treatise on Prayer and Meditation*, 99.

29. Guigo II, *Ladder of the Monks and Twelve Meditations,* 73.

30. Guigo II, *Ladder of the Monks and Twelve Meditations*, 130–31.

31. Beguines were lay women contemplatives who flourished primarily in the thirteenth century. The vitality of the movement and its beautiful literature came to an and with the burning of its most brilliant and courageous member, Marguerite Porete, in 1310.

32. Mechthild of Magdeburg, *The Flowing Light of the Godhead*, 62.

33. Marguerite Porete, *Mirror of Simple Souls*, trans. Ellen L. Babinsky (Mahwah, NJ: Paulist Press, 1993), 109.

34. Julian of Norwich, *Showings*, 259. As we will discuss later, this view of God as utterly good and permitting no permanent separation between humanity and God, no hell or eternity of suffering, could put contemplatives in tension with church teachings.

35. Marguerite Porete, *Mirror of Simple Souls*, 187.

36. John of the Cross, "The Dark Night," part 2, ch. 25.

37. Pseudo-Dionysius, "Mystical Theology," ch. 5, trans. John D. Jones.

38. Marguerite Porete, *Mirror of Simple Souls*, 201. This is my modification of Babinsky's translation.

39. These translations are from Robert Alter, *The Hebrew Bible: A Translation with Commentary*, vol 3.

40. These are images from Pseudo-Dionysius who talks about the divine darkness in *Divine Names* and *Mystical Theology*, in *The Complete Works*, trans. Colm Luibheid; the anonymous author of the *Cloud of Unknowing*, Anonymous, translated by Carmen Acevedo Butcher; and Nicholas of Cusa, "The Vision of God," in *Selected Spiritual Writings*, translated and introduced by H. Lawrence Bond.

41. Maximus of Tyre, Dissertation 38, *Five Stages of Greek Religion,* trans. Gilbert Murray, 74–75. Maximus of Tyre was a second-century Greek philosopher, a precursor to Neoplatonism.

## Chapter 3: Awakening to Beauty

1. Alice Walker, *The Color Purple* (Orlando: A Harvest Book, 1992), 197.

2. John O'Donohue, *Beauty: The Invisible Embrace*, 13.

3. O'Donohue, *Beauty*, 3–4.

4. Simone Weil, "Forms of the Implicit Love of God," *Waiting for God*, 162.

5. When I am feeling down, sometimes I just look at the photographs on the Hubble site. The beauty of the cosmos puts a good deal in perspective, https://hubblesitc.org/images/gallery.

6. Gregory of Nyssa, *The Great Catechism,* ch. 21. Plato extolls beauty in a number of places. The *Symposium* and the *Phaedrus* are both extended dialogues on the philosophy of beauty.

7. Pseudo-Dionysus, *The Divine Names*, in *The Complete Works*, trans. Colm Luibheid, 77. John D. Jones translates the Greek as "charmed," Colm Luibheid translates the term as "beguiled" in the Paulist Press edition.

8. John O'Donohue, *Beauty*, 236.

9. Patrick Pearse, "Ideal," quoted in John O'Donohue, *Beauty,* 235.

10. Patty Griffin, "Icicles," on *Impossible Dream* (New York: ATO Records, 2004).

11. At a meeting recently, J. Kameron Carter reminded me of the resonance of this phrase with Audre Lorde's essay, "Poetry Is Not a Luxury." I read this long ago and am happy to give her credit for implanting this idea deep in my brain. Audre Lorde, *Sister Outsider: Essays and Speeches.*

12. This phrase began to circulate in 1911, but it was the women of the textile strike in Lawrence, Massachusetts, in 1912 that used it as a rallying cry.

13. Trevor Noah, *Born a Crime: Stories from a South African Childhood* (New York: Spiegel & Grau, 2016).

14. Amineh Abou Kerech, "Lament for Syria." The poet recites her poem on YouTube: https://www.youtube.com/watch?v=VOCtYxbtpFU.

15. This last example is a scene in Delia Owens's *Where the Crawdad's Sing* (New York: G. P. Putnam's Sons, 2018), 128: "Tate eased more power to the winch, and the boat crawled up the track into dry dock. They secured her with cables and set about scraping blotchy barnacles from her hull as crystal-sharp arias of Miliza Korjus rose from the record player."

16. Paul Tillich *On Art and Architecture*, 234–35

17. Elizabeth Alexander, "Ars Poetica #100: I Believe," in *American Sublime*, 35.

18. Robert Burns, "Soldier Laddie," in *The Complete Works of Robert Burns*, 18; sung by Dervish on *Spirit*.

19. Elizabeth Alexander, *Praise Song for the Day: A Poem for Barack Obama's Presidential Inauguration.*

20. Walt Whitman, quoted in the frontispiece of Natasha Trethewey's collection of poetry, *Monument: Poems New and Selected.*

21. Imogen Lycett Green, Director of the Betjeman Poetry Award for Children, quoted in Killian Cox, "The 13-Year-Old Syrian Refugee Who Became a Prizewinning Poet," *The Guardian* (October 1, 2017): https://www.theguardian.com/books/2017/oct/01/the-13-year-old-syrian-refugee-prizewinning-poet-amineh-abou-kerech-betjeman-prize. Green's reference to "telling the truth

slant" is an allusion to Emily Dickinson, who described poetry this way: "tell the truth but tell it slant," https://www.poetryfoundation.org/poems/56824/tell-all -the-truth-but-tell-it-slant-1263.

22. "On June 24, 2018, in an unprecedented gesture, the host of Sirius XM Radio followed a playing of the Zinman/Upshaw recording by asking the listeners to consider parallels between the theme of the texts referencing the separation of mothers and children to the then current political situation." Online article at Wikipedia:  https://en.wikipedia.org/wiki/Symphony_No._3 _(G%c3%b3recki).

23. Hildegard of Bingen, quoted in *Favourite Heroes and Holy People*, ed. Deborah Cassidi (London: Continuum, 2008), 215.

24. Rainer Maria Rilke, *Sonnets to Orpheus*, part 2.2 (my translation).

25. Trethewey's recent volume, *Monuments: Poems New and Selected,* is a monument in words to much that has been lost and violated.

26. Quoted by Erin Vanderhoof, "Former Poet Laureate, Natasha Trethewey, on Why Poetry Unites Us," *Vanity Fair* (online), November 8, 2018, https:// www.vanityfair.com/style/2018/11/natasha-trethewey-monument-interview.

27. Rilke, *Sonnets to Orpheus*, 2.10 (my translation).

28. Simone Weil, "Beauty," in *Gravity and Grace*, trans. Arthur Wills, 205.

29. Walt Whitman, quoted in Maria Popova, "The Wisdom of Trees," BrainPickings.org,  https://www.brainpickings.org/2017/11/06/walt-whitman -specimen-days-trees/?mc_cid=6c1d7c6198&mc_eid=2546e719d4.

30. Simone Weil, "Beauty," 204.

31. William Blake, "Auguries of Innocence," in *The Poems of William Blake* (London: Basil Montagu Pickering, 1874), 145

32. Randall Jarrell, *Pictures from an Institution: A Comedy*, 4.

33. Gerard Manley Hopkins, "As Kingfishers Catch Fire," in *Gerard Manley Hopkins: Poems and Prose,* ed. W. Gardner, 51, emphasis in the orginal.

34. William Wordsworth, "Lines Composed a Few Miles Above Tintern Abbey." This poem is available online and is anthologized many places, including *The Collected Poems of William Wordsworth*, 1998.

35. William Wordsworth, "The World Is Too Much with Us," Poetry Foundation,  https://www.poetryfoundation.org/poems/45564/the-world-is-too -much-with-us.

36. See, for example, Charles Hartsorne, *Born to Sing: An Interpretation and World Survey of Bird Song*; Ferris Jabr, "How Beauty Is Making Scientists Rethink Evolution," *New York Times Magazine*.

37. Walker, *The Color Purple*, 197.

38. Lucille Clifton, "won't you celebrate with me?" in *The Book of Light*, 25.

39. Simone Weil, "Beauty," *The Simone Weil Reader*, 378.

40. Simone Weil, *The Notebooks of Simone Weil*, trans. Arthur Wills, 449.

41. Howard Thurman quoted in Gil Bailie, *Violence Unveiled: Humanity at the Crossroads* (New York: Crossroads, 1997).

42. Rosemarie Freeney Harding and Rachel Harding, *Remnants: A Memoir of Spirit, Activism and Mothering*, 69.

43. *Kenōsis* is a Greek word for self-emptying. It is associated with Paul's letter to the Philippians. In chapter 2, he encourages his readers to imitate Christ's compassion and mercy, putting on the "same mind" that was Christ, who emptied himself of the form of God to become a servant to all.

## Chapter 4: Practice

1. Evagrius Ponticus, "Chapters on Prayer," ch. 20, *The Praktikos and Chapters on Prayer*, 58.

2. Rosemarie Freeney Harding and Rachel Harding, *Remnants*, 120.

3. Christian contemplatives employed many disciplines to cultivate unitive experience and integrate it in their daily life. Friedrich Schleiermacher, a nineteenth-century German theologian, may have had something like this in mind when he used phrases like "living fellowship with Christ" or "the touch and taste of the infinite" or "immediate self-consciousness." They described their experiences in many ways but had a different vocabulary for this than we find in eastern religions. Certain schools of Buddhism as well as various schools within Indian religion, for example, the *Yoga Sutra* of Patanjali, propose ways of influencing the subtle body as part of meditation and transformative practices. In considering the role of the subtle body in prayer, one need not adopt any particular metaphysical or even religious point of view. For whatever reason, thematizing this aspect of the human person is less robust in modern European-American Christianity.

4. Gregory Palamas describes the use of energy in prayer in the fourteenth century in "The Hesychast Method of Prayer, and the Transformation of the Body," *The Triads*, 41–55. *The Way of the Pilgrim*, trans. R. M. French, describes a nineteenth-century version of this type of prayer.

5. Cynthia Bourgeault, "Psalmody as Christian Yoga," *Chanting the Psalms: A Practical Guide with Instructional CD*.

6. Cynthia Bourgeault, *The Holy Trinity and the Law of Three: Discerning the Radical Truth at the Heart of Christianity*, 153.

7. Bourgeault, *The Holy Trinity*, 155. This description of the divine presence in creation resonates with the thought of Pseudo-Dionysius in *Divine Names*. This sixth-century text by an anonymous monk influenced Thomas Aquinas and other medieval theologians very deeply.

8. Bourgeault, *The Holy Trinity*, 179.

9. Bourgeault, *The Holy Trinity*, 181.

10. The Didache 1.1–2. This is an ancient handbook for Christian practice. Scholars disagree about its date, but the consensus places it in the first century, roughly contemporary with the synoptic Gospels (Matthew, Mark, Luke). The title means teaching, especially in the sense of trainings. That is, not teaching about Jesus' sayings or life story but training in the way to follow Christ.

11. Didache 1.3.

12. To enter into prayer one must begin by "forgiving everyone who has wronged him, with the passion of anger banished from his soul and in wrath with none. And again, to prevent his mind from being made turbid by irrelevant thoughts, he must while at prayer forget for the time everything outside prayer—surely a state of supreme blessedness!" Origen, "On Prayer," in *Origen: An Exhortation to Martyrdom, Prayer, and Selected Works,* 98. Origen lived from 184–253. His father was martyred when Origen was a young man, who himself was tortured as an old man during another wave of persecutions. He was a generous and beloved teacher, a theologian, and an indefatigable writer of homilies and Scripture commentary.

13. Marguerite Porete, *Mirror of Simple Souls,* 81.

14. The German word *geist* can be translated as either spirit or mind. The New Testament has a variety of words for the complex interactions of mind, spirit, heart, psyche, soul, body. Hebrew uses *lev* or *levav* as a word for heart, but it does not mean emotion as much as interior sense, heart, and mind. Chinese *xin* can be translated as mind or heart. In Greek *nous* or *gnōsis* refer to forms of knowledge or intellect that perceive ultimate reality and therefore are not merely discursive or informational but transformative. *Hokmah* (Hebrew) or *sophia* (Greek) are words for wisdom that are similarly reality-oriented while having also a spiritual or existential orientation.

15. John Eudes Bamberger, OCSO, "Introduction," in Evagrius Ponticus, *The Praktikos and Chapters on Prayer,* 9. "Apatheia" does not correspond to our word, apathy. It means to be without passions, that is, without habitual afflictive emotions and negative mental patterns. It is closer to what Buddhists mean by equanimity.

16. Evagrius Ponticus, "Praktikos," 14.

17. Hesychasm promoted inner stillness, calm, silence. It included the recitation of the Jesus prayer, visualization, meditation with breath, apophatic theology and meditation, and some severe ascetical disciplines. It was and is practiced by Orthodox monks in the Middle East. I have been influenced by this style of contemplation but have not attempted to replicate the practices of a male, Eastern Orthodox monk of this century or of one thousand years ago.

18. Symeon the New Theologian, "The Three Methods of Prayer," *The Philokalia,* vol. 4, 71.

19. See, for example, Cynthia Bourgeault, part 3, *Centering Prayer and Inner Awakening*; Thomas Keating, *Open Mind, Open Heart: The Contemplative Dimension of the Gospel,* ch. 9; James Finley, *Christian Meditation: Experiencing the Presence of God.* All three have teachings recorded on YouTube.

20. James Finley, *Christian Meditation,* 144.

21. Finley, *Christian Meditation,* 281.

22. Finley, *Christian Meditation,* 279.

23. See, for example, Elizabeth Liebert, *The Way of Discernment: Spiritual Practices for Decision Making.*

24. Marguerite Porete, *Mirror of Simple Souls*, 142.

## Chapter 5: Contemplative Dispositions

1. Albert Einstein, quoted in Maria Popova, "Einstein on Widening Our Circles of Compassion," https://www.brainpickings.org/2016/11/28/einstein -circles-of-compassion/.

2. Anais Nin quoted in Mark Nepo, *The Book of Awakening: Having the Life You Want by Being Present to the Life You Have*, 161.

3. Henri-Frédéric Amiel, *Amiel's Journal*, https://www.gutenberg.org/files /8545/8545-h/8545-h.htm. The Gutenberg PDF does not have page numbers, but the date is Berlin, July 16, 1848.

4. Anne Porter, "A Song of Fear and Fire," in *Living Things: Collected Poems*, 27.

5. Ancient Christian contemplatives were very preoccupied with this hazard of the life of prayer. They considered it a commonplace but terrible temptation that vitiated all the gains of an ascetical life. They called this spiritual pride "vain-glory" or *prelest*—a state of spiritual delusion and self-deception based in pride or arrogance over one's spiritual accomplishments. One can also think of Paul's first letter to the Corinthians—though you speak the tongues of angels or give your body to be burned, without love, these spiritual accomplishments are nothing.

6. Julian of Norwich, *Showings*, ch. 7. My translation.

7. Elie Wiesel, *Souls on Fire*, 20.

8. Dorotheos of Gaza, "On Refusal to Judge Our Neighbor," in *Discourses and Sayings*, trans. Eric Wheeler, 135.

9. Dorotheos of Gaza, "On Refusal to Judge Our Neighbor," 132, 135.

10. Rosemarie Freeney Harding with Rachel Elizabeth Harding, *Remnants: A Memoir of Spirit, Activism, and Mothering*, 262.

11. Harding and Harding, *Remnants*, 260, emphasis in the original.

12. Fannie Lou Hamer, quoted in Rosetta Ross, *Witnessing and Testifying: Black Women, Religion, and Civil Rights*, 115.

13. Patanjali, "Yoga Sutra," 2.1.a, trans. T. K. V. Desikachar, *The Heart of Yoga*, 165.

14. "The Letter of Peter to Philip," 140:15–25, ed. James Robinson, trans. Frederick Wisse in *The Nag Hammadi Library in English*, 437.

15. The Gospel of Mary, 9:10–20, trans. George W. MacRae and R. McL. Wilson, in *The Nag Hammadi Library in English*, 525. This text translates the word for human beings as "men," but more recent translators, including Karen King, translate it as human beings.

16. *Bhagavad Gita: A New Translation*, trans. Stephen Mitchell, 2.43–47, p. 54.

17. This lovely expression is found in several beguines' writing. Marguerite Porete uses it, as does Meister Eckhart.

18. Leonard Cohen, "Hallelujah," on *Various Positions*.

19. Angela of Foligno, *Complete Works*, trans. Paul Lachance, OFM, 170.

20. Edward Farley, *Requiem for a Lost Piety: The Contemporary Search for the Christian Life*, 125.

21. Simone Weil, "On the Right Use of School Studies for the Love of God," *Waiting for God*, 64. Parzival was the grail knight who initially failed the quest because he neglected to ask the wounded king why he suffered. After many adventures, his ethics matured into compassion. He returned to the Fisher King and was able to ask the right question, "What are you going through," in this way liberating the king from his wound, the land from its barrenness, and Parzival from his endless questing. He was able to pay attention to the king and not be preoccupied with his own emotional landscape.

22. Elizabeth Johnson, *Ask the Beasts: Darwin and the God of Love*, 42.

23. Johnson, *Ask the Beasts*, 42.

24. Johnson, *Ask the Beasts*, 42.

25. Fay Keys, *A Particle of Light*, 31.

26. Edward Farley, *Requiem for a Lost Piety*, 125.

27. Fay Key, *A Particle of Light*, 146.

28. "The Letter of Peter to Philip," 140:25, in *The Nag Hammadi Library*, 437.

29. Pseudo-Dionysius, "The Divine Names," in *The Complete Works*, trans. Colm Luibheid, 712B.

## Chapter 6: Watching the Mind

1. Naomi Shihab Nye, *Voices in the Air: Poems for Listeners*, xiv.

2. Henri-Frédérick Amiel, *Amiel's Journals*, https://www.gutenberg.org/files/8545/8545-h/8545-h.htm. There are no page numbers in this text, but the date is December 2, 1851.

3. Quoted by Martin Buber in *Tales of the Hasidim*, 251.

4. Amiel, *Amiel's Journals*.

5. There are interesting similarities and differences between these ancient Christian practices and mindfulness-based stress reduction (MBSR) made popular by Jon Kabat-Zinn. MBSR is a secularized version of Buddhist meditation practices.

6. Symeon the New Theologian, "The Three Methods of Prayer," 71.

7. Symeon the New Theologian, "The Three Methods of Prayer," 71.

8. Evagrius Ponticus was a sensitive and profound scientist of the psyche. He was a fourth-century desert ascetic who spent most of his adulthood in the

Egyptian desert where he was a monk and beloved spiritual director. His under-standing of the psyche knew nothing about Freud, Jung, or modern psychol-ogy. He usually refers to negative mental habits ("passions") as the work of the demons. If we transpose his metaphors for our own time, he describes the work-ing of difficult thoughts and habits quite insightfully. Like most monastics of his time, he conceived of the contemplative life as a combat against the assault of evil thoughts and impulses. For whatever reason, these martial metaphors seemed helpful to these communities, though they are less common today.

9. Evagrius Ponticus, "Praktikos," Ch. 50, *Praktikos & Chapters on Prayer.*

10. Dorotheos of Gaza, "On the Need for Consultation," in *Discourses and Sayings,* 123. We met Dorotheos in the last chapter. He was a sixth-century monk in Palestine.

11. David Foster Wallace, *This Is Water: Some Thoughts, Delivered on a Significant Occasion, about Living a Compassionate Life,* 85–86. This essay is one of the most brilliant and moving descriptions of compassionate watching of the mind I have read. It was written as a commencement address at Kenyon College in 2005. It is also available on YouTube: https://www.youtube.com/watch?v=8CrOL-ydFMI.

12. Wallace, *This Is Water,* 93.

13. Evagrius Ponticus, *Praktikos and Chapters on Prayer,* ch. 15, 17, 91.

14. Plato, *Phaedrus,* 278D.

15. Karl Jaspers, *Tragedy Is Not Enough,* 105.

16. Hannah Arendt, *Men in Dark Times,* viii.

17. Hannah Arendt, *Eichmann in Jerusalem,* 86.

18. *Satya* (truth) *agraha* (holding firmly) is a term used by Gandhi to describe the spiritual force of nonviolence. It concerns the power of truth and ethical reality to prevail over injustice, however entrenched its lies or violent its methods.

19. Hans Christian Anderson, "The Snow Queen." This story is present in many collections of Anderson's fairy tales as well as in stand-alone picture books. A PDF (without any publication information) is available online: https://andersen.sdu.dk/moocfiles/snowqueen.pdf.

20. Rosemarie Freeney Harding and Rachel Harding, *Remnants,* 263.

21. Naomi Shihab Nye, from "Kindness," https://poets.org/poem/kindness.

22. For example: Matthieu Ricard, *Altruism: The Power of Compassion to Change Yourself and the World,* trans. Charlotte Mandell and Sam Gordon; His Holiness the Dalai Lama and Archbishop Desmond Tutu, *The Book of Joy: Last-ing Happiness in a Changing World*; Pema Chodron, *The Places That Scare You: A Guide to Fearlessness in Difficult Times*; Karen Armstrong, *Twelve Steps to a Compassionate Life.*

23. Oscar Wilde, *De Profundis,* 47–48.

24. Madeleine L'Engle, quoting Ellis Peters, *Two Part Invention: The Story of a Marriage,* 186.

25. Evagrius Ponticus, "Chapters on Prayer," *Praktikos and Chapters on Prayer*, paragraph 34, 60.

26. See Cheryl Kirk-Duggan, "African-American Spirituals: Confronting and Exorcising Evil through Song," in *A Troubling in My Soul: Womanist Perspectives on Evil and Suffering,* ed. Emilie Townes, 165.

27. Julian of Norwich, *Showings,* ch. 53, my translation.

28. Julian of Norwich, *Showings,* ch. 55, my translation.

29. This prayer is available various places. It is included in compline prayers in the Episcopal *Book of Common Prayer.*

## Chapter 7: Guarding the Heart

1. Karen Baker-Fletcher, *Dancing with God: The Trinity from a Womanist Point of View*, 1.

2. John Coltrane, *A Love Supreme.*

3. This is quoted in various places, more extensively in the "Jewish Women's Archive," online at https://jwa.org/media/quote-from-epistle-to-hebrews, Jewish Women's Archive, "A Quote from Epistle to the Hebrews," https://jwa.org/media/quote-from-epistle-to-hebrews. Emma Lazarus was a Jewish poet, writer, and activist. Lines from her poem, "The New Colossus," are on a bronze plaque at the base of the Statue of Liberty.

4. See for example, the Dalai Lama and Archbishop Desmond Tutu, *The Book of Joy: Lasting Happiness in a Changing World*, which records a week-long conversation between His Holiness and Archbishop Tutu; Sister Chân Không, *Learning True Love: Buddhism in a Time of War.*

5. Dorothy Day, *The Long Loneliness: The Autobiography of Dorothy Day*, 39: "I wanted life and I wanted the abundant life. I wanted it for others too. I did not want just the few, the missionary-minded people like the Salvation Army, to be kind to the poor, as the poor. I wanted everyone to be kind. I wanted every home to be open to the lame, the halt and the blind, the way it had been after the San Francisco earthquake. Only then did people really live, really love their brothers. In such love was the abundant life and I did not have the slightest idea how to find it."

6. I may have gained particular sensitivity to this from my father. He lived it but also wrote about it various places, including the "Opinions" section of his lovely memoir. Noticing a red-tailed hawk flying by, he knows something, but fails to perceive the whole reality of the hawk: "Nor do I apprehend in any specific or direct way what is the red tail hawk's flow of perception and experience. . . . First, our knowing (experience) is always partial (abstract), always running to catch something whose constant process or change can never be caught. Second, to reduce anything to what language (knowing) can express is not only a cognitive mistake but may be a kind of violation of that thing, a refusal to recognize it as itself, a deprivation of its being. Third, all actual things—planets, cells,

molecules, and atoms—have a certain impenetrability. They do in a way show themselves to us, yield something of their make-up, but at the same time they retain their secrets," *Thinking About Things and Other Frivolities*, 82, 83.

7. Michael Yandell, "Do Not Torment Me: The Morally Injured Gerasene Demoniac," in *Moral Injury: A Guidebook for Understanding and Engagement*, ed. Brad Kelle, 2020.

8. In Greek mythology, Hercules was tricked into putting on a poisoned shirt that he could not remove but caused him excruciating agony. It is an image for a suffering that cannot be evaded.

9. Fay Keys, *A Particle of Light*, 145–46.

10. Pema Chodron has written many helpful books on this topic. She emphasizes that suffering can be worked with fruitfully rather than transcended or avoided or repressed. See, for example, Pema Chodron, "Becoming Pema," *Lion's Roar Collector's Edition: Pema Chodron.*

11. Robert Alter, *The Hebrew Bible: A Translation with Commentary*, 108.

12. Alter, *The Hebrew Bible*, 66–68.

13. Philip Browning Helsel, "Witnessing the Body's Response to Trauma: Resistance, Ritual, and the Nervous System Activation," *Pastoral Psychology* 64, no. 5 (October 2015). The online version of this article did not include page numbers. This quotation is from the section "The Spirituality of Freezing, Fight-or-Flight, and Resting."

14. Peter A. Levine, *In an Unspoken Voice: How the Body Releases Trauma and Restores Goodness;* Bessel van der Kolk, *The Body Keeps the Score: Brain, Mind, and Body in the Healing of Trauma.*

15. Simone Weil, "The Love of God and Affliction," *Waiting for God*, 69. When I first read this passage, I thought Weil was being unduly cynical. But I came to realize she was not talking about ordinary suffering, which often does evoke pity, charity, or compassion. She is talking about the repellent quality of what we would now call trauma and its isolating effects. She is a rare person who writes about both afflictive suffering and contemplation from inside them both.

16. I am grateful to Michael Yandell, an Iraq war veteran and PhD student in theology for teaching me this idea of a "negative revelation." The revelation of the harm our country was doing to innocent people and the participation of soldiers in that harm shatters the moral universe that had made soldiering patriotic, heroic, self-sacrificing, and courageous. But this very revelation uncovers the sacred humanity of the "enemy" and with it a glimpse of another world, a more authentic witness of Good. I am hoping that his dissertation on this topic will be published soon. A shorter version of his argument is available: "Moral Injury and Human Relationship: A Conversation," https://www.researchgate .net/publication/322663798_Moral_Injury_and_Human_Relationship_A _Conversation.

17. Simone Weil, "On the Right Use of School Studies for the Love of God," 59.

18. John of the Cross, "The Spiritual Canticle of the Soul and the Bridegroom Christ," XXXVI, trans. Kieren Kavanaugh, *Collected Works of St. John of the Cross.*

19. Elie Wiesel, *Souls on Fire: Portraits and Legends of Hasidic Masters*, 26. The Baal Shem Tov ("Master of the Good Name") was an eighteenth-century Jewish mystic and is considered the founder of the Hasidic movement. Most of what is known about him is legends and stories passed through an oral tradition.

20. Joy R. Bostic, *African American Female Mysticism: Nineteenth-Century Religious Activism*, 83.

21. See Catherine of Sienna, "Consumed in Grace," *Love Poems from God: Twelve Sacred Voices from the East and West*, 183.

22. See Beverly Lanzetta, *Radical Wisdom: A Feminist Mystical Theology.*

23. Bonnie Thurston, "The Tradition of Wisdom and Spirit: Wisdom in Thomas Merton's Mature Thought." Online PDF at the Merton.org website: http://merton.org/ITMS/Seasonal/20/20-1Thurston.pdf.

24. Thurston, "The Tradition of Wisdom and Spirit."

25. The Wisdom of Solomon is one of the books of the Bible that Catholics count as part of the canon of the Hebrew Bible (Old Testament) that Protestants do not. We Protestants miss out on a number of wonderful texts!

26. St. Anselm, "A Song of Anselm," https://www.churchofengland.org /prayer-and-worship/worship-texts-and-resources/common-worship/daily-prayer /canticles-daily-prayer/82-song-anselm.

27. Julian of Norwich, *Revelations of Divine Love,* ch. 60, *The Writings of Julian of Norwich: A Vision Showed to a Devout Woman and a Revelation of Love*, edited by Nicholas Watson and Jacqueline Jenkins. Julian's riff on God the Mother runs from Chapter 57–63. Translation mine.

28. Julian of Norwich, *Revelations of Divine Love,* ch. 63, *The Writings of Julian of Norwich: A Vision Showed to a Devout Woman and a Revelation of Love*, edited by Nicholas Watson and Jacqueline Jenkins, translation mine.

29. This is quoted in many places, including at Paul Vasile's Advent website. Vasile has composed a song, "We Are All Meant to Be Mothers of God," based on this quotation, which is also available on his blog: https://www.paulvasile.com /blog/2015/12/23/we-are-all-meant-to-be-mothers-of-god

30. This is the Memorare, for some Catholics the first prayer they learn.

31. Clarissa Pinkola Estés, *Untie the Strong Woman: Blessed Mother's Immaculate Love for the Wild Soul,* frontispiece.

32. Estés, *Untie the Strong Woman,* 47, 46.

33. Estés, *Untie the Strong Woman,* 66.

34. Estés, *Untie the Strong Woman,* 128.

35. Rebecca Jackson, *Gifts of Power: The Writings of Rebecca Jackson, Black Visionary, Shaker Eldress,* ed. Jean McMahon Humez (Amherst: University of Massachusetts Press: 1981), 72, quoted in Joy Bostic, *African American Female Mysticism: Nineteenth-Century Religious Activism* (Palgrave Macmillan: 2013), 96–97, 102, 117.

## Chapter 8: Contemplative Practices

1. T. K. V. Desikachar, *The Heart of Yoga: Developing a Personal Practice* (Rochester, VT: Inner Traditions, 1995), xviii.

2. The list is very long. A few examples include: the writings and daily reflections of Richard Rohr (https://cac.org/sign-up/); James Finley's recordings on Christian meditation and his beautiful books, including *Christian Meditation: Experiencing the Presence of God*; Cynthia Bourgeault's book on centering prayer, *The Heart of Centering Prayer: Nondual Christianity in Theory and Practice*; John Main's accounts of Christian mantra, including *Word Into Silence: A Manual for Christian Meditation*; Ineda Adesanya's edited volume on spiritual direction for people of color, *Kaleidoscope: Broadening the Palette in the Art of Spiritual Direction*; Susan Phillips on spiritual direction, *Candlelight: Illuminating the Art of Spiritual Direction*; Elizabeth Liebert on discernment: *The Way of Discernment: Spiritual Practices for Decision Making* and *The Soul of Discernment: A Spiritual Practice for Communities and Institutions*; and Beverly Lanzetta on lay monasticism and the role of the feminine, *The Monk Within: Embracing a Sacred Way of Life*. In addition to these there are countless teachers, websites, and books introducing practices from different religious traditions into lay, secular, or interfaith contexts, including Spiritual Directors of Color Network, https://sdcnetwork.org/.

3. Gerard Manley Hopkins, "Thou Art Indeed Just Lord, if I Contend," in *Gerard Manley Hopkins: Poems and Prose,* ed. W. Gardner, 67.

4. Symeon the New Theologian, Hymn 15, *Divine Eros: Hymns of Saint Symeon the New Theologian*, 89.

5. Gregory Palamas, *The Triads*, 51.

6. See, for example, Thomas Ryan, *Prayer of Heart and Body: Mediation and Yoga as Christian Spiritual Practice;* Thomas Matus, *Yoga and the Jesus Prayer Tradition: An Experiment in Faith.*

7. God who created the sun, you are the Sun of my soul, and you make me glad. Light of the Sun, be with me today. Scotty, my oldest child, translated this for me.

8. Thomas H. Green, *Celtic Daily Prayer: Prayers and Readings from the Northumbria Community*, February 16, p. 334.

9. Evagrius Ponticus, ch. 122, "On Prayer," in *Praktikos and Chapters on Prayer.* See also, "Happy is the spirit that attains to perfect formlessness at the time of prayer" (ch. 117, p. 75). This theme is repeated through the next several chapters.

10. The Contemplative Outreach website is full of good information about this practice as well as listing many of the places where people gather to practice together. Many churches offer this prayer. Cynthia Bourgeault and Thomas Keating are among those who have written many helpful books on this practice. These teachers can also be found on YouTube. The primary classical text describing this

kind of prayer is *The Cloud of Unknowing* (author unknown), available in many translations, https://www.contemplativeoutreach.org/.

11. Anonymous, *The Cloud of Unknowing*, ch. 7.

12. Cynthia Bourgeault, *The Heart of Centering Prayer*, 36. Bourgeault emphasizes that the trajectory of centering prayer is not mystical experiences or a calmer attitude but a restructuring of consciousness itself, "putting the mind in the heart," as she explains in the second half of *The Heart of Centering Prayer*.

13. Thomas Keating, *Open Mind, Open Heart*, 93.

14. There are many books about this: Matthieu Ricard, *Altruism: The Power of Compassion to Change Yourself and the World*; the Dalai Lama, *An Open Heart: Practicing Compassion in Everyday Life*. Jean-Yves Leloup compares Christian and Buddhist forms of compassion meditation in *Compassion and Meditation: The Spiritual Dynamic between Christianity and Buddhism*. Frank Rogers has two wonderful books on Christian compassion meditation: *Practicing Compassion* and *Compassion in Practice: The Way of Jesus*. Karen Armstrong offers a more secular version: *Twelve Steps to a Compassionate Life*. Courage of Care provides online trainings in compassion meditation as well as workshops and retreats (courageofcare.org).

15. A classic source is Guigo II, *The Ladder of Monks and Twelve Meditations*. Christine Valters Paintner, *Lectio Divina—The Sacred Art: Transforming Words and Images into the Heart-Centered Prayer*, and M. Basil Pennington, *Lectio Divina: Renewing the Ancient Practice of Praying the Scriptures* are two among many modern examples.

16. To see an example of scientific research in this area, see Marc Russo, Danielle Santarelli, and Dean O'Rourke, "The Physiological Effects of Slow Breathing in the Healthy Human," *Breathe* 13, no. 4 (December 2017): 298–309.

17. The ancient prayer posture, the "orant," raises hands over one's head, palms facing outward. There are many pictures in catacombs and elsewhere of woman and men praying in this position. "He who prays must lift up holy hands," Origen, "On Prayer," 98.

18. The writings of John Main, *Words into Silence: A Manual for Christian Meditation* and Laurence Freeman, *Jesus the Teacher Within*, are good introductions to Christian mantra.

19. Fran Grace describes this as the "live current of energy from within" that is particularly potent in genuine teachers, in *The Power of Love: A Transformed Heart Changes the World*, 350.

20. Cynthia Bourgeault, *Chanting the Psalms*, 29.

# Bibliography

Adesanya, Ineda. *Kaleidoscope: Broadening the Palette in the Art of Spiritual Direction.* New York: Church Pub, Inc., 2019.

Aelred of Rievaulx. *Treatises and Pastoral Prayer.* Introduced by David Knowles. Spencer, MA: Cistercian Publications, 1971.

Alexander, Elizabeth. *American Sublime.* Minneapolis, MN: Graywolf Press, 2005.

———. *Praise Song for the Day: A Poem for Barack Obama's Presidential Inauguration.* Minneapolis: Graywolf Press, 2009.

Alexander, Michelle. *The New Jim Crow: Mass Incarceration in the Age of Colorblindness.* New York: The New Press, 2012.

Alter, Robert. *The Hebrew Bible: A Translation with Commentary.* 3 vols. New York: W. W. Norton, 2018.

Amiel, Henri-Frédéric. *Amiel's Journal.* Translated and introduced by Humphrey Ward. A Gutenberg Project eBook, 2005. Https://www.gutenberg.org /files/8545/8545-h/8545-h.htm.

Anderson, Hans Christian. "The Snow Queen." Https://andersen.sdu.dk /moocfiles/snowqueen.pdf.

Angela of Foligno. *Complete Works.* Translated by Paul Lachance, OFM. New York: Paulist Press, 1993.

Anselm. "A Song of Anselm." Website: Church of England: A Christian Presence in Every Community. Common Worship: Daily Prayer, material from which is included here, is copyright © The Archbishops' Council 2005 and published by Church House Publishing. Https://www.churchofengland.org /prayer-and-worship/worship-texts-and-resources/common-worship/daily -prayer/canticles-daily-prayer/82-song-anselm.

Arendt, Hannah. *Eichmann in Jerusalem: A Report on the Banality of Evil.* New York: Penguin Books, 1977.

———. *Men in Dark Times.* New York: Harcourt Brace Jovanovich, 1955.

Armstrong, Karen. *Twelve Steps to a Compassionate Life.* New York: Alfred A. Knopf, 2010.

Bailie, Gil. *Violence Unveiled: Humanity at the Crossroads.* New York: Crossroads, 1997.

Baker-Fletcher, Karen. *Dancing with God: The Trinity from a Womanist Perspective.* St. Louis, MO: Chalice Press, 2006.

Baptist, Edward E. *The Half Has Never Been Told: Slavery and the Making of American Capitalism*. New York: Basic Books, 2014.

Barnhart, Bruno. *The Future of Wisdom: Toward a Rebirth of Sapiential Christianity*. New York: Continuum, 2007.

*Bhagavad Gita: A New Translation*. Translated by Stephen Mitchell. New York: Three Rivers Press, 2000.

Berry, Thomas. *The Great Work: Our Way into the Future*. New York: Bell Tower, 1999.

Blake, William. "Auguries of Innocence." The Poetry Foundation. Https://www.poetryfoundation.org/poems/43650/auguries-of-innocence

Bostic, Joy R. *African American Female Mysticism: Nineteenth-Century Religious Activism*. New York: Palgrave Macmillan, 2013.

Bourgeault, Cynthia. *Centering Prayer and Inner Awakening*. Cambridge, MA: Cowley Press, 2004.

———. *Chanting the Psalms: A Practical Guide with Instructional CD*. Boston: New Seeds Books, 2006.

———. *The Heart of Centering Prayer: Nondual Christianity in Theory and Practice*. Boulder, CO: Shambala Publications, 2016.

———. *The Holy Trinity and the Law of Three: Discerning the Radical Truth at the Heart of Christianity*. Boulder, CO: Shambala Publications, 2013.

Brooks, Gwendolyn. "my dreams, my works must wait till after hell." *Selected Poems*. New York: Harper Perennial Modern Classics, 2006.

Brother Lawrence. *The Practice of the Presence of God*. Translated by John J. Delaney. New York: Image, 1977.

Buber, Martin. *Tales of the Hasidim*. Translated by Olga Marx, with a new foreword by Chaim Potok. New York: Schocken Books, 1991.

Burns, Robert. *The Complete Works of Robert Burns*. Edinburgh: William P. Nimmo, 1867.

Cassian, John. *The Conferences*. Translated by Boniface Ramsey, OP. New York: Paulist Press, 1997.

Catherine of Genoa. *Purgation and Purgatory, The Spiritual Dialogue*. Translated by Serge Hughes. Mahwah, NJ: Paulist Press, 1979.

Catherine of Siena. "Consumed in Grace." In *Love Poems from God: Twelve Sacred Voices from the East and West*. Edited by Daniel Ladinsky. New York: Penguin Compass, 2002.

*Celtic Daily Prayer: Prayers and Readings from the Northumbria Community*. Introduction by Richard J. Foster. New York: HarperSanFrancisco, 2002.

Chodron, Pema. "Becoming Pema." In *Lion's Roar Collector's Edition: Pema Chodron*. Escondido, CA: Lion's Roar Foundation, 2016.

———. *The Places That Scare You: A Guide to Fearlessness in Difficult Times*. Boulder, CO: Shambala Publications, 2018.

Clifton, Lucille. *The Book of Light*. Port Townsend, WA: Copper Canyon Press, 1993.

*Cloud of Unknowing.* Anonymous. Translated by Carmen Acevedo Butcher. Boston: Shambhala, 2009.

Cohen, Leonard. *Various Positions.* New York: Columbia Records, 1984, compact disc.

Coleman, Monica. *Making a Way Out of No Way: A Womanist Theology.* Minneapolis: Fortress Press, 2008.

Coltrane, John. *A Love Supreme.* Santa Monica, CA: Impulse! Records, 1965, compact disc.

Cox, Killian. "The 13-Year-Old Syrian Refugee Who Became a Prizewinning Poet. *The Guardian.* October 1, 2017. Https://www.theguardian.com/books/2017/oct/01/the-13-year-old-syrian-refugee-prizewinning-poet-amineh-abou-kerech-betjeman-prize.

Dalai Lama [14]. *An Open Heart: Practicing Compassion in Everyday Life.* Edited by Nicholas Vreeland. Boston: Little, Brown, and Company, 2001.

Dalai Lama [14], and Desmond Tutu. *The Book of Joy: Lasting Happiness in a Changing World.* New York: Avery, 2016.

Day, Dorothy. *The Long Loneliness: The Autobiography of Dorothy Day.* San Francisco: Harper & Row, 1981.

Dervish. "Soldier Laddie," *Spirit.* Whirling Discs. WHRL007 2003, compact disc.

*Desert Wisdom: Sayings from the Desert Fathers.* Translated and art by Yushi Nomura. Garden City, NY: Doubleday, 1982.

Desikachar, T. K. V. *The Heart of Yoga: Developing a Personal Practice.* Rochester, VT: Inner Traditions, 1995.

Dickenson, Emily, "Tell the truth but tell it slant," (1263). Poetry Foundation. Https://www.poetryfoundation.org/poems/56824/tell-all-the-truth-but-tell-it-slant-1263

*Didache: Text, Translation, Analysis, and Commentary.* Aaron Milavec. Collegeville, MN: Liturgical Press, 2003.

Dorotheos of Gaza. *Discourses and Sayings.* Translated and introduced by Eric Wheeler, OSB. Kalamazoo, MI: Cistercian Publications, 1977.

Dostoevsky, Fyodor. *The Brothers Karamazov.* Translated by Constance Garnett. New York: The Modern Library, Random House: 1996.

Douglas, Kelly Brown. *Stand Your Ground: Black Bodies and the Justice of God.* Maryknoll, NY: Orbis Books, 2015.

Ellsberg, Robert. *All Saints: Daily Reflections on Saints, Prophets, and Witnesses for Our Times.* New York: The Crossroads Publishing Company, 1997.

Estes, Clarissa Pinkola. *Untie the Strong Woman: Blessed Mother's Immaculate Love for the Wild Soul.* Boulder, CO: Sounds True, 2013.

Evagrius Ponticus, *The Praktikos and Chapters on Prayer.* Translated and introduced by John Eudes Bamberger, OCSO. Spencer, MA: Cistercian Publications, 1981.

Farley, Edward. *Requiem for a Lost Piety: The Contemporary Search for the Christian Life.* Philadelphia: Westminster Press, 1966.

———. *Thinking about Things and Other Frivolities: A Life.* Eugene, OR: Cascade, 2014.

Finley, James. *Christian Meditation: Experiencing the Presence of God.* San Francisco: HarperSanFrancisco, 2004.

Fletcher Hill, Jeannine. *The Sin of White Supremacy: Christianity, Racism, and Religious Diversity in America.* Maryknoll, NY: Orbis Books, 2017.

Floyd, Richard. *Down to Earth: Christian Hope and Climate Change.* Eugene, OR: Cascade, 2015.

Freeman, Laurence. *Jesus the Teacher Within.* London: Canterbury Press Norwich, 2010.

Grace, Fran. *The Power of Love: A Transformed Heart Changes the World.* Athens, GA: Inner Pathway Publishing, 2019.

Green, Thomas H. *Celtic Daily Prayer: Prayers and Readings from the Northumbria Community.* San Francisco: HarperCollins, 2002.

Gregory of Nyssa. *The Great Catechism.* In *Gregory of Nyssa Select Works, Letters: The Nicene and Post-Nicene Fathers.* Second Series, vol 5. Philip Schaff and Henry Wace. Grand Rapids, MI: Wm. B. Eerdmans Publishing Co., 1954.

Griffin, Patty. *Impossible Dream.* New York: ATO Records, 2004, compact disc.

Guigo II. *The Ladder of Monks and Twelve Meditations.* Translated and introduced by Edmund Colledge, OSA, and James Walsh, SJ. Kalamazoo, MI: Cistercian Publications, 1979.

Hample, Patricia. "Introduction." In *The Best Spiritual Writings of 1998.* Edited by Philip Zaleski. New York: HaperOne, 1999.

Harding, Rosemarie Freeney, with Rachel Elizabeth Harding. *Remnants: A Memoir of Spirit, Activism, and Mothering.* Durham, NC: Duke University Press, 2015.

Hart, David Bentley. *The New Testament: A Translation.* New Haven, CT: Yale University Press, 2017.

Hartsorne, Charles. *Born to Sing: an Interpretation and World Survey of Bird Song.* Bloomington: Indiana University Press, 1992.

Hayes, Diana L. *Standing in the Shoes My Mother Made: A Womanist Theology.* Minneapolis: Fortress Press, 2011.

———. "Standing in the Shoes My Mother Made." In *Deeper Shades of Purple: Womanism in Religion and Society.* Edited by Stacey M. Floyd-Thomas. New York: New York University Press, 2006.

Helsel, Philip Browning. "Witnessing the Body's Response to Trauma: Resistance, Ritual, and the Nervous System Activation." *Pastoral Psychology* 64, no. 5 (October 2015): 681–93.

Hopkins, Gerard Manley. *Gerard Manley Hopkins: Poems and Prose.* Edited by W. Gardner. London: Penguin Books, 1985.

Jabr, Ferris. "How Beauty Is Making Scientists Rethink Evolution," *New York Times Magazine*. January 9, 2019. Https://www.nytimes.com/2019/01/09/magazine/beauty-evolution-animal.html.

Jackson, Rebecca. *Gifts of Power: The Writings of Rebecca Jackson, Black Visionary, Shaker Eldress*. Edited by Jean McMahon Humez. Amherst: University of Massachusetts Press, 1981.

Jarrell, Randall. *Pictures from an Institution: A Comedy*. Chicago: University of Chicago Press, 1986.

Jaspers, Karl. *Tragedy Is Not Enough*. Boston: Beacon Press, 1952.

John of the Cross. *A Spiritual Canticle of the Soul and the Bridegroom of Christ*, trans. David Lewis. Stanza 1. Http://www.documentacatholicaomnia.eu/03d/1542-1591,_Ioannes_a_Cruce,_A_Spiritual_Canticle_Of_The_Soul,_EN.pdf. There are many good translations of John of the Cross's poetry, but this one is available online.

"A Spiritual Canticle," *The Collected Works of St. John of the Cross*. Translated by Kieran Kavanaugh, OCD, Otilio Rodriguez, OCD. Washington, DC: ICS Publications, 1979.

———. "The Dark Night of the Soul." *The Collected Works of St. John of the Cross*. Translated by Kieran Kavanaugh, OCD, Otilio Rodriguez, OCD. Washington, DC: ICS Publications, 1979.

Johnson, Elizabeth. *Ask the Beasts: Darwin and the God of Love*. London: Bloomsbury Publishing, 2014.

Jordon, June. "These Poems." The June M. Jordan Literary Estate, 2017. Https://poets.org/poem/these-poems.

Julian of Norwich. *The Complete Julian of Norwich*. Father John-Julian, OJN. Brewster, MA: Paraclete Press, 2009.

———. *Showings*. Translated and introduced by Edmund Colledge, OSA, and James Walsh, SJ. Mahwah, NJ: Paulist Press, 1978.

———. *The Writings of Julian of Norwich: A Vision Showed to a Devout Woman and a Revelation of Love*. Edited by Nicholas Watson and Jacqueline Jenkins. University Park: The Pennsylvania State University Press, 2006.

Keating, Thomas. *Open Mind, Open Heart: The Contemplative Dimension of the Gospel*. New York: Continuum, 2002.

Kerech, Amineh Abou. "Lament for Syria," Read by Amineh Abou Kerech. March 11, 2019. Https://www.youtube.com/watch?v=VOCtYxbtpFU.

Keys, Fay. *A Particle of Light*. Independently published, 2019.

Kinnell, Galway. "Flying Home." Poetry Soup, https://www.poetrysoup.com/famous/poem/from_flying_home_444

Không, Sister Chân. *Learning True Love: Buddhism in a Time of War*. Berkeley, CA: Parallax Press, 2007.

Kirk-Duggan, Cheryl A. "African-American Spirituals: Confronting and Exorcising Evil through Song." In *A Troubling in My Soul: Womanist Perspectives on Evil and Suffering.* Edited by Emilie Townes. Maryknoll, NY: Orbis Books, 1993.

Kolk, van der Bessel. *The Body Keeps the Score: Brain, Mind, and Body in the Healing of Trauma.* New York: Penguin Books, 2015.

Lanzetta, Beverly. *The Monk Within: Embracing a Sacred Way of Life.* Sebastopol, CA: Blue Sapphire Books, 2018.

———. *Radical Wisdom: A Feminist Mystical Theology.* Minneapolis: Fortress Press, 2005.

Lazarus, Emma. Jewish Women's Archive. "A Quote from Epistle to the Hebrews." Online at https://jwa.org/media/quote-from-epistle-to-hebrews, Jewish Women's Archive.

Leloup, Jean-Yves. *Compassion and Meditation: The Spiritual Dynamic between Christianity and Buddhism.* Translated by Joseph Rowe. Rochester, VT: Inner Traditions, 2009.

L'Engle, Madeleine. *Two Part Invention: The Story of a Marriage.* New York: Farrar, Straus and Giroux, 1988.

Levine, Peter A. *In an Unspoken Voice: How the Body Releases Trauma and Restores Goodness.* Berkeley: North Atlantic Books, 2010.

Liebert, Elizabeth. *The Soul of Discernment: A Spiritual Practice for Communities and Institutions.* Louisville, KY: Westminster John Knox Press, 2015.

———. *The Way of Discernment: Spiritual Practices for Decision Making.* Louisville, KY: Westminster John Knox Press, 2008.

Lorde, Audrey. *Sister Outsider.* Berkeley, CA: Crossing Press, 2007.

Main, John. *Word into Silence: A Manual for Christian Meditation.* London: Canterbury Press Norwich, 2006.

Matus, Thomas. *Yoga and the Jesus Prayer Tradition: An Experiment in Faith.* Ramsey, NJ: Paulist Press, 1984.

Maximus of Tyre. *Five Stages of Greek Religion.* Translated by Gilbert Murray. Garden City: Doubleday Anchor Books, 2011.

Mbiti, John S. *African Religions and Philosophy.* Portsmouth, NH: Heinemann Educational Publishers, 1999.

Mechthild of Magdeburg. *The Flowing Light of the Godhead.* Translated and introduced by Frank Tobin. Mahwah, NJ: Paulist Press, 1998.

Meister Eckhart. *Meister Eckhart: A Modern Translation.* Translated by Raymond B. Blakney. New York: Harper Torchbooks, 1941.

Merton, Thomas. *The Collected Poems of Thomas Merton.* New York: New Directions, 1980.

———. *Thoughts in Solitude.* New York: Farrar, Straus and Cudahy, 1958.

Mitchell, Stephen. *The Enlighted Heart: An Anthology of Sacred Poetry.* New York: HarperPerennial, 1989.

Nepo, Mark. *The Book of Awakening: Having the Life You Want by Being Present to the Life You Have.* San Francisco: Conari Press, 2000.

Nicholas of Cusa. "The Vision of God." In *Selected Spiritual Writings*. Translated and introduced by H. Lawrence Bond. New York: Paulist Press, 1997.

Noah, Trevor. *Born a Crime: Stories from a South African Childhood*. New York: Spiegel & Grau, 2016.

Norgaard, Kari Marie. *Living in Denial: Climate Change, Emotions, and Everyday Life*. Cambridge, MA: The MIT Press, 2011.

Nye, Naomi Shihab. *Voices in the Air: Poems for Listeners*. New York: Greenwillow Books, 2018.

———. "Kindness," online: https://poets.org/poem/kindness.

O'Connor, Sinead. *Gospel Oak*. London: Chrysalis Records, 1997, compact disc.

O'Donohue, John. *Beauty: The Invisible Embrace: Rediscovering True Sources of Compassion, Serenity, and Hope*. New York: Perennial, 2003.

Origen. *Origen: An Exhortation to Martyrdom, Prayer, and Selected Works*. Translated by Rowan A. Greer. Mahwah, NJ: Paulist Press, 1979.

Owens, Delia. *Where the Crawdads Sing*. New York: G.P. Putnam's Sons, 2018.

Paintner, Christine Valters. *Lectio-Divina—The Sacred Art: Transforming Words and Images into the Heart-Centered Prayer*. Woodstock, VT: SkyLight Paths Publishing, 2011.

Palamas, Gregory. *The Triads*. Translated by Nicholas Gendle. Mahwah, NJ: Paulist Press, 1983.

Patanjali. "The Yoga Sutras." Translated by T. K. V. Desikachar. In *The Heart of Yoga: Developing a Personal Practice*. Rochester, VT: Inner Traditions, 1995.

Pennington, M. Basil. *Lectio Divina: Renewing the Ancient Practice of Praying the Scriptures*. New York: A Crossroads Book, 1998.

Peter of Alcantara. *Treatise on Prayer and Meditation*. Translated by Dominic Devas, OFM. Charlotte, NC: TAN Books, 2012.

Plato. *Phaedrus*. Translated by Alexander Nehamas and Paul Woodruff. Cambridge: Hackett Publishing Co, 1995.

Phillips, Susan. *Candlelight: Illuminating the Art of Spiritual Direction*. Harrisburg, PA: Morehouse Publishing, 2008.

Popova, Maria. "The Wisdom of Trees: Walt Whitman on What Our Silent Friends Teach Us about Being Rather Than Seeming." Brainpickings.org. Https://www.brainpickings.org/2017/11/06/walt-whitman-specimen-days -trees/?mc_cid=6c1d7c6198&mc_eid=2546e719d4.

Porete, Marguerite. *Mirror of Simple Souls*. Translated by Ellen L. Babinsky. Mahwah, NJ: Paulist Press, 1993.

Porter, Anne. *Living Things: Collected Poems*. Hanover, NH: Steerforth Press, 2006.

Pramuk, Christopher. *Sophia: The Hidden Christ of Thomas Merton*. Collegeville, MN: Liturgical Press, 2009.

Pseudo-Dionysius. *The Complete Works*. Translated by Colm Luibheid. Mahwah, NJ: Paulist Press, 1987.

———. *The Divine Names and Mystical Theology.* Translated John D. Jones. Milwaukee: Marquette University Press, 1980.

Rascal Flatts. "Bless the Broken Road," *Feels Like Today.* Nashville: Lyric Street Records, 2004, compact disc.

Ricard, Matthieu. *Altruism: The Power of Compassion to Change Yourself and the World.* Translated by Charlotte Mandell and Sam Gordon. New York: Little, Brown, and Company, 2015.

Rilke, Rainer Maria. *Sonnets to Orpheus: Bilingual Edition.* Translated by Edward Snow. New York: North Point Press, 2004.

Robinson, Frank, ed. *The Nag Hammadi Library in English.* Translated and introduced by Members of the Coptic Gnostic Library Project of the Institute for Antiquity and Christianity, Claremont, California. San Francisco: Harper & Row, 1988.

Rogers, Frank. *Compassion in Practice: The Way of Jesus.* Nashville, TN: The Upper Room Books, 2016.

———. *Practicing Compassion.* Nashville, TN: The Upper Room Books, 2015.

Rohr, Richard. "Richard Rohr's Meditation, Week Forty-one, Franciscan Way: Part Two." October 9, 2019. Center for Action and Meditation daily email.

Ross, Rosetta. *Witnessing and Testifying: Black Women, Religion, and Civil Rights.* Philadelphia: Fortress Press, 2003.

Russo, Marc, Danielle Santarelli, and Dean O'Rourke. "The Physiological Effects of Slow Breathing in the Healthy Human." *Breathe* 13, no. 4 (December 2017): 298–309.

Ryan, Thomas. *Prayer of Heart and Body: Meditation and Yoga as Christian Practice.* Mahwah, NY: Paulist Press, 2001.

Salzberg, Sharon. *Loving Kindness: The Revolutionary Art of Happiness.* Boulder, CO: Shambala Publications, 2018.

Sauvage, Pierre. *Weapons of the Spirit: The Astonishing Story of a Unique Conspiracy of Goodness.* Le Chambon-sur Lignon, France: The Chambon Foundation, 2007, DVD.

Shantideva. *The Way of the Bodhisattva.* Translation by the Padmakara Translation Group. Boston: Shambala Publications, 2006.

Sheldrake, Philip. *Julian of Norwich: In God's Sight.* Hoboken, NJ: Wiley-Blackwell, 2018.

Steindl-Rast, David. "Praying the Great Dance." In *The Best Spiritual Writing: 1998.* Ed. Philip Zaleski. New York: Dimensions, HarperSanFrancisco, 1998.

Stithatos, Nikitas. "On the Practice of the Virtues," *Philokalia,* Vol. 4. Compiled by St Nikodimos of the Holy Mountain and St. Mkrarios of Corinth. Translated from the Greed by G. E. H. Palmer, Philip Sherrard, Kallistos Ware. London: Faber and Faber, 1995.

Symeon the New Theologian. *Divine Eros: Hymns of Saint Symeon the New Theologian.* Translated and introduced by Daniel K. Griggs. Yonkers, NY: St. Vladimir's Seminary Press, 2010.

———. *The Philokalia: The Complete Text.* Vol. 4. Translated and edited by G. E. H. Palmer, Philip Sherrard, Kallistos Ware. London: Faber and Faber, 1995.

———. *Writings from the Philokalia on Prayers of the Heart.* Translated by E. Kadloubovsky and G. H. H. Palmer. London: Faber & Faber, 1992.

Teresa of Avila. *The Interior Castle.* Translated by E. Allison Peers. New York: Image Books, Doubleday, 1989.

Thurman, Howard. *The Inward Journey.* Richmond, IN: Friends United Press, 2000.

Thurston, Bonnie. "The Tradition of Wisdom and Spirit: Wisdom in Thomas Merton's Mature Thought." *The Merton Seasonal* 20, no. 1. (Winter 1994). The Thomas Merton Center at Bellarmine University. Http://merton.org /ITMS/Seasonal/20/20-1Thurston.pdf.

Tillich, Paul. *On Art and Architecture.* New York: Crossroad, 1987.

———. "Shaking the Foundations," *The Essential Tillich: An Anthology of the Writings of Paul Tillich.* Edited by Fr. Forrester Church. Chicago: University of Chicago Press, 1987.

Tirman, John. *The Deaths of Others: The Fate of Civilians in America's Wars.* Oxford: Oxford University Press, 2011.

Tolstoy, Leo. "The Death of Ivan Ilyich." Translated by Ian Dreiblatt. New York: Melville House Publishing, 2008.

Trethewey, Natasha. *Monument: Poems New and Selected.* Boston: Houghton Mifflin Harcourt, 2018.

Tuggy, Dale. "History of Trinitarian Doctrines." Supplement to "Trinity: *Stanford Encyclopedia of Philosophy.* Winter 2016 edition. Https://plato.stanford .edu/archives/win2016/entries/trinity/trinity-history.html.

Vanderhoof, Erin. "Former Poet Laureate, Natasha Trethewey, on Why Poetry Unites Us." *Vanity Fair.* November 8, 2018. Https://www.vanityfair.com /style/2018/11/natasha-trethewey-monument-interview.

Voss Roberts, Michelle. *Body Parts: A Theological Anthropology.* Minneapolis: Fortress Press, 2017.

Walker, Alice. *The Color Purple.* Orlando: A Harvest Book, 1992.

———. *In Search of Our Mothers' Gardens: Womanist Prose.* Orlando: A Harvest Book, 1983.

Wallace, David Foster. *This Is Water: Some Thoughts, Delivered on a Significant Occasion, about Living a Compassionate Life.* New York: Little, Brown, and Company, 2009.

*Way of the Pilgrim and the Pilgrim Continues His Way.* Translated by R.M. French. Pasadena: Hope Publishing, 1989.

Weil, Simone. *Gravity and Grace.* Translated by Arthur Wills and introduced by
    Gustave Thibon. New York: G.P. Putman's Sons, 1952.
————. *The Notebooks of Simone Weil.* Translated by Arthur Wills. Routledge:
    New York, 2004.
————. *Simone Weil Reader.* Edited by George A. Panichas. London: Moyer
    Bell, 1994 (second printing).
————. *Waiting for God.* Translated by Emma Craufurd. New York: Harper-
    Perennial, 2009.
Wiesel, Elie. *Souls on Fire: Portraits and Legends of Hasidic Masters.* Translated by
    Marion Wiesel. New York: A Touchstone Book, 1972.
Wilde, Oscar. *De Profundis, The Ballad of Reading Gaol, and Other Writ-
    ings.* Notes and Introduction by Anne Varty. Ware, Hertfordshire: Words-
    worth Classics, 1999.
Wordsworth, William. "Lines Composed a Few Miles above Tintern Abbey."
    *The Collected Poems of William Wordsworth.* Introduced by Antonia Till.
    Ware, Hertfordshire, Wordsworth Editions, 1998.
Yandell, Michael. "Do Not Torment Me: The Morally Injured Gerasene Demo-
    niac." In *Moral Injury: A Guidebook for Understanding and Engagement.*
    Edited by Brad Kelle. New York: Lexington Books, 2020.
————. "Moral Injury and Human Relationship: A Conversation. *Pastoral Psy-
    chology* 68, no. 1 (January 2018): 3–14.
Yeats, William Butler. *The Collected Poems of W. B. Yeats.* Edited by Richard
    Finneran. New York: Scribner, 1996.
Zaleski, Philip. *The Best Spiritual Writing: 1998.* New York: HarperSanFran-
    cisco, 1998.

# Index

Printed in the USA
CPSIA information can be obtained
at www.ICGtesting.com
JSHW011043010823
45757JS00005B/41